JUN   2011

The Philanthropy of George Soros

THE
PHILANTHROPY
OF
GEORGE SOROS

BUILDING OPEN SOCIETIES

CHUCK SUDETIC

With an Essay by
GEORGE SOROS

and an Afterword by
ARYEH NEIER

PublicAffairs

NEW YORK

PublicAffairs books are available at special discounts for bulk purchases in the U.S. by corporations, institutions, and other organizations. For more information, please contact the Special Markets Department at the Perseus Books Group, 2300 Chestnut Street, Suite 200, Philadelphia, PA 19103, call (800) 810-4145, ext. 5000, or e-mail special .markets@perseusbooks.com.

Book design by Lisa Kreinbrink
Set in 11-point Janson by Eclipse Publishing Services

Library of Congress Cataloging-in-Publication Data
Sudetic, Chuck.
  The philanthropy of George Soros : building open societies / Chuck Sudetic ; with an introduction by George Soros, and an afterword by Aryeh Neier.
    p. cm.
  Includes bibliographical references and index.
  ISBN 978-1-58648-822-2 (hbk.) — ISBN 978-1-58648-859-8 (electronic)
  1. Soros, George. 2. Open Society Fund (New York) 3. Capitalists and financiers—Conduct of life. 4. Humanitarianism. I. Title.
  HG172.S63S83 2011
  361.7'6092--dc22

                                    2011005156

First Edition
10 9 8 7 6 5 4 3 2 1

Contents

Part IV

Minority Empowerment: The Roma

Part V

U.S. Open Society: Drugs, Crime, and Two Cities

The Philanthropy of George Soros

My Philanthropy

George Soros

I am both selfish and self-centered and I have no qualms about acknowledging it; yet over the past thirty years I have established a far-reaching philanthropic enterprise—the Open Society Foundations—whose annual budget used to hover around $500 million and is now climbing towards a billion. (Total expenditures since 1979 are about $8 billion.) The activities of the Open Society Foundations extend to every part of the globe and cover such a wide range of topics that even I am surprised by it. I am, of course, not the only one who is selfish and self-centered; most of us are. I am just willing to admit it. There are many truly charitable people in the world, but few of them amass the kind of wealth that is necessary to be a philanthropist.

I have always been leery of philanthropy. In my view, philanthropy goes against the grain; therefore it generates a lot of hypocrisy and many paradoxes. Here are some examples: Philanthropy is supposed to be devoted to the benefit of others, but philanthropists are primarily concerned with their own benefit; philanthropy is supposed to help people, yet it often makes people dependent and turns them into objects of charity; applicants tell foundations what they want to hear, then proceed to do what the applicant wants to do.

Given my critical attitude towards philanthropy, why do I devote such a large part of my wealth and energies to philanthropy? The answer is to be found partly in my personal background and history, partly in the conceptual framework that has guided me through my life, and partly in sheer happenstance.

*   *   *

The formative experience of my life was the German occupation of Hungary in 1944. I was Jewish and not yet fourteen years old. I could have easily perished in the Holocaust or suffered lasting psychological damage had it not been for my father, who understood the dangers and coped with them better than most others. My father had gone through a somewhat similar experience in the First World War, which prepared him for what happened in the Second.

As I like to tell the story, he joined the Austro-Hungarian army as a volunteer and was captured by the Russians. He was taken to Siberia as a prisoner of war. In the camp he became the editor of a handwritten literary magazine which was displayed on a plank, and it was called *The Plank*. The writers of the articles used to gather behind the plank and listen to the comments of the readers. My father brought home the handwritten pages, and I remember looking at them as a child. *The Plank* made him very popular, and he was elected the prisoners' representative. When some prisoners of war escaped from a neighboring camp, their representative was shot in retaliation. Instead of waiting for the same thing to happen in his camp, my father collected a group of prisoners and organized a break-out. They built a raft with the intention of drifting down to the ocean. But their knowledge of geography was deficient, and they did not realize that all the rivers of Siberia empty into the Arctic Ocean. When they recognized their mistake, they got off the raft and made their way back to civilization across the uninhabited taiga. They got caught up in the lawlessness of the Russian Revolution and went through some harrowing adventures. That was *his* formative experience.

Eventually my father made his way back to Hungary, but he came home a changed man. When he volunteered for the army he was an ambitious young man. As a result of his adventures in Russia, he lost his ambition and wanted nothing more from life than to enjoy it. Bringing up his two children was one of his chief joys. That made him a very good father. He also liked to help and guide other people and had a knack for striking up acquaintance with strangers. He held his own insights and judgment in high regard, but in other respects he was genuinely not a selfish or self-centered man.

When the Germans occupied Hungary on March 19, 1944, my father knew exactly what to do. He realized that these were abnormal times and people who followed the normal rules were at risk. He arranged false identities not only for his immediate family but also for a larger circle. He charged a fee, sometimes quite an exorbitant one, to those who could afford it and helped others for free. I had never seen him work so hard before. That was his finest hour. Both his immediate family and most of those whom he advised or helped managed to survive.

The year of German occupation, 1944, was *my* formative experience. Instead of submitting to our fate, we resisted an evil force that was much stronger than we were—yet we prevailed. Not only did we survive, but we managed to help others. This left a lasting mark on me, turning a disaster of unthinkable proportions into an exhilarating adventure.* That gave me an

---

* My father wrote an eminently readable memoir of our adventures in 1944. Tivadar Soros, *Masquerade: Dancing around Death in Nazi-Occupied Hungary* (New York: Arcade Publishing, 2001 and 2010).

appetite for taking risk, and under my father's wise guidance I learned how to cope with it—exploring the limits of the possible but not going beyond the limits. I positively relish confronting harsh reality, and I am drawn to tackling seemingly insoluble problems. Helping others never lost its positive connotation for me, but for a long time I had few opportunities to practice it.

After the heady adventures of the war and immediate postwar period, life in Hungary became very drab. The country was occupied by Russian troops, and the Communist Party consolidated its rule. I wanted out and, with my father's help, I managed to get out. In September 1947, I left for England to study.

Life in London was a big letdown. Aged seventeen with very little money and few connections, I was lonely and miserable. I managed to work my way through college, but it was not a pleasant experience. All students whose parents were resident in England were entitled to a county council stipend. I was an exception because my parents were not with me. Working one's way through college was not a well-trodden path, but that is what I had to do.

I had two encounters with philanthropy during that difficult period, and they have colored my attitude towards charity ever since. Shortly after I arrived in London I turned to the Jewish Board of Guardians to ask for financial support. They refused me on the grounds that their guidelines called for supporting only young people who were learning a trade, not students. Later on, when I was already a student at the London School of Economics, I took on a temporary job at Christmas time as a railroad porter and I broke my leg. I came out of the hospital on crutches, and I thought this was a good opportunity to get some money out of the Jewish Board of Guardians. I climbed two flights of stairs on my crutches and asked them for temporary support. They repeated their mantra about helping only apprentices, but they couldn't refuse me. They gave me three pounds, hardly enough to live on for a week. This continued for several weeks. Each time I had to climb the stairs on crutches to collect the money.

In the meantime, my roommate, having heard my story, decided to go to the Jewish Board of Guardians and declare himself ready to learn a trade. He didn't last long in the jobs they found him, but they kept supporting him. After a while, they wanted to send me to the Industrial Injuries Board for assistance, but I said I could not go there because I was working illegally and did not want to endanger my student visa. That was not true. My temporary job on the railroad was perfectly legal, but they did not know that. They had sent a social worker to check on me, but he did not find out. So, when they refused me further assistance, I felt morally justified to write an impassioned letter to the chairman of the board in which I said that "I will manage to survive but it makes me sad that the board of which you are the chairman is unwilling to help a young Jewish student who had broken his leg and was in need." That had the desired effect. The chairman arranged for me to receive three pounds a week by mail without having to climb the stairs. After I no longer needed the crutches and after taking a hitchhiking holiday in the south of France, I wrote to the chairman telling him that I no longer needed his assistance and thanked him for it. Although I had deceived the foundation, I felt morally justified because they had investigated and, having checked out my story, they should have been willing to help me.

My next encounter with philanthropy was when I was working nights as a waiter in a nightclub while studying during the day. When my tutor found out about it she turned to the Quakers, who sent me a questionnaire. After I filled it out, they sent me a check for forty pounds without any strings attached. That impressed me as the right way to help people. After the crash of 2008, I was able to arrange for nearly a million New York school children whose families were on welfare or food stamps to receive a check for two hundred dollars, no questions asked. I put up 20 percent of the cost on behalf of New York State so it could qualify for a grant from the federal government as part of the economic stimulus package. The Quakers' generosity bore ample dividends sixty years later, and I felt good about that in spite of the attacks by the *New York Post* decrying "welfare handouts."

After finishing college, I had a difficult time finding my way in the world. I had a number of false starts in England and eventually ended up in New York, first as an arbitrage trader, then as a security analyst and institutional salesman, and finally as the manager of one of the first hedge funds. During that period I was not particularly philanthropic. The only venture worth mentioning was an attempt to restore Central Park. In partnership with Dick Gilder, a broker and investor, we set up the Central Park Community Fund, but it was not particularly successful. Another organization, the Central Park Conservancy, established a close working relationship with the park administration and made much greater progress in restoring the park. My greatest accomplishment was to dissolve our organization and merge it into the successful one. During the process I discovered that charitable organizations have a life of their own which is independent of their stated mission, and it is easier to set up a charity than to wind it down.

*   *   *

Starting as a student at the London School of Economics and continuing in New York, I developed a conceptual framework, the theory of reflexivity, which served to guide me both in making money as a hedge fund manager and later in spending it as a policy-oriented philanthropist. Let me summarize its main components briefly because it played such an important role in my life, and it is difficult to understand my career as a hedge fund manager and philanthropist without it.

My theory seeks to explain the relationship between thinking and reality. It draws a distinction between human events and natural phenomena. What distinguishes them is that the former have thinking participants; the latter do not. In human events the participants' thinking plays a dual role: On the one hand, human agents seek to understand the situation in which they participate; this is the cognitive function. On the other hand, their understanding informs their decisions and through their actions influences the course of events; this is the causative or manipulative function. The two functions connect thinking and reality in the opposite direction, and when both are operating at the same time they interfere with each other. In the cognitive function reality is supposed to determine the participants' view of reality; in the causative function the participants' actions are supposed to determine the course of events. But that is the case only if the cognitive function deals with a reality that is independently given; it is clearly not the case when the course of events is contingent on the participants' view of reality. When the two functions operate concurrently and the supposedly independent variable of one function is the dependent variable of the other, neither function has a truly independent variable; and in its absence neither function provides a determinate result: The participants' views do not correspond to reality, and the outcome of their decisions will not correspond to their expectations. I call the interference between the two functions reflexivity.

By contrast, natural phenomena do not have thinking participants, only outside observers, and there is no manipulative function to interfere with the cognitive function. As a consequence, reality constitutes an independent criterion by which an outside observer's views can be judged and the cognitive function does yield determinate results. This does not mean that observers necessarily form the correct views; it means only that there is an independent criterion by which the truth or validity of their statements can be judged. The existence of an independent criterion has allowed natural science to produce remarkable results.

The success of natural science has encouraged scientists to seek to produce similarly conclusive results in the study of human affairs, but their endeavors have not been crowned by success. The discipline that advanced the furthest in that direction is economics, but it had to do violence to its subject matter in order to do so. Instead of studying reality, it established a hypothetical framework based on certain postulates. That was the method established by Euclid for the study of geometry, but Euclid's postulates closely resembled reality except for ignoring the curvature of the earth, whereas economics became further and further removed from reality. The uncertainties introduced by the participants' thinking had to be assumed away. Economics started with the assumption of perfect knowledge and ended up with the theory of rational expectations: a make-believe world in which the participants' expectations converge around a future which would prevail only if the participants' views converged around it. The closest analogy is with medieval theology, which debated how many angels can dance on the point of a needle. This whole economic edifice came crushing down in the crash of 2008.

Agents base their decisions not on reality but on their interpretation of reality, and the two are never identical. It is possible to obtain knowledge—natural science is the best example— but knowledge cannot cover all of reality because human beings are part of the world and in their endeavor to understand the world in which they live they have to introduce simplifications: analogies, metaphors, frames, decision rules, and the like. These simplifications themselves become part of reality. As a consequence, the complexity of reality will always exceed the understanding of reality. Nevertheless, people are obliged to act. In the absence of perfect knowledge they are guided by their emotions and illusions as well as knowledge, and their behavior introduces an element of uncertainty into the course of events. Imperfect knowledge or fallibility is not the only source of uncertainty, but it is an important one, particularly in human affairs, and it distinguishes social situations from natural phenomena. I attribute the difference to what I call the "human uncertainty principle."

Since perfect knowledge is unattainable, the degree and extent of people's misconceptions becomes all-important. The closer their interpretation comes to reality, the greater the likelihood that the outcome of their decisions will resemble their expectations. Judged by this criterion, recognizing fallibility and reflexivity—the two pillars of my conceptual framework— would constitute a major step forward in our understanding of human affairs.

Unfortunately, mankind has not yet taken that step. Ever since the Enlightenment, it has pursued knowledge instead. That is how the methods of natural science came to be applied to the study of human affairs. It was a logical step to take, but it was pushed too far. I call that the Enlightenment fallacy.

The Enlightenment saw reason as something apart from reality, like a searchlight illuminating reality. Setting reason apart from reality was appropriate to the Age of Enlightenment when there was so much to be discovered: Even the earth had not been fully explored. That was a fallacy, but it produced remarkable results. By putting statements into a separate universe from the facts to which they relate, it allowed the development of natural science. That works for natural phenomena but not for the study of human affairs.

I call fallacies that produce worthwhile results fertile fallacies, and I contend that civilizations are built on fertile fallacies. I do not mean to say that all knowledge is fallacious. What I mean is that our knowledge is limited, and in our search for better understanding we are liable to push what limited knowledge we have beyond the limits of its validity. That is what happened to economic theory. In the early stages it provided valuable insights; only after I left college did it take the wrong turn. I was reared on John Maynard Keynes and I read Frank Knight's seminal book *Risk, Uncertainty, and Profit*. That was the book that latter-day macroeconomic theorists and financial engineers forgot.

My conceptual framework was not as developed in my college days as it is today. But the core ideas were already there, and they extended not only to economics but also to politics and human affairs in general. My thinking was greatly influenced by Karl Popper, the Austrian-born philosopher, first through his book *Open Society and Its Enemies*, and then through his theory of scientific method. I finished my undergraduate courses a year early, and I had a year to kill before I would earn my degree. I chose Karl Popper as my tutor and wrote a couple of essays for him. After college I had to earn a living, but I never lost my interest in the complicated relationship between thinking and reality. I submitted an essay entitled "The Burden of Consciousness" to Popper several years after I left college. It was the first formulation of my conceptual framework and it is not all that different from the current one, only less complete.

My business career followed a tortuous path with many false starts and missteps, but eventually I ended up in charge of one of the first hedge funds in New York. Running a hedge fund was an all-absorbing activity. I started in 1969 with about $3 million. By 1979 the fund reached $100 million, mostly from retained earnings. About $40 million of that belonged to me. That was more than enough for me and my family, I felt. The strain of risk-taking on a leveraged basis was enormous. On one occasion, I subscribed to a very large amount of a new issue of British government bonds on short notice without previously arranging the necessary financing. I was rushing around the city of London trying to find a credit line, and walking down Leadenhall Street I thought I was having a heart attack. "I took on this risk to make a killing," I told myself, "but if I die now I end up as the loser. It doesn't make sense to risk my life to make money." That is when I decided to do something worthwhile with my money and set up a foundation. I thought long and hard about what I really cared about. I relied on my rather abstract conceptual framework for guidance and I honed in on the concept of open society, which is one of the cornerstones of that framework.

As far as I know, the term *open society* was first used by Henri Bergson, the French philosopher, in his book *The Two Sources of Morality and Religion*. One source was tribal and led to a closed society; the other was universal and it was associated with an open society. Karl Popper pointed out that open societies can be turned into closed ones by universal ideologies that claim to be in possession of the ultimate truth. That claim is false; therefore such ideologies can prevail only by using methods of compulsion. By contrast, open societies recognize that different people have different views and interests; they introduce man-made laws to enable people to live together in peace. Having experienced both Nazi and Communist rule in Hungary, I was deeply impressed by Popper's ideas. I defined the mission of my foundation as (1) opening closed societies, (2) making open societies more viable, and (3) promoting a critical mode of thinking. That was in 1979.

*   *   *

The foundation had a slow start. I was aware of the pitfalls and paradoxes of philanthropy, and I wanted to avoid them. I undertook an apprenticeship at Helsinki Watch—a fledgling human rights organization which later became Human Rights Watch. I attended the Wednesday morning meetings where current events and activities were discussed. I also went on a fact-finding trip to El Salvador and Nicaragua, which were at that time in the midst of civil war. I learned a lot but did relatively little on my own. I did get involved with a Russian refugee, Vladimir Bukovsky, who was active in Afghanistan, but I drew the line at financing activities that might result in people killing or getting killed. Later I went to Russia on another fact-finding trip, and there I struck up an intimate relationship with a refusenik* and started sending him cash through a Swissair stewardess for distribution to other dissidents in Russia. Eventually, my foundation became a major source of financial support for dissident movements throughout Eastern Europe.

My first major independent undertaking was in South Africa. I had a Zulu friend in New York, Herbert Vilakazi, who was a university lecturer in Connecticut. He returned to South Africa to take up a post at the University of Transkai—one of the homelands under the apartheid system. I visited him in 1980 and gained insight into South Africa from an unusual angle. Here was a closed society with all the institutions of a first world country,

---

* A person who was refused an exit visa.

but they were off limits to the majority of the population on racial grounds. Where could I find a better opportunity for opening up a closed society? I met with the vice chancellor of Cape Town University, Stuart Saunders, who was eager to open the university to black students. All students accepted by the university had their tuition paid by the state. I jumped at the opportunity to use the resources of the apartheid state for opening it up and offered to pay the living expenses for eighty black students.

I traveled to South Africa again the next year, but that trip was less successful. I wanted to support African arts and culture, so I asked Nadine Gordimer, who would go on to win a Nobel Prize for literature, to arrange a meeting with African cultural leaders to discuss how best to do it. But the meeting was a flop. My cover was blown by then. Everyone knew that I was a wealthy philanthropist from New York, and the meeting's participants saw a pot of gold sitting in the middle of the room; all they could discuss was how to divide it amongst themselves. I decided to abandon my project, disappointing everyone.

I visited Cape Town University and discovered that the number of black students had increased by less than eighty, either because some of the Open Society scholarships were given to students already enrolled or because some students had dropped out. The students I met seemed thoroughly disaffected. They felt unwelcome, discriminated against, and forced into an alien culture, and they had difficulties meeting the academic requirements. I also met with the faculty and found them far less open-minded than the vice chancellor.

I decided to discontinue the scheme; I would, however, see the first cohort through. In retrospect, that turned out to be a bad decision. The vice chancellor engaged a black mentor for the black students—it happened to be my friend Herbert Vilakazi—and subsequently they did much better. It would have been great to have a larger number of black university graduates when the apartheid system was abolished. But at the time I made my decision the apartheid system seemed firmly established. I tried a few other projects as well, but I came to feel that nothing I did would change the system. The fact that they tolerated my activities merely served to demonstrate how tolerant they were. Instead of me taking advantage of the apartheid state, the apartheid state seemed to be taking advantage of me. In retrospect, I wish I had been more persistent. This experience taught me that it is worth fighting seemingly hopeless battles.

My next major venture was in my native Hungary. In the early 1980s, the Communist regime in Hungary was eager to be accepted by the IMF and the World Bank, offering me an opportunity to bring out a group of Hungarian dissidents to spend a year at New York University. They were allowed to leave the country. This gave me a knowledge base about Hungary on which I could build.

In 1984, I approached the Hungarian government about setting up a foundation there, and somewhat to my surprise they responded positively. We engaged in protracted negotiations in which I was guided by my dissident friends. It was agreed that my foundation would support Hungarian culture in general and not only dissidents. The Hungarian Academy of Sciences, then under the strict control of the political police, was designated as my partner.

I visited the country repeatedly and selected a group of people in whom I could have confidence and who were also acceptable to the government. Together with the vice president of the academy, they would constitute the board of our joint venture. So far so good. But the authorities insisted that the decisions of the board should be carried out by a secretariat controlled by the political police, and that was a deal breaker. I went to see the cultural czar of the Communist Party, George Aczel, to inform him that we had reached an impasse. "I hope you won't leave with bad feelings," he said. I answered: "I can't help it, having put so much effort into it." I was already at the door when he said, "What would it take for you to go ahead?" "An independent secretariat," I replied. We agreed to have two secretaries, one nominated by the academy and one by me. Every document would have to be countersigned by both to be valid.* That is how the Hungarian foundation came into existence. I also hired my first employee, a Hungarian émigré, in New York at what eventually became the headquarters of the Open Society Foundations. Until then, the staff had consisted of my wife, Susan Weber.

The foundation in Hungary worked like a charm. It was exempt from all the pitfalls which beset normal foundations because civil society adopted it as its own. We relied on a simple precept I derived from Karl Popper's concept of open society: The state dogma, promoted by the ruling Communists, was false; by providing an alternative we could expose its falsehood. Accordingly, the foundation supported every cultural initiative that was not an expression of official dogma—from zither clubs to farmers' cooperatives. The amounts awarded were very small because most of the initiatives used state facilities and the people engaged in them drew salaries from the state. We used the state's own resources to undermine it.

The Hungarian forints needed for these awards were generated by giving dollar grants to cultural and educational institutions. They were flush with Hungarian forints but devoid of foreign currency, so they were willing to make contributions to the Hungarian foundation at better than the official exchange

---

* I believe that is the formula the U.S. government ought to follow to distribute aid in Pakistan and other countries which cannot be fully trusted.

rate. Our most successful venture was to provide them with Xerox machines. This served a dual purpose. Not only did it secure Hungarian currency for the Hungarian foundation, but it also spread information that was not otherwise easily available. The Karl Marx Institute of Szeged, for instance, used the Xerox machines to print clandestine samizdat literature.

The foundation did not have to protect itself from applicants who wanted to take advantage of it because it was protected by those whom it supported. If there were any abuses, they were reported by those who regarded the foundation as their own. For instance, the foundation abandoned plans to support the Association of the Blind for the production and distribution of talking books when it was warned that the organization was corrupt. This network of information made the foundation extremely efficient. With a budget of $3 million a year, it actually could offer an alternative to the Ministry of Culture, which had a much bigger budget. Indeed, we became known as the alternative ministry of culture. One of our most successful initiatives was to support independent student-run colleges and an independent students' union which later became the kernel of one of the main political parties in Hungary, Fidesz.

Of course, the foundation was not without its problems—for instance, it developed a clientele which became used to receiving support, eventually making it less open to society at large than it should have been—but it escaped many of the defects that characterize normal foundations. Its success exceeded my expectations. That was the happenstance that gave me the appetite for philanthropy, which in turn provided me with a motivation to keep making money as a hedge fund manager.

*   *   *

In 1986, I set up a foundation in China. The Hungarian foundation had organized a highly successful exchange of economists between China and Hungary. Their Chinese counterpart, the Institute for Economic Reform, became my partner in China. I found a Chinese émigré, Liang Heng, to be my emissary. He had written a well-received autobiography, *Son of the Revolution*, and later published a periodical called *The Chinese Intellectual*. I visited China repeatedly and established personal contact with the prime minister, Zhao Ziyang, and his chief of staff, Bao Tong. The latter authorized the establishment of the foundation on his sole signature, without going through the routine of gathering the signatures of a large number of authorities. This cost him dearly later on.

The foundation was supposed to give grants based on merit, not connections. This was an alien concept in China, where connections are paramount, and it caused a lot of friction with our institutional partner, which kept favoring its own staff. China practiced what I called the "feudalism of the mind": Those who received support felt indebted to their benefactor, and the benefactor was in turn obliged to take care of those whom it supported because their fate reflected on his own standing. In retrospect it was a mistake to impose an alien concept on the foundation; it would have been better simply to support my institutional partner, which was in the forefront of economic and political reform.

My foundation in China had an unfortunate history: It became the subject of factional infighting within the Communist Party. Bao Tong was attacked by the hardliners for allowing on his sole signature the establishment of a foundation which was accused of being a subversive organization. He and the prime minister protected themselves against an investigation by the internal political police by placing the foundation into the hands of the external political police. Since the two organizations were co-equal, this protected them, but it left the foundation in the hands of the political police. When I found out about it, I closed the foundation. That was just before the Tiananmen Square massacre. Subsequently, Bao Tong was one of the few people who was actually put in prison.

It was more than a decade after I closed down the foundation that it was rehabilitated in China. This took the form of my being invited to address a government-sponsored conference on China's future in Beijing in 2001. In 2005, the Chinese again grew suspicious of me when I was falsely accused by President Putin of masterminding the "color revolutions" in Georgia and Ukraine. These were popular uprisings against corrupt and oppressive regimes. My foundation did support the criticism, but did not mastermind or finance the uprisings. Relations have remained ambivalent ever since. That is a pity. I regard China as a rising power and I attribute great importance to closer cooperation between China and the rest of the world.

In 1987, I tried to replicate the Hungarian foundation model in Poland. I was already supporting a program for visiting Polish academics at Oxford University, and sent money to the cultural arm of Solidarity, so we had good connections within Polish civil society. With the help of Zbigniew Pelczynski, who ran the Oxford program, we obtained the permission of the Polish authorities.

Right from the beginning, the board of the Polish foundation refused to follow the Hungarian model. It insisted that the foundation should take a more targeted approach, focusing on selected program areas instead of opening its doors wide to all kinds of proposals. I decided to give them some rope to hang themselves, but they turned out to be right, and subsequently we adopted the Polish model in other countries as well. That also taught me a lesson. I realized that the people living in the countries where I had foundations understood their countries better than I did, and from then on I deferred to the judgment of the local boards. If I seriously disagreed with their judgment, I changed the board.

*   *   *

I also started a foundation in the Soviet Union in 1987. In December 1986, Prime Minister Mikhail Gorbachev made an unprecedented phone call to the nuclear scientist and human rights activist Andrei Sakharov, who had been exiled to the city of Gorky (now Nizhni-Novgorod). Gorbachev invited him to return to Moscow "to resume your patriotic activities." I took that as a signal that something had fundamentally changed. If it had been business as usual, Sakharov might have been allowed to leave the Soviet Union but not to return to Moscow. I flew to Moscow as soon as I could.

Not long after my arrival I identified the newly established Cultural Foundation, of which Gorbachev's wife Raisa was the patron, as a potential partner. I visited Sakharov and asked him to be my personal representative on the board, but he refused. "You will be merely lining the coffers of the KGB with dollars," he warned me. He took me for a naive American, and I was proud to have proved him wrong. Even so, my counterparties at the Cultural Foundation turned out to be associated with the KGB, as they informed me in confidence when they took me for a stroll in the open air. Sakharov did advise me on potential board members. I had already established contact with Tatyana Zaslavskaya, an independent-minded sociologist from Novosibirsk. Sakharov recommended Yuri Afanasiev, the historian, and Grigory Baklanov, the editor of *Znamya*; I also identified Daniil Granin and Valentin Rasputin, writers, Tengiz Buachidze, a philologist from Georgia, and Boris Rauschenbakh, a space scientist and religious philosopher, as board members in whom I could have confidence.

I made a deal with the head of the Institute of Personal Computers, who paid me for imported computers at five times the official exchange rate. And that is how my foundation in the Soviet Union, the Cultural Initiative, came into existence.

We started operating right away, without waiting for official permission. I remembered what my father had told me as a child about his experiences during the Russian Revolution: In turbulent times the impossible becomes possible. Other Western foundations insisted on getting permission from the authorities before they started operating. For the next year or two the Cultural Initiative was practically the only game in town, so we could make a big impact. Perhaps our most successful effort was to commission and distribute new textbooks in the social sciences, history, and law to high schools and universities. We also kept alive the so-called thick journals, famous literary magazines, which would have perished without our support.

I came up with a plan to reform the Soviet economy. Instead of geographically defined free trade zones, I proposed freeing up a particular segment of the Soviet economy, notably the food processing industry. I envisioned it as the embryo of a market economy embedded in the womb of the planned economy. I brought in a group of Western economists led by Wassily Leontief, a Nobel Laureate of Russian origin. To my amazement, Premier Nikolai Ryzhkov, chairman of the Council of Ministers, ordered the heads of the various state agencies to attend our first meeting. This shows how eager the authorities were for Western assistance. I was little known at that time; yet the heads of the most powerful state agencies were lined up to meet the experts I brought. The discussions went on for a while, but it soon became clear to me that the planned economy was too diseased to support a healthy embryo.

We also brought in Western legal experts to help with the establishment of a civil code. But my ability to influence Western policy did not keep pace with the impact my foundation had in the Soviet empire. That may be attributed to a cognitive dissonance between East and West. The East was in the midst of a systemic collapse; in the West it was business as usual. When I proposed a new Marshall Plan for the Soviet empire at an East–West conference in the spring of 1989 in Potsdam, which was then still in East Germany, I was literally laughed at. (The proposal was greeted with amusement, the *Frankfurter Allgemeine* reported.) And that was not my only attempt to influence Western policy that fell flat.

The Soviet system was rapidly disintegrating, and it was beyond the capacity of the foundation on its own to lead the transformation from a closed to an open society. Instead, the foundation itself got caught up in the process of disintegration. We discovered that some officials of the foundation were corrupt and lost valuable time reorganizing the leadership. Who knows what we could have accomplished had the foundation functioned properly.

I was at the very heart of the political turmoil at the time—a strange position for a foreigner to find himself in. I was intimately involved in the power struggle between rival groups of economic reformers. I became very close to Grigory Yavlinsky, who tried to put my father's precept, that in revolutionary times one must attempt the impossible, into practice. He was the real force behind the Shatalin Plan and the 500 Days Program, which sought to replace the Soviet Union with an economic union modeled on the European Common Market. When I brought in a group of Western economists to advise him, they were captured and practically kept prisoners for a day in a rural retreat by a rival group of reformers. I ended up taking Yavlinsky and his team to the annual meeting of the World Bank and IMF in Washington, where they fought for recognition with the rival team. Although I managed to get them a hearing, they went home empty-handed, and Gorbachev rejected their program in favor of the less radical one. Shortly thereafter, Gorbachev himself was removed from power.

In the meantime, the Berlin Wall had fallen and the Soviet empire disintegrated. As the Communist regimes of Eastern Europe collapsed, I followed close on their heels and established foundations in one country after another. I was in Prague just before Christmas 1989, where I learned from the Communist Party's Marian Čalfa, who was then prime minister and acting president of Czechoslovakia, that he was determined to hand over power peacefully to Václav Havel. This came as news to Havel. I arrived in Bucharest early in January 1990, shortly after the Communist dictator Nicolae Ceauşescu was executed. I found the city under siege conditions. From there I went on to Sofia to open the Bulgarian foundation. I also traveled around in the constituent republics of the Soviet Union and established local foundations before they became independent countries.

My visit to Ukraine was particularly memorable. I attended a meeting in Kiev with the cultural elite of the country, and they proposed all kinds of ideas for the foundation. I found all of them impractical and said so. At the end of the meeting, I apologized for responding so negatively. But they did not mind at all. "You don't realize how refreshing it is to have someone say no outright; our authorities always say yes and then they don't do anything." That was a lesson for me. From then on, I had no hesitation in rejecting proposals which I found impractical.

These were hectic and euphoric times. I had a peculiar under-standing of far-from-equilibrium conditions which I derived from my father's experiences during the Russian Revolution and my own during the German occupation of Hungary. This enabled us to take advantage of the revolutionary situation.

I moved my family to London so I could be closer to the scene of action. I distributed funds without any coherent plan. I saw open society as a more complex form of social organization than the Communist system that was collapsing. To achieve a systemic transformation required a helping hand from the outside. Every-thing needed to be done at once. So when I received a proposal that seemed to be backed by an ability to deliver, I usually approved it. That is how the expenditures of my Open Society Foundations jumped from $3 million to more than $300 million in the space of a few years. It could not have been done according to a plan. We operated without a budget, and eventually the en-tire foundations network was running out of control. We were mired in the chaos in which we flourished. We urgently needed to introduce some order into the chaos.

I was fortunate to be able to recruit the executive director of Human Rights Watch, Aryeh Neier, to become president of the Open Society Foundations in 1993. He took charge. I was not allowed to travel on my own anymore; somebody had to accom-pany me and take note of all the commitments I was making, otherwise they would not be honored. That is when the founda-tions network started to take on its present shape. We established foundations under local leadership in practically every country of the former Soviet empire; these came to be known in our parlance as the network of national foundations. We also estab-lished what we called network programs, which cut across national boundaries and covered specific program areas such as justice, public health, and education. This created a matrix which combined local knowledge through the national foundations with professional expertise through the network programs. The matrix was open-ended: National foundations could have projects outside the fields covered by network programs, and network programs could be active in countries where we had no national foundations. The Soviet system continued to disintegrate, but our organization started to become more cohesive. The chaotic years had served their purpose. The foundations had been first on the scene and earned a reputation for their willingness to attempt the impossible. Now their work became more professional.

About a third of our budget was spent on education—bringing a child-centered approach emphasizing critical thinking to a region used to authoritarian methods and rote learning. I established the Central European University, a postgraduate institution, first in Prague and then in Budapest with a branch in Warsaw. I also set up a Higher Education Support Program, which spent about an equal amount of money on other newly established educational institutions. In addition, we supported systemic reform both in higher and general education. And we introduced "Step by Step" for preschool-age children, which was a modification of the Head Start program for kindergarten.

Another third or more of our budget went to support civil society in the broadest sense with particular emphasis on civil rights and the protection of vulnerable populations. We identified the Roma, or "gypsies" as most people pejoratively called them, as the worst case of social exclusion on ethnic grounds in Eastern Europe, and we devoted increasing amounts of money and energy to deal with the problem—at first supporting their culture and then their education. Our greatest achievement was to raise a new generation of educated young Roma who were proud to be Roma.

As the disintegration of the Soviet system continued and the suffering of the population increased, so did our budget. I devoted $100 million to establish an International Science Foundation whose objective was to preserve the best of Soviet science from destruction. It distributed emergency grants of $500 each to the most eminent scientists in the former Soviet Union. Due to runaway inflation, that was enough to support a family for a year. Selection was based on a simple and objective criterion: three citations in an internationally recognized scientific journal. More than 30,000 scientists qualified. The rest of the money was committed to research programs selected by an international jury of scientists, using the peer-review system. The scheme was an outstanding success: The entire amount was committed within a year. My objective was not only to save the best of Soviet science, which I considered a crowning achievement of the human intellect, but also to demonstrate that foreign aid could be administered efficiently.

In a *Wall Street Journal* article in 1992, I proposed that the aid offered by the International Monetary Fund should be administered along the same lines. Instead of providing budgetary support to the Soviet government and its successors, the aid should be earmarked for the payment of pensions and unemployment benefits and its distribution closely supervised. The idea was a good one, but it did not go anywhere. Generally speaking, when I implemented an idea on my own, it worked; when I tried to influence public policy, I did not get very far. This has changed with the passage of time: More recently I have been more successful in mobilizing public support. I firmly believe that if my *Wall Street Journal* proposal had been followed, history would have taken a different course. The people of the Soviet Union would have seen some practical and tangible benefits from Western aid, and their attitude towards the West would be quite different. Europe is paying a heavy price today for having failed to come to the assistance of the Russian people in their hour of need.

I also matured a lot in the course of these adventures. At first, I was carried away by the almost unlimited opportunities opened up by the collapse of the Soviet system and I was so eager to play a role in history that I did not hesitate to attempt the impossible. Gradually, I learned to discern between what could work and what could not. I became more discriminating, and less concerned with making myself important than with achieving something worthwhile. I remember a visit to Moscow when two of the most important people I was supposed to meet canceled their appointment with me because of the policy I was advocating. Earlier, I would have been upset; now I felt good about the stand I took. More recently, when people asked me whether I had met Putin I could honestly say I did not want to.

The year 1992 brought an important change in my status as a public figure. When the currency of the United Kingdom, the pound sterling, was forced out of the European Exchange Rate Mechanism, I became known as "the man who broke the Bank of England." This happened because I did not deny that my hedge fund had played a role in the event; the media then exaggerated my role. I deliberately allowed it to happen in order to establish a platform from which I could speak on other issues. And it worked. Suddenly I had a voice that could be heard.

That year Yugoslavia was caught up in war, and I used my platform to announce a $50 million fund for humanitarian assistance to the civilian population of war-torn Bosnia. My announcement at Christmas time drew attention to the plight of the civilian population. The original idea behind my donation was to get aid workers into the war zone, which in turn would compel the United Nations troops to adopt more aggressive rules of engagement to protect them. That is not what happened. UN troops did not intervene to prevent the massacre at Srebrenica. But a Texan genius of humanitarian assistance, Fred Cuny, used the money to provide gas, electricity, and water for Sarajevo as well as seeds for growing vegetables. The idea behind my contribution didn't work, but the way Fred Cuny used my money did. It may not be an exaggeration to say that it helped the people of Sarajevo to survive. Shortly thereafter Cuny was killed in Chechnya.

I visited Sarajevo in November 1993 when the city was under siege. I did it reluctantly because I was not eager to put my life at risk. It was a pretty scary trip flying in an Ilyushin-76, one of the world's largest planes. We were sitting next to stacks of gas pipes lying on the floor. The Ukrainian crew was tightening and loosening the straps that held the pipes together as the plane was banking and landing. Then we had ten minutes to clear the airport.

I went to Sarajevo for a ceremonial opening of the water plant that Fred Cuny had built. It had been flown in by plane in modules and installed into a road tunnel in the side of a mountain. But the local authorities did not give permission for the water to be turned on. We never found out why. Either somebody was making a lot of money selling water or the government wanted to continue having people killed by snipers while waiting for water in order to have pictures on TV generating sympathy for the city's plight. Or both. I had to threaten going public with my protest before permission to turn on the spigots was granted.

The task of putting a semblance of order to the foundations that had sprung up across Eastern Europe and the former Soviet Union was an arduous one, but not as all-absorbing or enjoyable as the revolutionary period. Our annual spending peaked around

$600 million before we started introducing fiscal discipline. The goal was to cut spending in half, but it was never reached because new opportunities arose elsewhere.

*   *   *

When the Duvalier regime was overturned in Haiti and American troops occupied the country in 1994, I felt this called for establishing a foundation there. Aryeh Neier knew just the right person, Michèle Pierre-Louis, to run it. Aryeh also knew a good person for Guatemala. We set up a foundation there whose board had a unique character: It combined urban liberal intellectuals with leaders of indigenous communities from the countryside. Then the apartheid system was abandoned in South Africa and Nelson Mandela became president. Given our principles, our history in South Africa, and our experiences in the former Soviet Union, I felt obliged to set up a national foundation in South Africa. From there we branched out to other parts of Africa, and our network programs also started to reach out to other parts of the world.

By 1995, I felt that we had done enough on the first point of our agenda, opening up closed societies, so that we could pass on to the second, making open societies more viable. The activities of the Open Society Foundations were concentrated in foreign countries; it was time to do something at home. I reflected on the deficiencies of open society in America and developed a strategic plan which I then submitted to a select group of social philosophers for critical examination.

Two ideas were novel. First, market values had penetrated into areas where they did not properly belong; most notably they had undermined professional values. Liberal professions like medicine, law, and journalism had been turned into businesses. The primacy of professional values needed to be reaffirmed. Second, in certain areas fear had stifled the critical process and had given rise to false dogmas characterized by prejudice and intolerance, which undermine the principles of open society. I identified two such areas: the American attitude towards death and the American government's drug policy. They have something in common: Both drug addiction and death constitute insoluble problems, and there is an understandable inclination to look for false solutions. The solutions make the problems worse than they need be. In both cases they involve a refusal to accept the existence of an insoluble problem: Doctors prolong life at all cost, and drug warriors advocate zero tolerance. Later on the two areas proved to be more intimately connected: In retrospect, the "war on drugs" could be seen as the precursor of the "war on terror."

The rest of our programs in the United States were the outgrowth of our programs in the rest of the world: social justice, vulnerable populations, civil rights, and the criminal justice system. The strategy passed critical examination and we started implementing it. I concerned myself mainly with the two ideas I had introduced. I was happy to delegate the other areas to Aryeh Neier, who knew a lot more about them than I did.

The Project on Death in America was perhaps our most successful domestic program. It gave life to a new field. The American attitude of denial applied both to the medical profession and to the general public. We found a group of experts who knew how to deal with dying patients, and they transformed the care of terminal patients as a medical discipline by establishing fellowships at various medical institutions. They helped enlighten the general public more indirectly. The most effective effort was a five-part television series on public television by Bill Moyers. That was not financed by the Open Society Foundations, but Moyers drew heavily on work sponsored by us. Dying ceased to be a taboo subject. We celebrated our success by withdrawing from the field. Other foundations moved in as we withdrew. But more recently we reentered the field by cosponsoring a second generation of projects which were spawned by the first one.

We made less progress on drug policy. It is a highly contentious field dominated by extremists. I don't know what the right drug policy is; I only know that the war on drugs has done more harm than drugs themselves. When I started opposing the war on drugs, I was denounced as a drug legalizer. Actually I do believe that it would be better to legalize drugs than to persist in the current policies, but I am reluctant to say so because that would play into the hands of the extremists who want to frame the issue as an either/or proposition: Either you support the war on drugs or you are a drug legalizer. I see drug policy more as a matter of trial and error.

The Open Society Foundations advocate harm reduction, provided harm is defined so that it includes not only the harm done by drugs but also the harm done by prohibition. Since legalization is not socially acceptable, using harm reduction as the goal allows for a process of trial and error to unfold. How far it will go depends on how public opinion evolves. I am also agnostic on how far it should go, but as I see the increasing damage wrought by the prevailing U.S. and UN policies, particularly in places like Afghanistan, Mexico, Haiti, Guatemala, and other parts of Latin America and Africa, I am increasingly in favor of pushing as far as possible.

The war on drugs cannot succeed because it violates the most elementary laws of economics—ones that were not discredited by the crash of 2008. Interdicting supply when demand is inelastic—and what could be more inelastic than addiction?—merely serves to increase prices and profit margins. High prices stimulate supply, and wide profit margins encourage drug pushing that generates addiction and inelastic demand. The tougher the law enforcement, the tougher the people attracted into the business. That is the trap in which we are currently caught. Fortunately attitudes in the U.S. are beginning to change. People who smoked pot and perhaps tried more serious drugs as children are becoming parents, and the costs and injustices of incarceration are beginning to sink in. The process is likely to accelerate under the impetus of the impending squeeze on state finances. I see better prospects for radical reform than at any time since I became involved in drug policy. Unfortunately, it may not come soon enough to save the situation in Afghanistan.

The project to reaffirm professional values has had mixed results. In the legal profession, we have been very successful in establishing individual fellowships for practicing public service law but much less successful in promoting professional standards in the selection of judges. The process has become even more politicized. In journalism, we sponsored several initiatives in investigative journalism, but otherwise we made little progress in addressing the problems of a profession that is essential to an open society and is in the midst of a technological transformation. In medicine, we established an institute for protecting the medical profession from the enticements of the pharmaceutical industry, but we have not been able to modify the mercenary attitude prevailing in professional associations and among some doctors. The recent debate on health care legislation has demonstrated how little public understanding there is about the meaning of health care. The American system provides payment for medical procedures, not health care. The national health care systems of Europe and Canada do a better job in spite of their imperfections, but national health care is a nonstarter in America; it is denounced as socialism. The influence of special interests is pervasive, and it has poisoned the legislative process.

My interest in the shortcomings of America as an open society and my concern about the failure of Western assistance to the former Soviet empire led me to study the deficiencies of global capitalism. In February 1997, I wrote an article for *The Atlantic Monthly* entitled "The Capitalist Threat" that questioned the precepts of the Washington consensus. After the emerging markets crisis of 1997, I expanded it into a book under the title *The Crisis of Global Capitalism*. In 2000, I wrote another book, *On Globalization*, where I advocated a set of reforms, but they were not taken seriously. One of these reforms, namely the use of Special Drawing Rights came into serious consideration only after the crash of 2008.

When Putin came to power in 1999, our foundation in Russia came under attack and was effectively chased out of the country. We had rented a building with an option to buy. However, the original owner sold the building to a Russian gangster landlord, who managed to replace the contract deposited at the court with a forged one without the option to buy. He then proceeded to take possession of our office when the lease expired. At the time I was not sure whether this was the work of a solitary Russian gangster, but in retrospect I am more inclined to believe that it had the connivance of the authorities. Anyhow, I concluded that the Russian government no longer needed or deserved my assistance and I closed the foundation.

It was rather a sad ending to a valiant philanthropic effort, but I have no regrets. The foundation could not have succeeded on its own in helping Russia to make the transition from a closed to an open society. And, as I said before, I believe that if the Western governments had followed its example, history would have taken a different course. I believe that in philanthropy one should do the right thing whether or not it succeeds. That is the big difference between philanthropic and business investments. I am certain that the work of the foundation was appreciated by the Russian people, and it will have a positive influence in the long run in spite of all the adverse propaganda directed against it by the Putin regime.

One of the reasons why President Putin came to regard me as a personal enemy was my support for Mikheil Saakashvili in Georgia. That is a truly sad story as far as I am concerned. During the presidency of Eduard Shevardnadze, Georgia became very corrupt. A major anticorruption campaign was launched by a group of reformers led by Saakashvili, who was the minister of justice at the time, and Zurab Zhvania, who was president of the Parliament. It was supported by my foundation and I became personally involved. It was also supported by President Shevardnadze, whom I considered a decent person but burnt out. The anticorruption program itself was well formulated and ambitious, but it could not get off the ground. Every time I visited Georgia, President Shevardnadze made a gesture of support, but he could never deliver because the main source of corruption was the Ministry of Interior, and his life literally depended on the security services. Eventually the reformers lost their patience. Saakashvili and Zhvania left the government and formed a political party in opposition to President Shevardnadze. I expressed my support for them by giving them the 2003 Open Society Prize on behalf of the Central European University. The opposition was successful at the polls. An independent exit poll, supported by my foundation among others, gave them a clear majority, but the official results declared the government party as the winner. The people believed the exit poll, not the official results, and there was a revolution. Saakashvili became president.

I was elated and did whatever I could to help him succeed. I donated several million dollars to a capacity-building fund set up by the United Nations Development Program, which paid supplemental salaries of a thousand dollars a month to members of Saakashvili's cabinet and a hundred dollars a month to personnel of the police force. This allowed Saakashvili to impose discipline on the police and order them to remove the roadblocks where they extorted bribes from the passing traffic. This was a tangible anticorruption measure which greatly enhanced his popularity. But the situation deteriorated when the Saakashvili administration arrested a large number of prominent businessmen on corruption charges and extorted large sums of money from them for their release. The monies went into a slush fund which was used for the purchase of arms to defend Georgia against an expected attack by Russia. Being a slush fund it eventually became a source of corruption.

My foundation in Georgia spoke out against this lawless behavior, and in the absence of a parliamentary opposition it became the most vocal critic of the new government. I personally was at first inclined to be more tolerant of the government's excesses, arguing that in revolutionary situations the normal rules don't apply, but when they did not cease I also became more critical. Saakashvili in power turned out to be much less of a paragon of open society values than he was in opposition.

In the meantime, I was accused by the Russian media of being Saakashvili's pay master, and Putin advised the rulers of the Central Asian republics to close down my foundations. Fortunately most of them decided against it, but the foundations felt the pressure, and there were adverse repercussions in other parts of the world as well. This painful lesson taught me to keep a greater distance from the internal politics of the countries where I have foundations.

That conclusion is easier to reach in theory than to implement in practice. The strategy we have developed to deal with individual countries greatly depends on internal political conditions.

We take a two-pronged approach. On the one hand, we help civil society to hold governments accountable. On the other, we try to work with those governments which are willing to accept our help to meet their obligations better. We can be more effective if we can exercise both functions, and we can be most effective at times of democratic regime change when a new government is eager to establish a more open society but does not have the capacity to do so. Strengthening their capacity is often our greatest contribution. That is what we did when the Soviet system collapsed. We brought in foreign expertise and provided financial support to qualified nationals of the countries concerned to return from abroad. And that is what we did a decade later in Georgia. When I look back on that difficult experience, I am not sure whether I would want to do anything differently.

The real lesson I learned in Georgia is that helping countries in transition is a difficult and thankless task. We have had similar experiences in other places where systemic reforms introduced by one government were systematically undone by the next one. Russia is the prime example. The freedoms that prevailed during the chaotic Yeltsin years have all but disappeared under Putin. Still, there is a more subtle lesson to be learned. It is dangerous to build systemic reforms on a close association with one particular government. Systemic reforms need broad public participation and support. That is what makes them irreversible.

*   *   *

In the twenty-first century the Open Society Foundations went global. It would have been unwieldy to establish national foundations all over the world, so we started establishing regional foundations, one for Southern Africa, covering the nine countries belonging to the Southern African Development

Community (SADC), one for the eighteen countries in Western Africa belonging to the Economic Community of West African States (ECOWAS), and one for Eastern Africa covering first Kenya and slowly expanding to the neighboring countries. When Suharto fell, we established a foundation in Indonesia in 2000. After the invasion of Afghanistan, we established a program there as well as in Pakistan. We now have a small number of grants in Iraq as well. In other parts of the world, notably the Middle East, Southeast Asia, and Latin America, our engagement is less formal but nevertheless real.

In addition to the matrix that combines national foundations with network programs, we opened up a new dimension which I call "the network of networks." This involves close cooperation and substantial financial support to independent organizations such as Global Witness, International Crisis Group, and more recently the European Council on Foreign Relations (ECFR) and the Institute for New Economic Thinking (INET). This has become my favorite formula for entering new fields of activity because the ability to raise funds from others establishes a quasi-objective standard of performance that we lack in our wholly owned foundations network. Our financial support ought in theory not to exceed one third of the total budget of the organizations we support so that they maintain their independence.

As I survey my foundations network, I cannot give a proper accounting of the far-reaching and varied activities going on inside because I am not aware of all of them. As I travel around I keep on discovering them, and they are a great source of satisfaction to me. The activities of which I am not aware are often the best; it is the problematic ones that are brought to my attention. Only Aryeh Neier and a few others who participate in the budget review process are familiar with the whole range of activities—and the budget process takes six weeks to complete.

The Open Society Foundations have grown organically by responding to needs and opportunities as they arise. In my opinion, that is the right way. Many other foundations are engaged in meeting their own institutional needs. We try to resist that. We pride ourselves, in that sense, as being a selfless foundation, and that has been a source of strength for us. We have been able to cooperate with other foundations, and we have accomplished a lot more by not claiming ownership of the projects. Other institutions need to claim success in order to raise funds; we satisfy our institutional requirements by actually accomplishing something whether it is recognized or not. Paradoxically this has gained us more friends and allies than beating our own drum.

A selfish man with a selfless foundation—how do the two fit together? Let me explain. I formed a rather negative view of foundations when I was a supplicant, and I have not changed my mind since I became an insider. There is something inherently self-contradictory in altruism, but most foundations see no need to recognize it and even less to resolve it. When you are giving away money, the recipients flatter you and do everything they can to make you feel good, so the contradictions are obscured by a thick layer of hypocrisy. That is what makes me leery of philanthropy. The foundations set the rules, and others have to live by them. Applicants can of course have their own way: They can tell the foundation what it wants to hear and then proceed to do what they want to do.

Well, I have resolved the seeming contradiction between a self-centered philanthropist and a selfless foundation. It is consciousness that has made me self-aware, and it has also made me aware how inadequate my mortal self is as the sole beneficiary of my consciousness. In other words, I have a very big ego—far too big for my mortal self. I can find sufficient scope for it only by identifying with humanity. Helping a few people around me as my father did is not enough; I aspire to make the world a better place. That is where my conceptual framework comes into play. It is both the source of my inflated ego and it is also the source of the systemic reforms I advocate. If I have indeed gained some special insights, then I am under a special obligation to put them to good use. The fact that I am rich adds to my sense of duty. There are people who are rich, people with insights, and people who care about humanity, but rarely are the three qualifications combined in one person. Only the combination satisfies my ambition.

I also need to explain the relationship between my philosophy and my ego. At first they were entangled in a knot. When I first started writing about reflexivity, I was inseparably attached to the idea because it was mine. I could not part with it. I kept on getting more and more convoluted in trying to articulate it until one morning I couldn't understand what I had written the night before. It took me most of my life to separate my ego from my philosophy, and both have benefited from the success of that effort. Today, my philosophy finds expression both in my writings and in my foundations, and my ego can sit back and enjoy them.

Since my philanthropy is a source of ego satisfaction, I feel I do not deserve any thanks for it. Indeed, I used to be embarrassed by expressions of gratitude. I felt that the enlarged ego which was responsible for my philanthropy would not have been socially acceptable if I had flaunted it; and therefore, it was embarrassing to be thanked for it. But I don't feel that way anymore. I realize that I have in fact helped a large number of people. That is what people see, not my enlarged ego. Therefore it is natural that they want to thank me. I have learned to accept gratitude. At the same time, I no longer see any reason to feel ashamed of having such a large ego because it turned out to be beneficial both to me and to many others. But a large ego is difficult to satisfy. Having seen through the hypocrisy that surrounds philanthropy, I cannot be satisfied by praise and flattery. They leave me cold. I need to see actual accomplishments. That is how a selfish man came to have a selfless foundation.

I still find the large gap between who I am and how I am seen by others both fascinating and disturbing. That is why I feel driven to go through with these explanations. I regard altruism and philanthropy not only as a duty but also as a pleasure and a source of satisfaction. It is a luxury that rich people can afford. I much prefer philanthropy to, say, collecting art. It has connected me with other people and allowed me to break out of my isolation. An art collection could not do that. The day I had a panic attack on Leadenhall Street, I did not think it was worth dying for the sake of amassing wealth. Since then, I have been occasionally exposed to mortal danger in connection with my foundation activities. I do not seek such danger, but I am willing to accept it. And it gives me a sense of satisfaction to be engaged in an activity for which it would be worth dying.

I occupy an exceptional position. My success in the financial markets has given me a greater degree of independence than most other people. This allows me to take a stand on controversial issues: In fact, it obliges me to do so because others cannot. Taking controversial positions gives me the added satisfaction of feeling that I have achieved an exceptional position. In short, my philanthropy has made me happy. What more could one ask for? I do not feel, however, that I have any business imposing my choice on others. That is why I did not join Bill Gates and Warren Buffet in their campaign urging rich people to give away half their wealth, especially as I believe that the value of philanthropy lies in *how* the money is spent, not in *how much* money is spent.

Clearly, I am not a saint, nor do I aspire to be one. I cannot think of anything more unnatural and unrewarding than to be selfless. By contrast, I consider a selfless foundation extremely valuable.

Most people participate in public affairs with selfish motives. They tend to cling to whatever power and influence they have attained and it is often difficult to remove them when they stand in the way of a satisfactory solution. There are two obstacles to finding the optimum arrangements: One is imperfect understanding; the other is the influence of special interests which are in conflict with the common interest. A selfless foundation is subject to the first limitation but it is exempt from the second. And that gives it great scarcity value.

I have made it a principle to pursue my self-interest in my business, subject only to legal and ethical limitations, and to be guided by the public interest as a public intellectual and philan-thropist. If the two are in conflict, the public interest ought to prevail. I do not hesitate to advocate policies which are in conflict with my business interests. And I firmly believe that our democ-racy would function better if a few more people adopted this principle. And if they care about a well-functioning democracy, they ought to abide by this principle even if others do not. Even a few spirited public figures could make a big difference.

Let me contrast the theory of reflexivity I have been pro-pounding and the market fundamentalist ideology that has prevailed since the presidency of Ronald Reagan and prime ministership of Margaret Thatcher in the UK. My theory of reflexivity sought to explain how financial markets work irrespec-tive of my interests as a participant; the market fundamentalist ideology also provided an explanation, but it served the interests of its proponents. No wonder that the theory of reflexivity was studiously ignored until the financial system collapsed. And when it comes to advocating policies, compare my activities with those of the Koch brothers or the American Chamber of Commerce. They are pursuing their business interests, I am pursuing the public interest even at the cost of my business interests—subject, of course, to our mutual fallibility. No wonder that they can mobilize more money on their side.

*   *   *

As I survey the foundations network, I am on the whole satisfied, but I have two big concerns. First, what will happen to the Open Society Foundations when the president, Aryeh Neier, and I are no longer around? Second, and more importantly, what more could we still accomplish during my lifetime?

When I established the Open Society Foundations, I did not want them to survive me. The fate of other institutions has taught me that they tend to stray very far from the founder's intentions. But as the Open Society Foundations took on a more substantial form, I changed my mind. I came to realize that terminating the foundations network at the time of my death would be an act of excessive selfishness, the equivalent of an Indian maharajah's wives being burned on his funeral pyre. A number of very capable people are devoting their lives to the work of the Open Society Foundations; I have no right to pull the rug from under them. More importantly, we have identified a sphere of activity that needs to be carried on beyond my lifetime and whose execution does not really require either Aryeh's presence or mine. That niche consists in empowering civil society to hold government accountable. In the United States, there are a number of institutions, such as the American Civil Liberties Union, which are devoted to making sure that the government upholds the rights of all people and adheres to the restrictions on state power established by the Constitution. In most other countries, there are no such institutions. In many countries wealthy people are too dependent on the government to be in a position to provide such support, and in developing countries there is not enough wealth. Hence the niche for the Open Society Foundations. I have also identified some other activities, such as protecting vulnerable populations and providing legal protection for the poor, that fall in the same category. These are worthwhile objectives, and the foundations network will be able to serve them beyond my lifetime.

What will be missing when I am gone is the entrepreneurial and innovative spirit that has characterized the Open Society Foundations. I have tried to deal with problems as they arose through a process of trial and error. I was able to move fast and take big risks. The governing board that will succeed me will not be able to follow my example; it will be weighed down by fiduciary responsibilities. Some of its members will try to be faithful to the founder's intentions; others will be risk averse; but the founder is anything but risk averse.

The structure of the Open Society Foundations is far too complicated to be preserved in its present form. Our growth was entirely unplanned. As I explained earlier, during the period of explosive growth, when our spending jumped from $3 million to $300 million, we didn't even have a budget. Then Aryeh Neier came on board and he brought some order into the chaos. We now have a very elaborate budget process, which takes a long time to prepare and has to start much in advance. I never took much interest in it. I was much more interested in rising to the occasion when the opportunity presented itself. As a result, we now have two very different types of foundations combined in one: The initiatives in which I am directly involved are still running on a very elastic budget, and the organization headed by Aryeh runs on a very tight budget. As the initiatives mature, they tend to pass from my hands into his. At the same time, the human and civil rights and criminal justice areas have been fully in his hands since inception.

Ours has been a very productive partnership, but it has resulted in a very untidy structure which would be unmanageable in our absence. We must reorganize it while we are around. As things stand now, a new president would have to spend several years just to get to know the organization. I should like to appoint six to eight vice presidents who could take charge of discrete portions of the organization and report to an incoming president—that would leave him or her time to formulate strategy and consider new initiatives. But we must avoid a centralized structure at all cost. At present most of the innovative ideas come from within the network of networks, not from the top. The best people working in the Open Society Foundations take a proprietary interest in their sphere of activities, and I am constantly surprised by how much they accomplish. I don't want to lose that spirit.

That is the main reason why I have decided to set up a School of Public Policy at the Central European University. An institution of learning can keep abreast of developments and identify both problems and solutions as they arise in a way that the board of a foundation cannot.

I have great hopes for the School of Public Policy. It has the potential to become the leading institution of its kind. It can combine the practical experience of the foundations network and the network of networks, which are engaged in practically all the burning issues of our day, with the theoretical knowledge that resides in a university. Currently our practical engagement in these burning issues exceeds our theoretical understanding; in other words, we have more money than ideas. We need to generate more ideas in order to use our money more effectively. If we outsource the process to the school, the school will produce public goods which count as output; if we did it internally, as most foundations do, that would count as overhead.

Like most ideas, this one also has a flaw: The best thinking cannot all be found in the same place. Therefore, the school has to go where the ideas are. It has to be a new kind of global institution dealing with global problems. It has to have a critical mass in Budapest, where CEU is located, but it has to have a global outreach. That is the formidable challenge it has to meet. The combination of theoretical knowledge with practical experience could then offer an excellent introduction to those who wish to enter the field. Those who are already engaged in the network of networks could take a sabbatical at the school, improving their career paths and contributing both to research and teaching. To fulfill my hopes, the school would have to institutionalize the entrepreneurial and exploratory spirit that currently imbues the Open Society Foundations. That would involve taking a critical look at our prevailing beliefs and practices.

While the foundations network seems as well run as it can be in its present form, it is not a form that can be perpetuated beyond the working lifetimes of Aryeh Neier and myself. Aryeh is a workaholic who has a great number of people reporting to him directly. My management style can only be described as chaotic. I engage in trial and error to an extent that no board aware of its fiduciary responsibilities could possibly replicate. Neither of us believes in quantitative measures for evaluating programs. I for one would find it difficult to spell out the value system I apply in deciding between various alternatives.

I like to innovate, but at the same time I recognize the importance of persistence and follow-through. So I try to strike a balance between the two. The result is a mixture of what I call "legacy" and "cutting edge" programs. This is as it should be.

Without an appropriate follow-through many promising initiatives would fail to realize their potential.

We have been successful in moving where the action is. In each country we start with supporting critical thinking or dissident activity, and we move in quickly when a new government comes to power and has good intentions but lacks the capacity to deliver. And we have been more persistent than official aid agencies, maintaining a presence long after they have moved on to greener pastures. The same is true of issues of global governance: We were not always the first to recognize them, but once we became aware of them, we remain committed to them, be it the Global Fund to Fight AIDS, Tuberculosis and Malaria, drug policy, or climate change.

Our main difficulty has been in keeping our network of national foundations and "legacy" programs from going stale because that requires almost as much effort as starting new ones; yet my bias has been to focus on the cutting edge. That is where I look for relief from the School of Public Policy. It is meant to be exploring new frontiers; therefore it should be able to keep the legacy programs up to date even in my absence.

Going forward, I favor the "network of networks" format. Supporting a network of formally self-governing institutions where we contribute less than a third of the budget avoids the governance problems we would have to face in initiatives that are wholly dependent on our support. Most of our recent initiatives belong to the network of networks, even if we have not been able to reduce our support to a third or less. But we cannot convert ourselves entirely into a network of networks because there are many worthwhile initiatives that would not be able to receive support from other sources, and we cannot ignore them. That applies both to the existing network and to future initiatives. That means that we shall have to live with an untidy structure into the indefinite future.

I am looking for novel solutions in order to make an untidy structure manageable. For instance, we are experimenting in countries like Thailand and Malaysia with forming local advisory boards without establishing full-fledged foundations. The boards could provide advice on local conditions, and the programs would be carried out by independent grantees or one of our network programs. In that way the combination of local and programmatic knowledge would be preserved without maintaining expensive local organizations which tend to become preoccupied with distributing money to a clientele. If that works, we could convert existing national foundations to the new format; alternatively they could join the network of networks, especially if they can raise money from other sources.

Having decided to allow the Open Society Foundations to survive me, I have done my best to prepare them for my absence. But it would contradict my belief that all human constructs are flawed if I had fully succeeded. Therefore, I bequeath my successors the task of revising any of the arrangements I shall have left behind in the same spirit in which I have made them.

*   *   *

That leaves the second question: What more could the Open Society Foundations achieve during my lifetime? I see greater opportunities open to us than ever before. It is true that we have many enemies and detractors in many parts of the world, but we have established a solid track record as being genuinely concerned with the well-being of humanity, and we have an active involvement with many of the burning issues of the day. We are in a position to increase the scope of our activities in the sense that it would be better to spend the money I have in my lifetime than to add to the size of the endowment. And the problems confronting humanity are, in my view, greater than ever before.

The limitations are mainly internal. We cannot increase our activities along the lines we are currently following because we are already at the limits of our capacity. Moreover, most of our current efforts go into advocacy, and advocacy needs ideas more than money. I have an aversion to spending too much money on advocacy. I prefer to spend the money on services that benefit real people like scholarships or needle exchanges or public defenders. Money spent on advocating systemic reform can be entirely wasted. Money spent on helping people will at least benefit the people who receive support; it also provides a good platform for advocating systemic reform.

To make my point, I like to invoke an out-of-date Soviet joke about goose liver pâté. As the Soviet official explains, there is a slight shortage of goose liver, so it is necessary to supplement it with horse meat. The ratio however is very respectable: one to one—one goose liver to one horse. That is how advocacy ought to be mixed with services that benefit real people: one goose liver to one horse. Yet it would not satisfy me to simply step up the money we spend on providing services because I am acutely conscious of the unprecedented problems that currently confront our civilization, and I feel that the foundations network is now in a position where it ought to be addressing those problems.

As I see it, mankind's ability to understand and control the forces of nature greatly exceeds our ability to govern ourselves. Our economy has become global; our governance has not. Our future and, in some respects, our survival depend on our ability to develop the appropriate global governance. This applies to a variety of fields: Global warming and nuclear nonproliferation are the most obvious, but the threat of terrorism and infectious diseases also qualify; so do global financial markets. In the aftermath of the financial crisis of 2008, it is not enough to stabilize and restart the financial markets; we must reinvent a global financial system that has broken down. Having reached this insight, I cannot afford not to address these issues. That is where my sense of duty kicks in.

I have two top priorities. One is personal; the other is for my foundations. On the personal level my primary interest is to develop my conceptual framework. I had been working on it in the privacy of my own mind. Although my books, articles, and public appearances reached a wide audience, I did not have the benefit of much assistance or even feedback from the outside until quite recently, and without it I made very slow progress. My interpretation of financial markets resonated with the hedge fund community and other practitioners, but they are not in the habit of engaging in theoretical discussions; so I got no feedback from them. The theory of reflexivity was studiously ignored or disparaged by academic economists and to a lesser extent by financial regulators. Mervyn King, the governor of the Bank of England, dismissed my theory without even considering it.

All this has changed as a result of the financial crisis. Mervyn King radically revised his views: He recognized that the instability of financial markets is endogenous, not exogenous. Lord Adair Turner, head of the Financial Stability Authority (FSA), publicly embraced reflexivity. So did Alan Greenspan, but only in private conversation. Paul Volcker had been my friend and supporter before; now we grew much closer.

I passionately disagreed with Treasury Secretary Hank Paulson's plan to bail out the banks by using a public fund called TARP to take toxic assets off their balance sheets. I argued that it would be much better to put the money where the hole was and replenish the equity of the banks. I worked closely with the democratic leadership in Congress to modify the TARP Act so as to allow the money to be used for the purchase of equity interests. I had many other ideas I hoped to put into practice when Obama became president, including a fundamental reform of the mortgage system, but that did not happen. I published a series of articles in the *Financial Times* but got little response from the Obama administration. I had many more discussions with Larry Summers before he became the president's economic adviser than after. My greatest disappointment was that I was unable to establish any kind of personal contact with President Obama himself.

The change of attitude among academic economists was much more gratifying. There was a widespread recognition that the prevailing paradigm had failed and a willingness to rethink the basic assumptions. At the instigation of Anatole Kaletsky, I agreed to become the sponsor of the Institute for New Economic Thinking, whose mission was to break the monopoly that the efficient market hypothesis and rational expectations theory enjoyed in academic and official circles. I convoked a group of distinguished economists, including several Nobel Prize winners, and they responded enthusiastically. A board was formed under the chairmanship of Joe Stiglitz. My friend and former colleague Rob Johnson became president of INET and provided inspired leadership. An initial workshop at King's College, Cambridge (John Maynard Keynes' home), was a resounding success.

I found a cosponsor in Jim Balsillie, of Blackberry fame, and we are on the way to the one-third match. I consider this essential to ensure the independence of INET, since I am the protagonist of an alternative paradigm as well as a sponsor.

This will give me an excellent opportunity to develop my conceptual framework further, although I see limits to how far I can go. I am too old to learn economic modeling, especially as I was no good at math even when I was young. I am also interested in the issues of global regulation and the international currency system. As I immerse myself in the subject, however, I realize that it would be a misuse of my limited time and energy to get bogged down in the details. Now that I can work with others I can be more productive by sticking to the big picture.

Reflexivity and initially self-reinforcing but eventually self-defeating processes play a role in politics as well as in finance. Fertile fallacies have the same dynamics as financial bubbles. I detect a strange similarity in the Bush and Obama presidencies, in spite of their being at opposite ends of the political spectrum: Both presidencies followed the boom-bust pattern commonly found in financial markets. I have not worked this out as a general theory, but I may have an opportunity to do so now.

*   *   *

This brings me to my top priority for the Open Society Foundations: What can we do to preserve and reinforce open society? I believe that open society is endangered worldwide. Of course, open society is always endangered and people must constantly reaffirm their commitment to the idea for open society to endure; what I fear is that we are closer to failing the test than on previous occasions.

For present purposes I shall focus on the United States because it would take too long to cover every part of the world. The United States has been a democracy and open society since its founding. The idea that it will cease to be one seems preposterous; yet it is a very likely prospect. After 9/11, the Bush administration exploited the very real fear generated by the terrorist attack, and by declaring war on terror was able to unite the nation behind the commander-in-chief, lead it to invade Iraq on false pretenses, and violate established standards of human rights in pursuing terrorists.

The war on terror forced me to reconsider the concept of open society. My experiences in the former Soviet Union had already taught me that the collapse of a closed society does not automatically lead to an open society; the collapse may be seemingly bottomless, to be followed by the emergence of a new regime which has a greater resemblance to the regime that collapsed than to an open society. Now I had to probe deeper into the concept of open society which I had adopted from Karl Popper in my student days, and I discovered a flaw in it.

Popper had argued that free speech and critical thinking would lead to better laws and a better understanding of reality than any dogma. I came to realize that there was an unspoken assumption embedded in his argument, namely that the purpose of democratic discourse is to gain a better understanding of reality. It dawned on me that my own concept of reflexivity brings Popper's hidden assumption into question. If thinking has a manipulative function as well as a cognitive one, then it is not necessary to gain a better understanding of reality in order to obtain the laws one wants. There is a shortcut: "spinning" arguments and manipulating public opinion to get the desired results. Democratic political discourse is primarily concerned with getting elected and staying in power. Popper's hidden assumption that freedom of speech and thought will produce a better understanding of reality is valid only for the study of natural phenomena. Extending it to human affairs is part of what I have called the "Enlightenment fallacy."

As it happened, the political operatives of the Bush administration became aware of the Enlightenment fallacy long before I did. People like me, misguided by the Enlightenment fallacy, believed that the propaganda methods described in George Orwell's *1984* could prevail only in a dictatorship. They knew better. Frank Lunz, the well-known right-wing political consultant, proudly acknowledged that he used *1984* as his textbook in designing his catchy slogans. And Karl Rove reportedly claimed that he didn't have to study reality; he could create it. The adoption of Orwellian techniques gave the Republican propaganda machine a competitive advantage in the political arena. The other side has tried to catch up with them but has been hampered by a lingering attachment to the pursuit of truth.

Deliberately misleading propaganda techniques can destroy an open society. Nazi propaganda methods were powerful enough to destroy the Weimar Republic. Those methods have been imported into the United States and further refined. Although democracy has much deeper roots in America than in Germany, it is not immune to deliberate deception, as the Bush administration has demonstrated. You cannot wage war against an abstraction; yet the war on terror remains a widely accepted metaphor even today.

How can open society protect itself against deceptive arguments? Only by recognizing their existence and their power to influence reality by influencing people's perceptions. People's thinking is part of the reality people need to understand, and that makes the understanding of reality much harder than the philosophers of the Enlightenment imagined. They envisioned reason as something apart from reality, acting as a searchlight illuminating it. That is true for natural science but not human affairs. In political discourse we must learn to give precedence to the understanding of reality, the cognitive function over the manipulative function; otherwise the results will fail to conform to our expectations. Popper took it for granted that the primary purpose of political discourse is the pursuit of truth. That is not the case; therefore we must make it so. What was a hidden assumption in Popper's argument must be turned into an explicit requirement for open society to prevail.

I thought I had a convincing argument in favor of open society. Look at the results of the Bush policies: They were designed to demonstrate America's supremacy, and they achieved the exact opposite; American power and influence suffered a precipitous decline. This goes to show, I argued, that it is not enough to manipulate perceptions; it is important to understand how the world really works. In other words, the cognitive function must take precedence over the manipulative function. That is the additional requirement I put into my definition of open society. Unfortunately that was easier said than done: My seemingly watertight argument did not sway the public. President Bush was reelected in 2004.

The election of President Obama in 2008 sent a powerful message to the world that the U.S. is capable of radically changing course when it recognizes that it is on the wrong track. But the change was temporary: His election and inauguration were the high points of his presidency. Already the reelection of President Bush had convinced me that the malaise in American society went deeper than the leadership. The American public was unwilling to face harsh reality and was positively asking to be deceived by demanding easy answers to difficult problems.

The fate of the Obama presidency reinforced that conviction. Obama assumed the presidency in the midst of a financial crisis the magnitude of which few people appreciated, and he was not among them. But he did recognize that the American public was averse to facing harsh realities and he had great belief in his own charismatic powers. He also wanted to rise above party politics and become—as he put it in his campaign speeches—the president of the *United* States of America. Consequently, he was reluctant to put any blame on the outgoing administration and went out of his way to avoid criticism and conflict. He resorted to what Akerlof and Shiller called the "confidence multiplier" in their influential book *Animal Spirits*. Accordingly, he painted a rosier picture than justified of the economic situation in the hope of moderating the recession. The tactic worked in making the recession shorter and shallower than would have been the case otherwise, but it had disastrous political consequences. The confidence multiplier is, in effect, one half of a reflexive feedback loop: A positive influence on people's perceptions can have a positive feedback in the underlying reality. If reality fails to live up to expectations, confidence turns to disappointment and anger; that is the other half of the reflexive feedback loop, and that is what came to pass.

The electorate showed no appreciation of Obama for moderating the recession because it was not aware of what he had done. By avoiding conflict Obama handed the initiative to the opposition, and the opposition had no incentive to cooperate. The Republican propaganda machine was able to convince people that the financial crisis was due to government failure, not market failure. According to the Republican narrative, the government cannot be trusted and its role in the economy—regulation and taxation—should be reduced to a minimum.

The Republicans had good reason to take this line: It is a half truth that advanced their political agenda. What is surprising is the extent of their success. The explanation lies partly in the power of Orwell's Newspeak and partly in the aversion of the public to facing harsh realities.

On the one hand, Newspeak is extremely difficult to contradict because it incorporates and thereby preempts its own contradiction, like Fox News calling itself fair and balanced. Another trick is to accuse your opponent of the behavior of which you are guilty, like Fox News accusing me of being the puppet master of a media empire. Skillful practitioners always attack the strongest point of their opponent, like the Swiftboat ads attacking John Kerry's Vietnam war record. Facts do not provide any protection, and rejecting an accusation merely serves to repeat it; but ignoring it can be very costly, as John Kerry discovered in the 2004 elections.

On the other hand, the pursuit of truth has lost much of its appeal. When reality is unpleasant, illusions offer an attractive escape route. In difficult times the unscrupulous manipulators enjoy a competitive advantage over those who seek to confront reality. Nazi propaganda prevailed in the Weimar Republic because the public had been humiliated by military defeat and disoriented by runaway inflation. In its own way, the American public has been subjected to somewhat similar experiences, first by the terrorist attacks of 9/11, which touched a weak nerve, namely the fear of death, and then by the financial crisis, which not only caused material hardship but also sealed the decline of the United States as the dominant power in the world. With the decline of the United States and the rise of China occurring concurrently, the shift in power and influence has been dramatic.

The two trends taken together—the reluctance to face harsh reality coupled with the refinement in the techniques of deception—explain why America is failing to meet the requirements of an open society. Apparently, a society needs to be successful in order to remain open.

What can we do to preserve and reinvigorate open society in America? First, I should like to see the public develop an immunity to Newspeak. Those who have been exposed to it from Nazi or Communist times have an allergic reaction to it; but the broad public is highly susceptible.

Second, I should like to convince the American public of the merits of facing harsh reality. I have been privileged not only to have survived Nazi occupation but to have emerged victorious: My father was able to help other people and I assisted him. This has given me an appetite for confronting harsh reality and tackling seemingly insoluble problems. Those in charge of Fox News, Rupert Murdoch and Roger Ailes, have done well in identifying me as their adversary. They have done less well in the methods they used to attack me: Their lies shall not stand and their techniques shall not endure.

But improving the quality of political discourse is not enough. We must also find the right policies to deal with the very real problems confronting the country: high unemployment and chronic budget and trade deficits. The financing of states and local governments is heading for a breakdown. The Republicans have gained control of the agenda, and they are promoting a misleading narrative: Everything is the government's fault. The Democrats are forced into fighting a rearguard battle, defending the other half of the truth.

We need to undertake a profound rethinking and recognize that half truths are misleading. The fact that your opponent is wrong does not make you right. We must come to terms with the fact that we live in an inherently imperfect society in which both markets and government regulations are bound to fall short of perfection. The task is to reduce the imperfections and make both private enterprise and government work better. But who is going to develop that agenda? That is the message I should like to find some way to deliver.

*   *   *

I have outlined my two top priorities. I am engaged in many other issues. Some of these engagements are purely personal and do not involve my foundations. I am also connected with innumerable other projects through my foundations. Rather than trying to enumerate them I have asked the Open Society

Foundations to provide some samples of their work. As I have pointed out earlier, we have two very different types of foundations combined in one. Accordingly, the following chapters were prepared independently of me, and I added my personal comments where appropriate. This will give the reader a sense of what I mean when I speak of two foundations in one.

PART I

Global Movements:
Resource Curse, Justice,
and Economic Development

A fisherman with his nets near Bibi-Heybat, a village in an oil-rich region of Azerbaijan. Over the past decade, the Open Society Foundations have fostered a global movement to reform how countries manage revenues from oil, gas, and minerals, and to more efficiently direct natural resource wealth toward development. (© Rena Effendi)

CHAPTER 1

Fighting the Curse
of Natural Resources

Many countries and regions of the world possess an abundance of oil, diamonds, timber, and other valuable natural resources. Yet the struggles to control and siphon off the revenues generated by the extraction of these resources are a driving force behind wars, intercommunal violence, rampant official corruption and repression, and poverty that is both abject and widespread. Since 1970, half of the world's oil-producing nations have experienced violent conflicts. Accounts of the bloodshed over the past thirty years in oil-rich Iraq or oil- and diamond-rich Angola show the savagery and hardship that a zero-sum game for control of natural resource wealth can produce in countries with governments that lack transparency and accountability and institutions strong enough to safeguard human rights and the rule of law. Since the outbreak of war in the Democratic Republic of the Congo in 1998, a violent rush for metals and diamonds has contributed to the deaths of millions of people and sexual assaults on untold numbers of women, many of them in their early teens. Control of profits from diamonds, metals, and timber were the driving force behind the killing, maiming, rape, and abduction of children into military units during the turmoil in Sierra Leone and Liberia in the 1990s. Burma's military junta is a bona fide natural resources mafia whose revenues flow from natural gas, timber, jade and other gemstones, and another cash export that drives economic and social pathologies: heroin.

It is paradoxical and tragic that so many people in countries with abundant natural wealth suffer violence, penury, government oppression, and human rights abuses while political leaders make off with stacks of money that could be used to mitigate poverty and foster economic growth. More than in sociology, anthropology, psychology, political science, or history, the explanation for much of this brutality can be found in economics—and an economic phenomenon known as the "resource curse." Inflows of petrodollars and other hard currency derived from exports of natural resources produce powerful economic side effects that make it difficult for even honest, well-meaning government officials to manage these revenues in a way that will promote economic growth and social development. Significant amounts of revenue derived from extraction of natural resources pervert interest rates and currency exchange rates, increase inflationary pressures, dampen competitiveness, destroy jobs, inspire futile government efforts to use subsidies to prop up unprofitable enterprises, and weaken ties between the state and its citizens.

The resource curse can warp political life and stifle development. In most countries, subsoil minerals belong to the state, and the central government negotiates the contracts and collects the revenues for their extraction. Large resource revenue flows can obviate the need for governments to tax their citizens, making the governments less responsive to the demands and needs of the general public. Expansion of the extraction of natural resources in an unstable country often coincides with the rise or entrenchment of an authoritarian government or dictatorship that maintains power by police repression, secrecy, patronage, and blaming foreign enemies for social and economic problems.

The resource curse is not, however, an inevitability in countries with abundant natural wealth. Developing countries such as Botswana, Chile, and Trinidad and Tobago have shown that the right combination of policies and engaged citizens can transform natural resource abundance into a driver of development that can benefit the broad population. Yet for many other countries, the resource curse remains a formidable challenge.

Over the past decade, George Soros, Aryeh Neier, and the Open Society Foundations have played key roles in fostering the growth of a global movement to reform the business of natural resource extraction. This movement's goal is to dampen the destructive force of the resource curse and help the developing world mobilize its natural wealth for development.

Soros and Neier channeled the Open Society Foundations' financial resources and influence to help build coalitions for increased transparency and accountability in the natural resources business, both on the part of governments of resource-exporting countries and companies involved in extracting these resources. They have also directed support to grassroots watchdog and advocacy organizations in resource-rich countries to strengthen their capacity to demand transparency and accountability from their governments. By 2010, the global movement to defeat the resource curse had enlisted the governments of key developed countries and resource-rich states, hundreds of nongovernmental organizations, the World Bank, the European Bank for Reconstruction and Development, and other multilateral organizations, as well as oil and natural gas companies, mining corporations, and investment managers. This effort has significantly altered the way governments approach the management of their countries' resources and how oil and mining companies from developed countries do business in developing countries and deal with government officials, nongovernmental organizations, and other stakeholder groups.

The Open Society Foundations began supporting efforts to defeat the resource curse in 1999 by providing funding for a project in Angola by Global Witness, a London-based nongovernmental organization that investigates links between extraction of natural resources and environmental damage, corruption, armed conflict, and human rights abuses.[1]

In December 1999, Global Witness's project yielded a groundbreaking report, *A Crude Awakening*, which exposed how corruption and lack of transparency in Angola contributed to a humanitarian disaster. Each year, the report revealed, as much as $1 billion of Angola's $3 to $5 billion in oil revenues disappeared.

The report had significant impact. In February 2001, two weeks after Global Witness appealed directly to oil companies active in Angola to disclose the payments they were making to the country's government, BP, the London-based multinational oil giant, pledged to reveal information on the payments it had made to Angola's government. The government responded by threatening to terminate BP's license to extract oil. This controversial response drew significant attention to the revenue transparency issue in Angola and beyond and demonstrated that mechanisms for increasing transparency would only be effective if all companies were compelled to disclose payments.

Aryeh Neier introduced several Global Witness leaders to George Soros, who had an interest in promoting revenue-monitoring work in successor states of the former Soviet Union, including Azerbaijan and Kazakhstan, where geologists had recently discovered sizable new oil and natural gas reserves. To undertake this work, in the autumn of 2001, the Open Society Foundations and their Central Eurasia Project, with Anthony Richter as director, launched Caspian Revenue Watch, a program that went on to produce a book-length analysis of the resource curse, the challenges Azerbaijan and Kazakhstan would face in managing their oil and gas revenues, and case studies showing how other states had managed, or mismanaged, such revenues. Revenue Watch, which later expanded its efforts beyond the Caspian region, also began working with grassroots civil society organizations in Azerbaijan and Kazakhstan, providing them with background information as well as training in analyzing contracts, budget materials, and financial transactions. In 2002, Soros and the Open Society Foundations helped establish two important elements of the global movement for transparency and accountability in the natural resource extraction industries: the Publish What You Pay coalition and the Extractive Industries Transparency Initiative.

*   *   *

Publish What You Pay (PWYP) and the Extractive Industries Transparency Initiative (EITI). During 2001 and 2002, a group of activists representing Global Witness, the Open Society Foundations, Save the Children, the Catholic Agency for Overseas Development, Transparency International, and Oxfam began meeting in London to discuss the impact of the resource curse in the developing countries where they were working. This discussion led them to develop strategies that would reduce the destructive power of the resource curse. From this discussion emerged the idea of forging a coalition to press for legal and regulatory changes that would require multinational, private, and state-owned oil, natural gas, and mining companies to publish what they were paying to governments in taxes, fees, royalties, bonuses, and other financial transactions. Such a coalition would also seek to require the governments of natural resource–exporting countries to publish what they were receiving from companies extracting oil, natural gas, and minerals from their territory; ensure that these governments would disclose how they dispersed revenue generated from oil, natural gas, and mineral extraction; push for public disclosure of all contracts between governments and oil, natural gas, and mining companies as well as the adoption of transparent licensing procedures; and strengthen civil society organizations in natural resource–exporting countries in ways that would assist citizen efforts to hold their governments accountable for the management and expenditure of revenues derived from the extraction of natural resources.

In March 2002, at an Open Society Foundations meeting in Johannesburg, George Soros and Global Witness's Simon Taylor agreed to organize a movement to promote revenue transparency in the extractive industries. At a press conference in London on June 13, 2002, Soros publicly launched the Publish What You Pay coalition. Its initial goal was to have natural resource extraction companies reveal how much they were paying to governments of resource-exporting countries. The coalition chose this approach because leverage existed to require such companies to disclose this information. Large natural resource extraction companies are generally publicly traded on national stock exchanges. They must abide by the accounting rules and regulations governing these exchanges. The coalition immediately called for amending these rules and regulations to require listed companies to disclose such payments.

Donations by George Soros and the Open Society Foundations gave members of the PWYP coalition significant financial security. Not having to raise funds freed the coalition to devote most of its energy to advocacy work. The core group of nongovernmental organizations developed and supported by the Open Society Foundations in Azerbaijan and Kazakhstan became key early members of the coalition. But perhaps Soros's most significant contribution to PWYP was the personal effort he made to give the coalition credibility.

Due to the celebrity he enjoyed from his success as a financier and philanthropist, Soros attracted significant media attention to the coalition and gave it immediate access to high places. Soros sent personal requests to executives of oil, natural gas, and mining companies to support revenue transparency in their dealings with resource-exporting countries. By helping to enhance political stability in these countries, he argued, the companies would reduce the risk of their investments and increase shareholder value. "It is in the enlightened self-interest of these companies to ensure that their payments are not misappropriated," Soros wrote in the *Financial Times*. "I recognize that oil and mining companies do not control how their payments are spent, or misspent. But if they are to be good corporate citizens in this age of globalization, they do have a responsibility to disclose these payments to the people of the countries concerned [so that they] can hold their governments to account."

On May 13, 2002, Soros wrote to Prime Minister Tony Blair of Great Britain to inform him about the formation of PWYP and enlist his backing for the coalition. "I want to alert you to a proposal being put forth by the London-based

NGO Global Witness and supported by a host of other groups including Oxfam, Save the Children, and Christian Aid," Soros wrote:

> The proposal calls for oil and other natural resource companies to disclose all payments to national governments as a condition of being listed on major stock exchanges. These payments could then be compared against national budgets to ensure that funds are not misappropriated.
>
> In Africa, resource companies do not disclose payments to governments, whereas in most developed countries they do. The result is that corruption is facilitated and money that could be directed to fighting poverty is stolen.
>
> Because individual companies may be disadvantaged if they disclose information that others keep hidden, calls for voluntary disclosure are doomed to failure. Yet companies would benefit collectively by a leveling of the playing field if disclosure requirements were imposed. In fact, my own private discussions indicate that support for such a proposal can be expected from the industries concerned.
>
> I would like to suggest that the UK take the lead on this issue during the G8 Summit in June. It could form a central part of the G8 response to the New Partnership for African Development (NEPAD). I am personally committed to seeing this proposal integrated into the developed world's effort to fight global poverty.

One of Blair's acquaintances, BP's chief executive, Lord John Browne, had already advised the prime minister about the potential benefits of making the business of natural resource extraction more transparent and holding the governments of the exporting countries more accountable. After a policy review, the Strategy Unit of the United Kingdom's Cabinet Office had also already informed Blair that volatility in resource-rich developing countries posed a threat to the United Kingdom's energy security and that promoting revenue transparency and good governance would dovetail with energy security policies his government might adopt to enhance stability in resource-exporting countries. Beyond energy security, Blair saw that promoting revenue transparency in the natural resources business would complement his government's other efforts to promote poverty reduction, good governance, and corporate social responsibility.

Blair was quick to act. On September 2, 2002, at the World Summit on Sustainable Development in Johannesburg, Blair announced the establishment of the Extractive Industries Transparency Initiative, a coalition of governments, natural resources companies, civil society groups, investors, and international organizations that promotes transparency and accountability by the companies that pay and the governments that receive revenues for extraction of natural resources.

Blair became EITI's early figurehead, which brought the initiative further prestige and credibility and attracted the support of nongovernmental organizations and executives at natural resource extraction companies such as BP and Royal Dutch Shell.

Influential organizations in Africa had already begun to support the movement to promote transparency and accountability. Two months before Blair's announcement in Johannesburg, the Roman Catholic Association of Episcopal Conferences of the Central African Region issued the first call by a major

African civil society organization for revenue transparency. "Most of our political leaders have ceased to dream of a better future for their people," the statement said:

> There is a rush to divide up the national pie, of which an important and secret portion comes from oil production. The quest for political power in our countries is less motivated by ideology and having a social agenda than by a willingness to become the all-powerful manager of the whole of our countries' resources. The social and economic well being of the people has become just campaign rhetoric. If not, why would the people continue to wallow in misery where oil is flowing?

This declaration had a huge impact. It put governments and natural resource extraction companies on notice that action was needed to dampen the effects of the resource curse and improve the lives of the poor. Nongovernmental organizations were at first skeptical that any voluntary initiative could attract the support of governments in greatest need of transparency. But Blair's decision to make joint management of the initiative by governments, companies, and civil society a core requirement had powerful appeal.

PWYP began to mobilize civil society groups across Africa and Central Asia to join the coalition and become advocates for EITI. Development agencies linked with the Roman Catholic Church, including the Catholic Agency for Overseas Development, Catholic Relief Services, and Secours Catholique/Caritas France, built support for PWYP in the countries where they were operating, and encouraged other civil society groups to work closely with the church in their efforts to introduce transparency and accountability.

In 2003, Francophone Africa's first national PWYP coalition was established in the Republic of the Congo. Nigeria's president, Olusegun Obasanjo, publicly committed his country to EITI. A year later, Nigeria became the first African country to begin formal implementation of EITI, and the first national PWYP coalition in Anglophone Africa was formed in Nigeria.

Azerbaijan joined Nigeria in pioneering EITI implementation. After concluding a review of the natural resource extraction industries, the World Bank committed itself to introducing transparency requirements for the extractive sectors of its clients and to support implementation of EITI at the country level. The European Union formally adopted the Transparency Obligations Directive to harmonize minimum disclosure requirements for listed companies across all European Union capital markets. The directive contained language encouraging the disclosure of payments made by listed companies in the natural resource extraction business.

In 2003, Open Society Foundations Executive Vice President Stewart Paperin and Karin Lissakers, then a consultant to George Soros, began discrete negotiations with Angola's finance minister and the head of its state oil company, Sonangol. Their goal was to persuade the government of Angola to agree to sweeping transparency measures for its oil sector in return for help from the Soros organizations in gaining international recognition and attracting foreign investment. The negotiations yielded a detailed agreement, for which a ceremonial signing was scheduled for Washington, D.C., with invitations issued to diplomats, Congress, and the press.

Two hours before the event, the Angolan ambassador informed the Soros team that the signing would not take place. Further efforts were to no avail. "The lesson for me," said Lissakers, "is that a top-down only approach will not work.

Citizens have to be engaged." The Open Society Foundations increased their support for Angolan civil society activists and sent Angolan journalists to Brazil for training in covering the oil sector.

The Open Society Foundations' Revenue Watch expanded its work beyond the Caspian, to West Africa and to the Middle East. It created the Iraq Revenue Watch, which exposed the opacity and mismanagement of Iraq's oil revenues by the U.S. occupation authority. Above all, it acted as mentor, trainer, and supporter of the growing Publish What You Pay movement.

In 2006, Soros formally launched the Revenue Watch Institute (RWI), which took over Open Society Foundations projects promoting revenue transparency and accountability. The government of Norway and the William and Flora Hewlett Foundation joined Soros in the endeavor.

The Revenue Watch Institute combined research with support for grassroots activism, advocacy, and technical assistance to governments to help them negotiate more effectively and collect a fair share of the resource rents from companies. Smita Singh of the Hewlett Foundation and a member of the Revenue Watch board called it a "do-tank." The institute continued to engage international financial institutions as well as government officials, legislators, media, and companies in natural resource–producing and –consuming countries, including Iraq, Georgia, Mexico, Indonesia, and Peru, and expanded work with grassroots organizations in resource-exporting countries. A year later, the Revenue Watch Institute launched a partnership with the Centre for the Study of Global Governance at the London School of Economics to promote transparency and accountability in the management of natural resource revenues in the Middle East and North Africa. In 2007, the Revenue Watch Institute worked to ensure that Iraq's draft law on hydrocarbons included language requiring transparency of revenues and contracts. In 2010, Iraq became the largest oil producer to adopt EITI disclosure rules.

Meanwhile, momentum continued to gather. In November 2007, the European Parliament adopted a resolution requiring country-by-country reporting by extractive companies. The International Accounting Standards Board also agreed in 2008 to consider the PWYP proposal that a new international financial reporting standard include the payments that companies in the extractive industries make to governments. The new standard would require natural resource extraction companies to report payments to governments on a country-by-country basis rather than as a lump sum; this would make it easier for civil society activists in individual countries to compare the companies' reports of these payments with reports of revenues each government had received. Once promulgated, this accounting standard would automatically become law in more than one hundred countries, eventually including even the United States, which is harmonizing its accounting rules with international standards.

The governments of some countries that endorsed EITI were slow to honor the commitments they made to disclose the revenues they receive. This generated concern that these governments were paying only lip service to the principle of transparency. Global Witness and other PWYP members threatened to leave EITI if it did not adopt criteria for implementation that prevented companies and governments from deriving the benefits of membership without honoring their commitments. Over the summer of 2007, the Revenue Watch Institute mobilized its civil society partners in natural resource–producing countries and joined forces with the World Bank, the UK Department for International Development, the German government's Society for Technical Cooperation (Deutsche Gesellschaft für Technische Zusammenarbeit, GmbH), the U.S. State Department, and other stakeholders in an effort to ensure that EITI candidate countries meet a validation test of compliance with the initiative. The representatives of the two countries that pioneered EITI, Azerbaijan and Nigeria, strongly backed the validation test. This helped spur EITI's first effort to distinguish those countries that were genuinely implementing the initiative's requirements from those that were not. In 2010, Equatorial Guinea was expelled from EITI for failing to meet the validation test, which includes the independent participation of civil society in the process.

The Revenue Watch Institute and PWYP's U.S. coalition also focused on promoting revenue transparency bills in the U.S. Congress. After several failed attempts, in September 2009, Senator Richard Lugar introduced the Energy Security Through Transparency Act, which would require companies regulated by the Securities and Exchange Commission to publish payments they make to foreign governments for oil, natural gas, and minerals. This mirrored an earlier House bill sponsored by Representative Barney Frank, the chairman of the House Financial Services Committee. In 2010, after an intense grass-roots and "grass tops" campaign by the U.S. PWYP movement, with support from George Soros as well as U2's Bono and his ONE campaign, the transparency movement secured its biggest victory. Included in the landmark Dodd–Frank financial regulatory bill was the Lugar–Cardin amendment that required company disclosure of payments by type and project by project as well as country by country. The SEC regulations will cover fourteen of the world's top fifteen publicly traded oil and natural gas companies, including Petrochina, China Petroleum, Lukoil of Russia, and ExxonMobil, as well as eight of the ten largest mining companies. The White House praised the bill and promised to press other countries to adopt similar legislation.

The Revenue Watch Institute also launched an alliance with the Project on Government Oversight, Friends of the Earth, and Taxpayers for Common Sense to promote royalty reforms in the United States as well as improvements in disclosure requirements for payments for mining and drilling undertaken on federal lands. PWYP promised to continue to press the United States to implement EITI. The Revenue Watch Institute, the European Bank for Reconstruction and Development, asset managers, and sovereign and quasi-sovereign debt issuers also worked to persuade investment rating agencies to factor transparency indicators, such as membership in EITI, into their risk assessments of national economies that are highly dependent on revenues from resource extraction and thus establish a direct link between good governance and the cost of capital.

While Revenue Watch concentrated on finding solutions to the "resource curse," the Open Society Foundations maintained their support for organizations like Global Witness, which continued to publish groundbreaking, headline-making reports about mismanagement of extractive resources, fueling the transparency movement and putting pressure on governments and companies to change their ways.

By 2010, the PWYP coalition included more than 350 local and international nongovernmental organizations working in almost seventy countries. EITI had thirty-two candidate countries and two countries, Azerbaijan and Liberia, in compliance with all of the initiative's requirements. The Revenue Watch Institute was working with grassroots organizations in more than twenty-five countries around the globe.

*   *   *

The Revenue Watch Institute. The global movement to promote transparency and accountability in the natural resources business includes a growing legion of activists and local and national nongovernmental organizations. Around the world, the Revenue Watch Institute has worked to initiate and develop the capacity of such grassroots organizations. It helped organize the first-ever EITI capacity-building workshop in Asia for sixty regional civil society organizations from Australia, Cambodia, China, Indonesia, Papua New Guinea, the Philippines, and Timor-Leste. With support from a local consultant, it helped more than forty civil society organizations launch a PWYP coalition in Indonesia and initiated projects to assist regional governments and local civil society organizations to promote the sound management of expected new flows of revenue from oil, gas, and mining from the central government in Jakarta to the country's provinces. In Trinidad and Tobago, the Revenue Watch Institute worked with a network of civil society organizations to establish and improve the monitoring of revenue flows from oil and gas exploitation. In 2009, it held training courses for activists from Ghana, Nigeria, Sierra Leone, and Tanzania. The Revenue Watch Institute began creating regional training hubs in partnership with local educational institutions that would gradually take over the capacity-building work. The first hub was established in Accra, Ghana, in 2009, the second in Lima, Peru, in 2010. Training increasingly focused on parliamentarians and journalists as well as civil society activists.

Technical assistance to governments emerged as another important part of Revenue Watch's work. Its lawyers and economists helped Mongolia and Sierra Leone obtain better terms in mining contracts, advised Iraq and Ghana on the structure of petroleum legislation, and helped Timor-Leste adjust its sovereign wealth fund to allow more investment in the domestic economy.

Provincial and other subnational governments also became a necessary focus. In Ghana, Indonesia, Nigeria, and Peru, regional and local governments get a large cut of resource revenues. Oversight and accountability is even weaker at this level, so the Revenue Watch Institute pioneered subnational projects that have brought greater public oversight where public services are delivered, or all too often are not.

With the assistance of the Revenue Watch Institute, Bayelsa became the first state in the Niger Delta to create a public disclosure and oversight mechanism for its oil revenues. Bayelsa produces 40 percent of the oil in the delta. By 2010, governors in neighboring states were inquiring about the possibility of emulating the Bayelsa Expenditure and Income Transparency Initiative.

The Revenue Watch Institute assisted Peru's legislature in assessing a formula for sharing mining revenues with regional governments and communities. Folded within the Andes of Peru are rich veins of metal ore, including gold. This natural wealth brought misfortune to the people of this land even before 1533, when Inca leader Atahualpa tried in vain to save his own life by paying his captor, the conquistador Francisco Pizarro, a ransom of gold and silver.

Today, revenues from mining account for about half of Peru's export earnings. Peru also has the fifth largest proven natural gas reserves in South America. One reason why Peru did not run afoul of the resource curse was the country's transparency laws, which guarantee its citizens access to basic information about oil, gas, and mining revenues, their distribution, and their use. With support from the Revenue Watch Institute, Grupo Propuesta Ciudadana created a system to monitor how extractive industries generate fiscal resources, how these resources are distributed between the central government and the producing regions and localities, and the use of these resources by subnational authorities. But activists in Peru still lacked sufficient information on contracts, corporate income tax payments, and corporate social contributions, particularly in the layers of government below the national level. Despite a commitment to EITI, Peru had not taken new steps since 2005 to implement the initiative's reporting requirements.

In September 2007, EITI's board gave Peru the status of candidate country, requiring Lima to demonstrate that it was implementing the initiative's principles. Local and regional governments were failing to invest all the transfers they received from the extraction of natural resources. The effective use of resources was being constrained by the limited capacity to identify and execute productive investment projects. "We have very good transparency laws and civil society is very active in monitoring and in advocacy to improve the quality of spending, but the picture is far from rosy, and I would not present Peru as an example of how to do things well from the perspective of inclusive and sustainable development," said Carlos Monge, a former board member of EITI and the Revenue Watch Institute's Latin America coordinator. "Poverty reduction is lagging far behind while income distribution figures are worsening. And mining is generating all kinds of environmental damage and fueling social conflicts." The Revenue Watch Institute undertook capacity-building and civil society monitoring projects in Peru to help improve this performance.

In countries without meaningful transparency laws, activists working in nongovernmental organizations face formidable obstacles in their efforts to ferret out official corruption and mismanagement in the natural resources business. These activists must go into offices and demand access to all contracts and licensing agreements between their countries' governments and resource extraction companies. They must demand access to their countries' budgets, including budgetary information on all revenues derived from resource extraction and the allocation and sequestering of these revenues. They must be EITI's local watchdogs if the initiative is to be implemented in their countries. They must mount public pressure to force their governments to negotiate and implement fair deals with the natural resource extraction companies and make it more difficult for the companies to leverage unfair deals or make secret payments to government officials. They must strive to see to it that the government disperses the revenues for the public good and not the enrichment of a few. These are all risky endeavors.

Marc Ona Essangui, coordinator of the PWYP coalition in Gabon, has been harassed and threatened for his work on government transparency and accountability. For decades, corruption, cronyism, and lack of accountability have marred the work of Gabon's government. Each year, billions of petrodollars enrich a tiny ruling elite that has largely neglected economic development beyond the natural resources extraction sector. Most of Gabon's people suffer in poverty and have no significant influence over management of their country's vast natural resource wealth.

Ona is the founder of the country's first national environmental organization. His efforts helped create Invindo National Park, whose equatorial rainforest, covering more than 10 percent of Gabon's territory, is the habitat of elephants, gorillas, chimpanzees, and buffalo, as well as the location of famous waterfalls.

However, after the park was established in 2002, government officials and the Chinese company CMEC secretly concluded a $3.5 billion project to build an iron ore mine, a dam, and a railroad line in the park, all of which violated the country's environmental laws. In 2007, without conducting any environmental impact study, the Chinese company began constructing a road to the waterfalls. Ona reported the illegal road construction, pointed out that it had already opened up once impenetrable areas to poachers, and warned that it might facilitate illegal and catastrophic logging in the park's virgin forest.

Ona also obtained a leaked copy of the mine agreement between the Chinese company and Gabon's government and announced that the deal gave Gabon a mere 10 percent of the mine's profits while allowing the Chinese company long-term tax breaks. "The law says that the minimum percentage the government must receive for such a project signed with a foreign entity is 25 percent," Ona said in an interview. "It is the Gabon authorities' responsibility and the responsibility of the companies involved to respect the law and complete an environmental impact study before commencing work."

Ona and his organization, Brainforest, worked to inform local communities about their rights and to complain about the road and the proposed mining project and dam. After Ona said he would disclose the contract's provisions, the country's president, Omar Bongo, agreed to revisit the mining agreement, divert the road to less environmentally sensitive areas, and reduce the scope of the dam project. Nevertheless, Ona continued to apply pressure on the government.

In January 2008, Gabon's interior minister complained that Ona's organization was "interfering in politics" and ordered it to suspend its activities. Burglars broke into Brainforest's office and made off with sensitive documents on the mining project. In 2008, Gabon's federal police barred Ona from leaving the country to attend a United Nations conference on climate change and a meeting of the World Bank. In December 2008, at the PWYP office in Gabon, the police took Ona into custody, where he was denied access to legal representation. After being transferred to a prison, Ona and activist Georges Mpaga, government employee Grégory Ngoua Mintsa, and journalists Gaston Asseko and Dieudonné Koungou were charged with "possession of a document for dissemination for the purpose of propaganda" and with "oral or written propaganda for incitement of rebellion against state authorities." Press attention and public pressure from the PWYP global coalition as well as European governments, the United States, and African nations prompted the authorities to release Ona two weeks after his arrest. The charges, however, were not withdrawn. Despite these challenges, Ona has continued his crusade for government accountability.

Such threats and abuse are all too common. To deal with them, the PWYP network has created a "rapid response" plan to quickly mobilize high-level international pressure on governments that threaten its members and, if need be, arrange legal support for them.

Some of Revenue Watch Institute's grassroots partners have received death threats. Some have been arrested and jailed. The government of the Republic of the Congo, for example, detained Christian Mounzeo, a member of EITI's international board, on trumped-up charges upon his return to his homeland from a high-level EITI conference in Oslo. In 2009, Nigerian authorities arrested a PWYP activist, Marou Amadou, for "regionalist propaganda" and "inciting disobedience," and placed him in a high-security prison where he was denied medical attention. In 2010, four members of the Niger Delta public monitoring coalition were stopped by the police, badly beaten, and held in jail overnight after they had attended a meeting. Police in the Democratic Republic of the Congo arrested Golden Misabiko, a leader of his country's PWYP coalition, and charged him with "undermining state security" and making "defamatory statements." He was detained after his organization, the African Association for the Protection of Human Rights, issued a report alleging corrupt mining practices and demanding disclosure of a contract between a nuclear power company in France and the government of the Democratic Republic of the Congo.

The authorities in Guinea and Madagascar violated the civil rights of other activists and journalists demanding greater transparency. In one of Indonesia's sprawling urban areas, a community activist received threatening text messages each night for a month: "If you want to live in this city, don't talk about budgets." "Informal conversations" with the local police came next, then interrogations, and then a colleague was injured in a traffic incident that scared the activist. Was it a warning or just an accident?

The community activist who received the threatening text messages is one of many local advocates trained by Pattiro, the Center for Regional Information and Studies, a grantee of the Open Society Foundations–supported TIFA Foundation in Indonesia and a key local partner of the Revenue Watch Institute. Headquartered in Jakarta, Pattiro has trained advocates to teach people how to demand access to information about budgets, government revenues, and the dispersal of revenues from natural resource extraction, including payments made by huge oil and mining companies. "It takes time to strengthen them and build their confidence," said Ilham Cendekia, who works for Pattiro. "We direct them to the local governments, to confront them. We find champions within the government." Success comes in fits and starts, and the Revenue Watch Institute has provided support to capitalize on it. One cooperative member of Indonesia's parliament passed Pattiro a copy of a contract between Indonesia's government and an oil company. "We sent the document to Revenue Watch's legal department," Cendekia said, "and used its expert opinion as an advocacy tool and in educational materials. It makes us stronger. It gives us greater credibility."

The Revenue Watch Institute has helped members of parliament in Ghana, Mongolia, Peru, Tanzania, and Uganda play a stronger role in overseeing extractive policies with training and advice, and actively promotes alliances with civil society activists.

Despite resistance in powerful quarters, activists managed to make transparency and accountable management of oil and mining revenues into national election issues in Indonesia and Ghana in 2009 and Brazil in 2010. By early 2010, Indonesia's president had an ambitious EITI implementation decree on his desk ready for signing. Ghana's new president pledged at his inauguration to include revenues from the country's new oil finds in the country's EITI program. Brazil's president, Luiz Inácio Lula da Silva, introduced legislation to devote most of the anticipated windfall from its huge new deep offshore oil discoveries to education and poverty reduction to help build popular support for his preferred successor.

*   *   *

Despite its successes in forging grassroots coalitions and gaining formal support from governments and natural resources companies, the global movement to improve transparency and accountability in the natural resources business faced formidable challenges in 2010. "There are two forces of resistance to the movement," said the director of the Revenue Watch Institute, Karin Lissakers. "The first is the force of competition for resources among the major consuming countries. While the G8 countries pledge strong commitment to transparency and accountability, they are all too willing to look the other way when competing with each other and with China, India, and other countries for access to natural resources."

One of the stiffest challenges facing the PWYP coalition, the Revenue Watch Institute, and its partners was to prevent the resource-hungry G8 countries from neglecting their commitments to revenue transparency. Signs of backsliding appeared in 2007, for example, when the European Union failed to mention good governance and transparency in its energy strategy. The United States later hinted that it might support Angola, with its notoriously corrupt government and its past as a source of blood diamonds, to become vice chair of the Kimberley Process Certification Scheme, the mechanism developed in 2003 to certify that exported diamonds have originated from areas that are free of conflict. In the scramble to win licenses to drill for oil and natural gas reserves in Turkmenistan, the European Union signed a memorandum of understanding on energy that did not mention transparency and accountability, even though a European Union country, the United Kingdom, had initiated EITI, and the European Union is one of EITI's strongest backers. "We caught the European Union policy strategy for Central Asia at the last minute and scrambled to get transparency included," said Lissakers. "We are making the point forcefully to governments and companies exploring possibilities of moving into Turkmenistan. These governments are perfectly willing to look away when assets are looted and are placed in Western accounts and in real estate in the United States and Europe."

The question is whether the support of EITI is mere lip service or legitimate. The emphasis President Obama and Secretary Clinton have given to EITI and their vocal support for transparency and accountability efforts such as the Lugar-Cardin amendment have encouraged the transparency movement. Yet U.S. policy toward notorious governments like that of Equatorial Guinea, which supplies the United States with oil and has long invested its looted wealth in the United States, will be another test of its commitment.

The second force of resistance to the movement, Lissakers said, is the argument of some natural resources–producing countries that the global campaign for greater transparency is a manifestation of imperialism by the European Union and the United States. "This makes it harder for us to draw in Chinese and Indian companies and other emerging markets that are increasingly important players in the global resource sector," she said. "Big Western companies, whether enthusiastically or not, are on board: Total, Chevron, Exxon, BP, Shell, and the big mining companies are active participants in EITI. Chinese companies have cooperated with the EITI process in implementing countries, but neither the companies nor the Chinese government have shown any interest in promoting transparency or participating in the international governance of the initiative." Despite the enthusiastic embrace of EITI by African leaders such as Liberia's president, Ellen Johnson Sirleaf, senior Chinese officials have dismissed EITI as "neocolonial."

Angola provided a stark example of this process at work after the end of its civil war in 2002. The international movement for transparency and accountability originally sprang from the Global Witness project to research and report on the resource curse in Angola. Foreign natural resource companies had made huge investments in the country. Corruption remained widespread and deeply rooted. The isolated, oil-rich Cabinda province continued to suffer from civil unrest. Environmental and social problems, among them heart-wrenching poverty, were severe even after economic growth began to skyrocket. Much of the economy was in ruins, and the country faced debt problems and financing needs. The World Bank and the International Monetary Fund were pushing for transparency reforms in return for financing.

Enter the Chinese government. In exchange for natural resource concessions, Beijing made huge low-cost loans and provided, as payment in-kind, multibillion-dollar construction projects built by Chinese companies with mostly Chinese laborers. China, however, refrained from becoming involved in what it called Angola's internal affairs.

China's "package deals" have obvious appeal for resource-exporting countries that have seen little local added value from their raw materials exports. But the complexity and lack of transparency make it difficult for governments to determine if they are getting a good deal or not.

Nevertheless, recent developments are encouraging. Like its neighbors Liberia and Sierra Leone, Angola has settled its civil war. While Angolan leaders continue to enrich themselves from the country's oil and diamond deposits, they have also begun to spend money on improving public services—health, education, infrastructure. And while continuing to resist the EITI, the government points with pride to the increasing professionalization of the state oil company, Sonangol, and to its new monthly disclosure of production and revenues from the country's oil fields.

The long-term goal of the Revenue Watch Institute and PWYP is to make transparency and accountability the global norm for extractive industries and government policy in all resource-rich countries, regardless of whether or not they are affluent. States need to have regulations requiring all extractive companies to publish what they pay for access to minerals, country by country, to have EITI-like transparency rules for both revenues and expenditures embedded in law in resource-producing countries, to have contracts and the fiscal terms for resource concessions made public and subject to parliamentary oversight, and to have export credit agencies and international financial institutions condition their support for minerals projects on full disclosure of terms and payments.

These aspirations are encapsulated in the Natural Resources Charter that the leading development economist Paul Collier,

Nobel Prize winner Michael Spence, and other tax, legal, and political economy experts concerned with ending the "resource curse" have drafted with the sponsorship of the Revenue Watch Institute. The charter points the way for policymakers, companies, and their sponsors to maximize the long-term public benefit of mineral resources.

The impetus that George Soros and the Open Society Foundations gave in 2002 in launching PWYP and inspiring the EITI has produced measurable results. Fewer resource-rich countries are active conflict zones, and the civil society movement has focused on making governments account for how much revenue they take in and how they spend it. All this increases the likelihood that peace can be sustained and that the people may finally begin to benefit from their countries' resource wealth.

*   *   *

GEORGE SOROS

Like many good ideas promoted by the Open Society Foundations, the idea of organizing a movement to promote revenue transparency in the extractive industries came from outside the organization. The Publish What You Pay campaign was developed by Global Witness, a tiny but innovative NGO based in London but active internationally. At the time I got to know them, it was basically a partnership of three people who had started out as environmentalists but became involved in fighting corruption when they tried to protect the forests of Cambodia. They were the inventors of the term "blood diamonds" and the originators of the Kimberley Process, which sought to prevent blood diamonds from coming to market. We were so impressed by their accomplishments that we adopted them and gave them a large grant that allowed them to expand.

As they grew, we continued to put up a third of their budget. They were one of the first members of our network of networks, but they remained entirely independent. We often disagree on specific issues, but we never interfere with their freedom of action.

The problem they were trying to solve was the resource curse, originally a term in economics describing how huge oil and gas revenues could lead to an overvalued currency and kill a country's employment-giving industries. But the real resource curse is political because in a poor country the attraction of gaining control of these valuable resources leads to corruption, oppressive governments, and very often civil war. So the resource curse can actually destroy countries rather than enrich them. If you think of places like the Congo or Sierra Leone or Liberia, they are all, basically, victims of the resource curse.

Curing the resource curse in a country with resources is more promising than trying to help improve countries that don't have resources. Since the resources are there, it is very attractive to try to make sure that they are properly used. The ultimate objective of the Publish What You Pay campaign was to hold governments accountable for how what they receive is spent.

I took the lead in launching the campaign in June 2002, but I soon discovered that the concept was flawed. The idea was to get oil and mining companies to disclose the amounts they paid to individual governments, not just in bribes but altogether. The amounts could then be added together and the governments held accountable for the spending of the money. The campaign was popular with civil society organizations because it tapped into the widespread distrust of multinational corporations. But the project was not realistic. The large integrated oil companies that were selling products to consumers were susceptible to public pressure, but there were many others that were not: national oil companies of nondemocratic states and fly-by-night operations.

I more or less fell in love with this project because it was a wonderful demonstration of what I call a fertile fallacy: a flawed idea that nevertheless proves to be successful. The British government embraced the idea before its flaws became more obvious and established the Extractive Industries Transparency Initiative (EITI), which brought together corporations, governments, and civil societies in pursuit of fair and transparent standards of behavior. My Open Society Foundations, and I personally, became active supporters of the initiative. After a while we spun off the various activities in which the foundations network was engaged into a separate organization, the Revenue Watch Institute. The Hewlett Foundation and the Norwegian government became equal partners. In addition, we received large contributions from the Gates Foundation among others. To head the Revenue Watch Institute we picked Karin Lissakers, who had represented the United States on the governing board of the International Monetary Fund. She brought both gravitas and energy to the institute, which grew by leaps and bounds under her leadership.

I was not involved in many of the activities described in this chapter and I was not even aware of some of them, but there were some others in which I was very actively engaged. Inspired by Joe Stiglitz, who was also actively involved, I developed my own theory of the resource curse. Why are people living in many resource-rich countries just as poor and even more miserable than those living in countries less well endowed with natural resources? To explain this phenomenon I identified three asymmetries between the governments of these countries and the oil and mining companies that exploited their resources: an asymmetric agency problem and an asymmetry in bargaining power in addition to the asymmetry in information that was Joe Stiglitz's contribution to economic theory. The asymmetric agency problem was by far the most important. The managements of the oil and mining companies were so devoted to the interests of their companies that they were often willing to engage in bribery and other illegal or unethical activities. By contrast, the rulers of the countries concerned were eminently amenable to using their public office for private gain.

One of the countries in which I was most involved was Nigeria. I first met Obasanjo in his capacity as vice chairman of Transparency International. When he became president of Nigeria he invited the Open Society Foundations to establish a branch there. On my way over to the opening of the branch in Abuja, I read a history of Nigeria and discovered that everything that could be done to turn Nigeria into a well-governed country had been tried and failed. I came to feel that Nigeria was one foundation too far. Yet, to my surprise, remarkable progress was made in President Obasanjo's second term. He put an anticorruption team in charge of the economy, led by Ngozi Okonjo-Iweala, who had returned to Nigeria from the World Bank. The team published not only the revenues that Nigeria received from the oil companies but also where the money went. Our foundation office advertised it in the newspapers, and civil society started asking the governments of individual states what they did with the money. Out of this grew a number of impeachment cases and a long list of corrupt officials, who were not allowed to participate in the next elections.

I had built up good personal relations with Obasanjo, and I was very disappointed when he decided to try to modify the constitution and run for a third term. I advised him against it but he persevered. I visited his successor in Abuja, who was a very decent person but sick and unable to provide leadership. Much but not all the progress made during Obasanjo's presidency was lost.

I was less involved in Angola. I was kept abreast of the negotiations and was prepared to pay a visit, but the proposed deal fell through. I was much more closely involved with the Caspian Revenue Watch in Kazakhstan and Azerbaijan. I met with the respective presidents several times, and we switched from providing services that should be provided by the state, like education or public health services, to using the resources of the Open Society Foundations to influence government expenditures in those areas. A few million from us could influence how a few hundred million is spent by the government.

Spinning off the Revenue Watch Institute as a freestanding organization was a very good move. The Norwegian government in particular proved to be a very strong partner given their expertise in the oil industry. For instance, they provided valuable assistance to Timor-Leste in their negotiations with the Australians. One project that deserves mention is a planning grant we gave to Jeff Sachs and his team to prepare a national development plan for Timor-Leste, which would involve a more liberal use of gas revenues than what is permitted by the currently operating wealth fund based on the Norwegian model.

Altogether, our efforts to bring transparency to the exploitation of natural resources made remarkable progress in a remarkably short period of time. One of the reasons for our success was the support EITI received from the international financial institutions; in order to obtain loans, they insisted, countries should meet the standards established by EITI. The more progress we made, the more it became a cat and mouse game. When you establish rules, there will always be private interests that benefit from circumventing the rules. If you have public auctions, how you set the terms for the auction may ensure that only a favored company can win that auction. Eliminating corruption is a never-ending process. Nevertheless, a lot of progress was made in a very short time. The difficulty we ran into in Africa is that China came in and became the spoiler. A country needing financing would have to abide by the terms set by the World Bank. China made loans without conditions, endangering the whole EITI effort. The challenge is to persuade China to join an international effort to fight the resource curse.

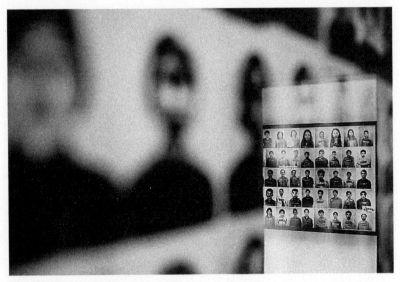

A former prison in Cambodia serves as a museum to help the public remember the Khmer Rouge genocide between 1974 and 1979. As part of its efforts to promote international justice and accountability, the Open Society Justice Initiative of the Open Society Foundations helped establish a tribunal to hold Khmer Rouge leaders responsible for their crimes. (© Jeff Hutchens/Getty Images)

CHAPTER 2

Promoting Justice

Aryeh Neier joined George Soros's Open Society Foundations in 1993 as president after directing the American Civil Liberties Union and Human Rights Watch. While at Human Rights Watch, he helped expand the mandate of the international human rights movement, which had previously limited its efforts to safeguarding the rights of individual victims of politically motivated abuse. Under Neier's leadership, Human Rights Watch began drawing attention to the direct responsibility governments sometimes bear for massive human rights abuses and, crucially, to the indirect responsibility of foreign governments and institutions that effectively support governments that commit wholesale rights abuses. Neier also led efforts to expand the work of the international human rights movement to address abuses that were not politically driven, including abuse of women, police brutality, and deplorable conditions in jails and prisons for persons awaiting trial or serving sentences for ordinary crimes.

Neier met George Soros in 1979, when Soros was just beginning his philanthropic activity. Soros became a strong supporter of Human Rights Watch, and he and Neier developed a friendship and a fruitful partnership.

Neier joined the Open Society Foundations at a particularly auspicious time for advancing open society and international

justice—a number of dictatorships and violent conflicts in different parts of the world were giving way to democratic governments and negotiated settlements. The revolutions of 1989
in Eastern Europe had brought fundamental change to countries
that had long suffered institutionalized repression. Nelson
Mandela had been freed from prison in South Africa in 1990, and
negotiations were under way to dismantle the apartheid system.

Neier made criminal justice and other human rights issues
a main thrust of the Open Society Foundations' work from his
first day as president, and he made sure that these efforts
included work in the United States, where the disastrous "war
on drugs" had filled detention centers, jails, and prisons with
inmates, a hugely disproportionate number of them African
American.

To attack slavery, torture, and the sexual exploitation of women;
to attack Kafkaesque criminal justice systems that allow people to
rot in jail for years without bringing them to trial; to attack systems
that strip individuals, and in some instances entire groups of
people, of their rightful citizenship and relegate them to the status
of legal nonentities, sometimes for generations; and to attack the
culture of impunity that has allowed political leaders and military
and police officers to organize massive acts of mass violence—
killings, rape, maiming, deportations: These were just some of the
aims Neier placed before the Open Society Foundations.

One early area of concern for the Open Society Foundations
was the Serbian government's violation of human rights in
Kosovo, including abuses committed during the early 1990s.
Belgrade had executed a campaign to introduce an informal
apartheid system by forcing all Albanians out of their jobs in local
hospitals, schools, and other public institutions. The Foundations worked to mitigate the damage this policy was causing.
Soros money, for example, funded a teacher-training program

and lesson materials to improve the effectiveness of a parallel system of schools the Albanians had established in homes, garages, and other private premises.

In their earliest days, the Open Society Foundations also supported the establishment, in South Africa, of Justice in Transition. Its director, Alex Boraine, a Methodist minister and former antiapartheid activist, oversaw the development of a proposal for a truth and reconciliation commission that would have the authority and capacity to produce a significant degree of acknowledgment of responsibility for crimes and gross violations of human rights by the apartheid authorities and by elements of the antiapartheid struggle. These crimes and human rights violations included the Sharpeville massacre of 1960, the Soweto riots of 1976, police killings of detained people, among them Steven Biko, who died in 1977, and the stoning and "necklacing" (immolation using burning tires) of political opponents and innocent victims of mob violence. Boraine submitted the proposal to Nelson Mandela a few days before Mandela became South Africa's president. Mandela then presented the proposal to South Africa's first postapartheid justice minister, Dullah Omar, a South African Muslim who had also participated in the antiapartheid struggle. Omar then presented it to the country's parliament. After heated debate, the commission was established. It went on to provide the first public forum for victims to share accounts of the trauma they had suffered under apartheid, and it arguably contributed to the remarkably low incidence of violence recorded during South Africa's transition from white minority rule. With Open Society Foundations support, Boraine went on to found the New York–based International Center for Transitional Justice, which, with the Foundations' continued support, has worked all over the world to confront the legacies of mass human rights abuses and to mitigate their effects.

From 2003, much of the Open Society Foundations' work in the area of human rights and justice was reorganized under the Open Society Justice Initiative. The Justice Initiative, under Executive Director James Goldston, who had previously served as legal director of the European Roma Rights Centre, launched projects to address issues along a broad front, including corruption, freedom of information and expression, and criminal justice.

In Mauritania, where slavery is still a reality, the Justice Initiative supported civil society groups that consulted with the government during the drafting and passage of a law prohibiting slavery and the sexual exploitation of women. In Latin America, the Justice Initiative has helped groups working to advance freedom of information and to challenge the use of government advertising contracts to control news organizations. In Europe, the Justice Initiative's documentation of discriminatory policing practices has brought new attention and urgency to the problem of racial profiling. In Kazakhstan, Kyrgyzstan, and Tajikistan, countries of the former Soviet Union where torture is widespread, the Justice Initiative collaborated with, and organized training programs for, lawyers litigating torture cases. In Moldova and Georgia, the Justice Initiative helped local non-governmental organizations draft and develop laws guaranteeing low-income people qualified legal assistance. The Justice Initiative supported nongovernmental organizations that use monitoring, litigation, and domestic and international advocacy to hold governments in Central and Eastern Europe, the former Soviet republics, and Mongolia accountable for corruption and violations of fundamental human rights.

Three major areas of concern for the Open Society Justice Initiative are abuses related to pretrial detention, governments denying or revoking the citizenship of individuals and groups,

and the culture of impunity for persons responsible for genocide and other war crimes.

*　　　　　*　　　　　*

Pretrial Detention. The problem of pretrial detention is
extraordinarily widespread and troubling in its ramifications. In
jurisdictions with healthy criminal justice systems, the law
strictly limits the amount of time that the authorities may hold a
person in custody pending the filing of charges and a trial.
Within a reasonable period, the authorities must inform accused
persons of their rights and the charges against them, and provide
decent living conditions and access to qualified legal counsel.

In too many jurisdictions with poorly functioning justice systems, however, pretrial detention can drag on for months or
years, leaving detained persons vulnerable to a broad range of
abuses. In some instances, detained persons have no knowledge
of their rights and no access to defense attorneys. In 2006,
about 7.4 million people worldwide found themselves in police
detention awaiting trial. Police and prosecutors exploit prolonged periods of detention to obtain confessions or guilty pleas
to crimes the accused may not have committed. Many detention
facilities are overcrowded and unsanitary and expose detainees to
tuberculosis, HIV, and other infectious diseases. Assault, mistreatment, and torture are a stark reality. (Tragically, in too many
instances, spurious arrests for minor crimes have effectively
carried sentences of death by disease or prison violence.)

The impact of a poorly functioning criminal justice system
falls disproportionately on poor people who cannot afford to
retain legal counsel. Spouses and children of detainees may suffer
through prolonged periods without a breadwinner and slip
deeper into penury. The scale of the danger and abuse faced by

many individuals awaiting trial across the world prompted the Open Society Justice Initiative to launch a global campaign for pretrial justice in 2009.

In July 2003, Mu'azu Ibrahim, fifty-one, and Isah Ibrahim, forty-nine, found themselves in pretrial detention in Sokoto prison, a gritty, sun-beaten place near Nigeria's far northern frontier. In the early 1990s, the Ibrahims, brothers who survived by fishing and farming, had been involved in a dispute over a plot of land. A villager had contested their claim to be the plot's rightful heirs but disappeared in about 1993. Ten years later, the missing man's nephew alleged to police that the Ibrahim brothers had killed his uncle. These allegations were enough for the police to lock the Ibrahims inside Sokoto prison and hold them without access to counsel or any other means of influencing the judicial process that had swept them up. No witness to any crime ever stepped forward. No body was ever found. No bail hearing was held. The Ibrahim brothers remained behind bars as the days and months passed.

Their plight was not unique. Three out of every four prisoners in Nigeria's jails are awaiting their day in court. On average, detainees have had to languish in custody for more than five years, and a few have waited more than a decade, before the charges against them were withdrawn or their cases went to trial. Never mind that Nigeria's constitution requires arraignment within forty-eight hours and a trial within a "reasonable time." Almost three-quarters of the detainees have no legal counsel, leaving them at the mercy of corrupt police officers and other officials. Several factors prolong pretrial detention in Nigeria. Responsibility for investigating crimes and managing evidence rests with the police, a federal-level agency. But 90 percent of the country's crime occurs at the state and local levels, and most trial courts are state-level institutions whose prosecutors rely heavily on supervision and authorization by federal officials and agencies. Slow interaction between separate bureaucratic entities frequently leads to miscommunication and loss of documents. In many instances, the police arrest a suspect based solely on an initial criminal investigation; they launch a thorough inquiry only after a suspect is in custody. The decision whether to prosecute or release a suspect, however, is the authority of the director of public prosecutions, who sometimes takes more than five years to decide. Nigeria's courts are not required to set time limits on investigations or to monitor the duration of pretrial custody. In 2005, 3.7 percent of all persons in pretrial detention were in custody because their case files were missing, 7.8 percent because the police officers assigned to investigate their cases had been transferred to other regions or states and no one had picked up their workload, and 17.1 percent as a result of delays in investigations. In 2005, a presidential committee found that 75 percent of suspects in pretrial detention in Nigeria had no legal representation. In too many cases, law enforcement officials fail or refuse to expedite investigation of an allegation and the filing of a charge in order to obtain bribes from detainees or their relatives.

In December 2004, the Legal Aid Council of Nigeria and the Open Society Justice Initiative launched a project to reduce the number of persons held in pretrial detention and to address the underlying causes of inordinately long detention. The project relied on trained lawyers who had been recently called to the bar as solicitors and advocates but were on compulsory service to the state for one year. The twenty lawyers participating in the early years of the project made numerous applications to the police, the director of public prosecution, and the courts calling for the release of detainees because they had no case to answer or because there had not been diligent prosecution. Periodic reports by the project team and its lawyers to the chief judges of the participating states led to the release of numerous detainees. Engagement with the police at both the national and state levels led to better monitoring of police behavior, reduced the incidence of abuse perpetrated by members of the police force, helped improve police investigations, and reduced delays. There were 3,011 detainees awaiting trial in the four participating states at the beginning of the project. Within one year, the project's lawyers had secured the release of 1,255 (42 percent) of these detainees. The project expanded to other states. As of 2010, it had secured the release of eight thousand detainees and reduced the average time of detention in these states to ten months.

In 2006, Mu'azu and Isah Ibrahim left Sokoto prison and returned to their farm and favorite fishing spots. It had taken three years for a court to finally free them—on bail.

*   *   *

Statelessness. In an effort to secure political power or pursue the idea of a mythical national identity, many governments have quashed the citizenship of members of particular ethnic, racial, religious, or social groups. Using the law to render citizens stateless has occurred in defunct multiethnic or multiracial countries like the former Soviet Union and the former Yugoslavia. It has happened in former colonies, like Kenya, as well as in countries like Burma and Nepal, which are torn by regional conflicts and have sizable populations of "refugees" who have yet to secure citizenship anywhere. Being deprived of citizenship is devastating, even if the victims are not physically expelled from their native land. Statelessness prevents people from sharing in the responsibilities that citizenship demands. It denies people access to public services, including health care, education, and housing. Many victims slip into extreme poverty. Too many

stateless people, especially women, become prey to human trafficking and slavery networks.

To take one example, the West African state of Côte d'Ivoire
was once a thriving trade center and a cocoa exporter, and its
prosperity attracted immigrants from poorer countries seeking
work. During the three-decade rule of its first postindependence
president, Félix Houphouët-Boigny, Côte d'Ivoire was not a
model democracy, but its government seemed stable. Then, in
1999, a military junta unseated Houphouët-Boigny's successor.
Junta leaders resorted to inciting the predominantly Christian
and animist people living in the southern half of Côte d'Ivoire
against Muslims who mostly inhabit the northern regions of
Côte d'Ivoire and can trace their roots to neighboring Burkina
Faso. The junta leaders declared that thousands of these Muslims
were not Côte d'Ivoire citizens, which effectively rendered them
stateless. The political conflict sparked a violent rebellion in
2002 that claimed thousands of lives. Côte d'Ivoire was split
between the North and the South, and its people faced an uncertain future.

The Open Society Justice Initiative played a leading role among
the few nongovernmental organizations working strategically to
establish citizenship as an inalienable human right. The Justice
Initiative worked to define the circumstances under which individuals have a right to claim citizenship of a specific country. It
developed statements of principle on statelessness and joined with
other organizations to promote their adoption by international
bodies, including the United Nations High Commissioner for
Refugees, the United Nations Committee on the Elimination of
Racial Discrimination, the African Commission on Human and
Peoples' Rights, and the African Union. The Open Society Justice
Initiative also supported local, regional, and international efforts
to help the world's stateless people gain or regain citizenship.

It participated in legal cases from Pakistan, where the authorities refused to accept residents of East Pakistan as citizens after it seceded to become Bangladesh in 1971, to the Dominican Republic, where the government in the 2000s declared that persons with a Haitian last name were no longer Dominican citizens no matter how many generations of their families had lived in the country.

Mauritania is another country where members of a minority group were rendered stateless. In 1989, the Arab-dominated government of Mauritania revoked the citizenship of approximately 90,000 Mauritanian blacks and physically expelled them from the country, asserting that these people, whose ancestors had lived in Mauritania for centuries, had never been Mauritanian in the first place. The expulsions of the black Mauritanians targeted primarily civil servants, prosperous merchants, and landowners, so the government found itself with a windfall of vacant jobs and unprotected assets to distribute to Arabic-speaking loyalists. The government had reconsidered the expulsions by 1994, and by 1997 about 35,000 of the exiles had returned, though many subsequently left because they could not regain their citizenship or their confiscated land. In 2000, the African Commission ruled that Mauritania had breached the African Charter when it undertook the deportations. This ruling and the installation of a new government in Mauritania during 2007 presented the Justice Initiative and its partners with an opportunity to press for the return of black deportees lingering in Senegal, which began under United Nations auspices in January 2008.

*   *   *

International Justice. In the time of Napoleon Bonaparte, making war became a markedly larger-scale and more violent endeavor than ever before. Ever larger armies of volunteers and conscripts armed with ever more powerful weapons carried out massive crimes against civilians and enemy combatants. But the political and military leaders of these armies directed the violence with the same impunity that such leaders had enjoyed since ancient times.

An orgy of violence commenced with World War I. Millions of civilians died during the Armenian genocide in Turkey and during massacres of civilians in territories occupied by the Ottoman Empire. In the 1930s, Japanese armies carried out massive atrocities in Manchuria. Germany's Nazi regime and its nationalist allies exterminated millions of Jews, Roma, members of unwanted ethnic minorities, homosexuals, political dissidents, Communists, and physically and mentally disabled persons. Millions more civilians died in Leningrad during the siege and in the massive aerial bombings of London, Plymouth, Dresden, Tokyo, Hiroshima, Nagasaki, and other cities during World War II. The United States killed large numbers of civilians with massive aerial bombings of North Vietnam and Cambodia. The people of Cambodia suffered mass slaughter during the late 1970s, and untold numbers of civilians died in conflicts all across Africa, including millions in the war that erupted in the Democratic Republic of the Congo in 1998.

Such affronts to human decency are not a local problem. Crimes of this magnitude affect everyone. National leaders too often lack the will, and national courts the authority and fortitude, to prosecute the highest-ranking individuals responsible. International input is required if justice is to trump impunity and create a deterrent to the most heinous crimes. The Nuremberg and Tokyo war crimes tribunals after World War II were a first attempt at ending the culture of impunity. Only after the Cold War did it become possible to attack the culture of impunity again.

The process gained traction in 1992. While Aryeh Neier was executive director of Human Rights Watch, the organization issued a report documenting the mass killing and uprooting of Muslims by Serb military forces in regions of Bosnia and Herzegovina. For the first time in its history, Human Rights Watch invoked the Genocide Convention and called for international intervention to halt the violence and for establishment of a war crimes tribunal to try the individuals most responsible.

Months of advocacy work followed the report. In early 1993, during a Serb attack on thousands of Muslim refugees herded into the Bosnian town of Srebrenica, the United Nations Security Council unanimously adopted a resolution authorizing the creation of the first international war crimes tribunal since Nuremberg and Tokyo. Three months later, the Security Council unanimously adopted a second resolution approving a specific plan for the tribunal's operation.

After the United Nations undertook inadequate measures to preempt the 1994 genocide in Rwanda, the Security Council established a second temporary international tribunal. The Security Council subsequently joined the government of Sierra Leone to form a court to try persons accused of directing the execution of civilians, the conscription of child soldiers, mass rape and maiming, and other crimes. Cambodia's government, together with the United Nations, established a mixed judicial body to try Khmer Rouge leaders accused of organizing the mass slaughter there during the 1970s. And, with adoption of the Rome Statute in July 1998, and its entry into force four years later, the International Criminal Court, the first standing court established to try accused war criminals, came into being.

For over fifteen years, the Open Society Foundations have significantly strengthened these institutions of international justice by funding efforts to enhance the quality of investigations and judicial decision making, to assist prosecutors in structuring criminal charges, to increase local participation and a sense of local ownership of the judicial process, and to promote the prosecution of rape, sexual slavery, and other gender-based crimes and encourage the appointment of more women prosecutors and judges.

The first of the international tribunals investigated war crimes in Yugoslavia. In early 1993, George Soros provided tens of millions of dollars to help in violence-ravaged Bosnia and Herzegovina. These funds, administered through the Open Society Foundations, gave Aryeh Neier an opportunity to launch work that would go beyond reporting on human rights abuses, and he saw to it that a significant amount went to support the effort to establish a war crimes tribunal. By the time of the Dayton peace conference of 1995, the United Nations Yugoslavia tribunal was up and running. The ranking Bosnian Serb political and military leaders, Radovan Karadžić and General Ratko Mladić, were facing international arrest warrants on war crimes charges, which disqualified them from participating in the Dayton negotiations and left the Bosnian Serbs to rely on representation by Serbia's president, Slobodan Milošević, who, though clearly responsible for much of the bloodshed that accompanied the breakup of the former Yugoslavia, was more willing to compromise because he assumed it would solidify his hold on political power in Serbia. "Some Western officials, including some in the government of Prime Minister John Major in Great Britain, feared that indictments would stand in the way of a settlement," Neier wrote in his memoirs, *Taking Liberties*. "The reverse turned out to be the case." Neier personally lobbied to ensure that crimes committed in Kosovo during 1998 and 1999 came within the jurisdiction of the United Nations Yugoslavia tribunal.

The 1994 genocide in Rwanda left the country with only a dozen or so attorneys. Tens of thousands of persons accused of participating in the genocide were taken into custody and held for years in squalid conditions, awaiting trial. The Rwandan authorities established local courts based on traditional tribunals to try about 50,000 of these accused, leaving about 7,000 of the higher-ranking and more notorious accused to face trials in Rwanda's national justice system. The Open Society Foundations participated in a needs assessment and urged foreign donors, including national governments, to support efforts to strengthen the International Criminal Tribunal for Rwanda and increase the capacity of Rwanda's judicial system to provide the accused fair trials.

In March 2003, the United Nations–sponsored Special Court for Sierra Leone indicted Charles Taylor, Liberia's former president, for war crimes and crimes against humanity arising out of his alleged backing of Sierra Leone rebels, including illegally conscripted child soldiers, who had killed, tortured, raped, and mutilated civilians and other combatants. The Open Society Justice Initiative provided significant assistance to local and international efforts to bring Taylor to justice. Taylor resigned the Liberian presidency in August 2003. Nigeria's president, Olusegun Obasanjo, welcomed Taylor to Nigeria and granted him asylum. In December, Interpol, the international law enforcement cooperation agency, issued a warrant for Taylor's arrest. The senior legal officer for the Justice Initiative's Africa program, Chidi Odinkalu, launched a legal action to revoke Taylor's asylum status in Nigeria, arguing that granting Taylor asylum was a violation of Nigeria's law. On December 10, 2003, a coalition of rights organizations, including the Open Society Justice Initiative, called on the Nigerian authorities to hand Taylor over for prosecution. In separate letters to Nigeria's national commissioner for refugees and its federal attorney general, human rights groups from Liberia, Nigeria, and Sierra Leone argued that granting asylum to the former Liberian president violated both international and Nigerian law. Even after he was called in for questioning by Nigeria's State Security Service, Odinkalu continued to push for Taylor's arrest. Ultimately, the Nigerian government relented and handed Taylor over to the government of Liberia, which transferred him to the custody of the Special Court for Sierra Leone. Taylor went on trial in The Hague in early 2008.

In order to bring West Africans and others news and information about the Taylor trial, the Justice Initiative helped create charlestaylortrial.org, a website that provides updates from the courtroom, including video streaming, background material, and expert analysis crucial to understanding the proceedings. The Justice Initiative has also undertaken assessments of the Special Court's operations and developed projects to focus on ways to ensure that the court will leave a positive legacy in West Africa and elsewhere.

The tribunals for Yugoslavia, Rwanda, and Sierra Leone, however, were onetime affairs. For many years, human rights advocates around the world campaigned for a permanent international criminal judicial body to try the highest-ranking leaders charged with war crimes. They saw a permanent criminal court as a formidable tool for ending the culture of impunity and introducing accountability into the decision making of political and military leaders involved in armed conflicts. The Open Society Foundations funded groups that campaigned for the establishment of the International Criminal Court.

One of the Foundations' collaborators was Emma Bonino, a member of Italy's Senate, a member of the European Parliament, and founder of No Peace Without Justice, an international nonprofit organization that promotes human rights, the rule of law, and international justice. Bonino had been instrumental in building support in the European Union for the United Nations Yugoslavia tribunal and took up the cause of establishing the International Criminal Court. With financial support from the Open Society Foundations, during the late 1990s she organized conferences in different parts of the world to garner government support for establishment of the International Criminal Court. She won significant support for the idea within the European Union and its member countries as well as the backing of key individual leaders, among them President Jacques Chirac of France, who altered his position to support the Court's establishment. Bonino and Neier together sought the backing of United Nations Secretary-General Kofi Annan. And it was because of Bonino that Rome became the venue of the conference to establish the International Criminal Court.

As Bonino worked in the European Union countries, Human Rights Watch amassed support for the International Criminal Court in countries across the world, and the Open Society Foundations sought backing from governments in Eastern Europe and in the countries that had emerged from the former Soviet Union. A third significant collaborator was South Africa's one-time justice minister, Dullah Omar. Without Omar's assistance in lobbying African governments, the Rome Statute would not have been adopted and the International Criminal Court would not have gathered ratifications from the required number of state governments to come into existence in 2002.

The Justice Initiative worked with human rights groups and other collaborators in several countries to investigate and build a series of cases documenting violations of international humanitarian law that could be forwarded to the prosecutor of the International Criminal Court. In the eight years since its founding, the Court opened investigations in the Central African Republic, the Democratic Republic of the Congo, Kenya, Uganda, and Sudan, where fighting in the Darfur region between government-backed militias and rebel forces led to the deaths of hundreds of thousands of people from violence and disease and to the displacement of about three million people; the United Nations has deemed this violence to be an act of genocide. In July 2008, the prosecutor of the International Criminal Court formally called on its judges to issue an arrest warrant for a sitting head of state, President Omar al-Bashir of Sudan, on charges related to crimes committed in Darfur. In March 2009, the Court issued an international warrant for President al-Bashir's arrest.

By 2009, the International Criminal Court had publicly issued arrest warrants against fourteen persons and launched two trials, the first against a militia leader from the Democratic Republic of the Congo, Thomas Lubanga Dyilo, who was charged with war crimes for using child soldiers in 2002 and 2003. The Open Society Justice Initiative launched a website in 2009 that provided people in Africa and across the globe with coverage and commentary about Lubanga's trial in The Hague.

Since it began over a decade ago, the conflict in the eastern regions of the Democratic Republic of the Congo has produced one of recorded history's most soul-destroying spates of violence against women. With each passing year, and despite the presence of the world's largest United Nations peacekeeping force, the rape, maiming, murder, child molestation, enslavement, and abduction for ransom seem only to worsen. Authorities at Panzi Hospital in South Kivu province registered forty-five cases of rape combined with severe bodily injury in 1999; the number of cases rose to 145 in 2000, 580 in 2001, and 3,500 in 2005. Many rapes are not tallied because the victims live in remote areas or do not lodge complaints against their attackers. According to the United Nations, 27,000 sexual assaults were reported during 2006 in South Kivu alone.

The Democratic Republic of the Congo's military, police, and justice system cannot cope with the overall security situation, much less attacks on women. Few of those who perpetrate gender crimes are ever brought to justice. Many victims do not approach the police because they fear retaliation by their attackers and lack confidence in the justice system. Many find themselves utterly alone while they struggle to cope with their trauma even as they deal with penury, unwanted pregnancies, raising their children (some of them also victims of sexual assault), HIV and AIDS, and ostracism by loved ones who have shunned them as "diseased" or "tainted."

The Open Society Justice Initiative has long urged both the International Criminal Court and the government of the Democratic Republic of the Congo to prosecute those persons responsible for the mayhem. Open Society Foundations programs, including the Open Society Justice Initiative, the International Women's Program, and the Public Health Program, collaborated with partners in the Democratic Republic of the Congo in efforts to halt the violence against women, to ease the victims' suffering, and to help enhance the capacity of local justice institutions. The Open Society Foundations secured the agreement of the Democratic Republic of the Congo's government to deploy three-judge mobile courts to South Kivu and other districts where crimes against women have been prevalent. Designed by Kelly Askin, the Justice Initiative's senior legal officer for international justice, these courts go to the victims, to remote areas where most people have never ridden in a car or ventured far from their home villages. The project has provided training for women judges and the placement of volunteer judges and lawyers from outside the

Congo to assist the mobile courts as mentors. On February 21, 2011, a mobile court sentenced a colonel of the army of the Democratic Republic of the Congo, three junior officers, and five soldiers to sentences ranging from ten to twenty years for carrying out the retaliatory rapes of dozens of people—women, men, and children—in the town of Fizi on New Year's Day.[1]

Cambodia represented another challenge for human rights advocates who wanted those responsible for crimes against humanity to be brought to justice. In 1975, the Khmer Rouge, the Cambodian Communist military force under the command of Pol Pot, captured the country's capital, Phnom Penh. By 1979, the Khmer Rouge bore responsibility for the deaths of as many as three million people by execution and starvation. Soldiers had violently uprooted millions of people from Phnom Penh and the country's larger towns and forced them to labor in rice paddies and undergo Communist indoctrination. The Khmer Rouge singled out educated people for execution. Persons who wore eyeglasses were suspect because the Khmer Rouge assumed that poor eyesight betrayed people who had spent time reading.

For years, Aryeh Neier and other rights advocates sought the establishment of a credible judicial body to try leading members of the Khmer Rouge indicted for crimes committed during the mass slaughter. In 1997, Cambodia's government requested assistance from the United Nations to establish a tribunal to prosecute former senior Khmer Rouge leaders. After a few years, however, it appeared that such a tribunal would be a nonstarter due to opposition from the country's prime minister, Hun Sen, who was a member of the Khmer Rouge before fleeing to Vietnam during the violence and returning to Cambodia with the Vietnamese forces who drove the Khmer Rouge from the country's capital.

Neier helped breathe new life into the idea of a tribunal to try the Khmer Rouge leaders responsible for the crimes in Cambodia. On his own initiative, Payam Akhavan, a former legal adviser at the prosecutor's office of the United Nations Yugoslavia tribunal, traveled to Cambodia and managed to convince the authorities to support a tribunal that would prosecute only a handful of former Khmer Rouge leaders. Akhavan subsequently approached Neier, who presented the idea to a number of experts on Cambodia, including Thomas Hammarberg, at the time the United Nations secretary-general's special representative for human rights in Cambodia. Later, in New York, Neier, Hammarberg, and a law professor from American University, Diane Orentlicher, put the case for a Cambodia tribunal to the ambassadors to the United Nations from Australia, France, Japan, and the United States. By 2001, Cambodia's national assembly had adopted a law creating the Extraordinary Chambers in the Courts of Cambodia. The law required the Extraordinary Chambers to be situated in Cambodia and to employ Cambodian judges and staff as well as foreign judges, prosecutors, investigators, and other personnel. International participation in the tribunal was important due to the weakness of the Cambodian legal system, the international nature of the crimes under scrutiny, and a desire by many to ensure that the Extraordinary Chambers met international standards of justice. Cambodia concluded an agreement with the United Nations in June 2003.

The Open Society Justice Initiative subsequently engaged international legal experts to provide technical assistance in Phnom Penh on a range of issues related to establishment of the Extraordinary Chambers. During the start-up phase, the Justice Initiative provided legal and technical training to local nongovernmental organizations and court staff. It had a resident fellow develop an outreach module for use in rural communities.

It engaged filmmakers to produce works on the victims of the Khmer Rouge's crimes. It spearheaded efforts to win government funding for the Extraordinary Chambers and secure the appointment of qualified international prosecutors, judges, administrative officials, and staff at all levels. It engaged local and international media on the significance of the Extraordinary Chambers and supported intensive court monitoring efforts.

After long delays and troubled negotiations, the Extraordinary Chambers began operating in July 2006. The Justice Initiative drew public attention to fundamental challenges confronting the Extraordinary Chambers, including a corrupt payback scheme involving some Cambodian staff, judicial independence and political interference, a failure to adopt internal rules of procedure and evidence, significant disagreements between the Cambodian and foreign judges and staff, an insufficient budget and overly cautious spending policies, and inadequately trained judges and staff.

In February 2007, the Justice Initiative called for an investigation of allegations that staff members of the Extraordinary Chambers were paying salary kickbacks to government officials. The Cambodian authorities responded with threats to expel the Justice Initiative from the country, but the result was a United Nations investigation and improved transparency at the Extraordinary Chambers. The Justice Initiative, which phased out technical assistance to the court in 2007, is continuing to monitor the Extraordinary Chambers. The Justice Initiative has provided training for the court's judges and other staff and pushed the court to improve its practice in areas such as victim services and administration.

The Justice Initiative also supported efforts to make the work of the Extraordinary Chambers comprehensible to those many Cambodians who are illiterate, who have never known the rule of law, who are not versed in the concept of a court or a witness, whose education has not included an examination of Cambodia's genocide, and who stand to benefit from a process that will make them more comfortable discussing the mass killing in a public forum and more confident that even once-powerful individuals responsible for atrocities can be held accountable for their actions. The magnitude of this task was apparent at one outreach session in October 2007. About sixty Cambodian peasants gathered inside a bamboo house. Most were curious to know more about the Extraordinary Chambers. Several expressed fear of a man living nearby who had been a member of the Khmer Rouge. One man, clearly afraid, articulated the challenge facing the effort to end the culture of impunity all over the world. "What use have we for this?" he asked. "We are Buddhists. This world means nothing. Justice for the guilty will be handed down with their next reincarnation."

*   *   *

GEORGE SOROS

Criminal justice is a field I have left entirely in the hands of Aryeh Neier because he knows it much better than I do. In my view, the International Criminal Court is a double-edged weapon. The threat of indictment can be a deterrent to the perpetrators of war crimes. On the other hand, once they have perpetrated the crime, the threat of prosecution may be a deterrent to a peace settlement. In fact, very often it is by breaking the rule that a settlement is reached. In the case of former Liberian President Charles Taylor, indicted for war crimes in Sierra Leone, President Obasanjo of Nigeria gave him asylum, claiming that he did it at the behest of the international community that wanted Taylor out of the way in order to reach a settlement in Liberia. That was another instance where the foundations network found itself straddling conflicting positions: The Open Society Initiative of West Africa (OSIWA) supported Nigerian civil society in attacking Obasanjo on Taylor's asylum while at the same time I was working closely with Obasanjo on the Revenue Watch issues. I had a hard time explaining to Obasanjo how we could be both with him and against him at the same time.

The only time I practically forced a project on the Open Society Justice Initiative is the issue of legal empowerment of the poor. This arose out of a report by the Commission on the Legal Empowerment of the Poor, created by Kofi Annan when he was secretary-general of the United Nations. It was the brainchild of Hernando de Soto, the charismatic Peruvian promoter of property rights, and it brought together left and right. Madeleine Albright, cochair with de Soto, and Justice Anthony Kennedy were the American members of the commission. The Justice Initiative was already engaged in many projects that qualified as legal empowerment of the poor. Employing paralegals in Sierra Leone to provide legal assistance using both the tribal and official but dysfunctional channels stood out as an ingenious innovation. I felt that the bipartisan support of the UN report made legal empowerment of the poor a politically neutral, universally acceptable concept that could be turned into a major movement. And so it is. A symposium on the subject organized by the European Commission drew large attendance. The British government is sponsoring an official launch in London in 2011.

Salamatu Kamara, whose husband was murdered by rebels in Sierra Leone, is rebuilding her life and providing for her two sons. A microcredit project supported by the Soros Economic Development Fund helped Kamara expand her business selling fish. She can now pay for food, clothes, and education for her family. She has opened a bank account and dreams of building a home. (© Aubrey Wade/Panos Pictures for the Open Society Foundations)

3

Alleviating Poverty Through Economic Development

Social entrepreneurship does not simply help individuals who have been excluded from jobs and other economic opportunities. It is an attempt to help stimulate the creation of profitable and sustainable businesses that will grow and employ increasing numbers of people and contribute significantly to the economic growth of a community or country.

Over the past fifteen years, the Open Society Foundations have played an increasingly significant role in encouraging social entrepreneurship worldwide. In 1995, the Open Society Foundations began supporting economic development efforts in South Africa by financing the construction of low-income housing. Two years later, with an initial investment of $50 million, George Soros and the Open Society Foundations established the Soros Economic Development Fund, a private, nonprofit foundation whose mission is to help alleviate poverty and strengthen communities by promoting access to financial services, developing small business and entrepreneurship, and enhancing economic opportunities for vulnerable populations.

By 2010, the Soros Economic Development Fund had $225 million in assets and was working in dozens of countries, providing credit guarantees and deposits, as well as equity financing and loans to more than three dozen microfinance institutions, cooperatives, banks, and social enterprise projects. In some cases, the aim was to provide loans, microcredit, and financial services to small, and in many instances minuscule, enterprises operated by people with few tangible assets and inadequate access to credit or financial services provided by commercial banks.

Small as these investments are, they can be effective. When poverty-stricken people seek to initiate and nurture small enterprises—if, say, a start-up house builder in South Africa needs funds to construct low-cost homes or a carpet weaver in Albania needs funds to buy a loom—they have generally had to rely on their own savings or turn to their friends, family members, or, worst of all, predatory moneylenders for credit. The poor have also lacked the ability to open savings accounts or to obtain insurance policies and money transfer services; without such tools, they have had few reliable means of building assets, managing emergencies, and planning for the future. The Soros Economic Development Fund and the policy and research center Consultative Group to Assist the Poor founded the Microfinance Management Institute, which has provided grants to support microfinance management education at selected business schools, training for people to manage and regulate these institutions, and grants to individual educators in order to develop new course curricula and case study materials. The fund has also invested in technological advancements for business, such as telecommunications systems that connect millions of people to markets and opportunities, mobile banking for the working poor, and effective organizational strategies for peasant farmers.

*   *   *

South Africa. In South Africa, the problem of inadequate housing, especially for low-income blacks and other people of color, festered for decades. Under the apartheid system, whole black populations were relegated to artificial "homelands." Blacks with permits to work in prosperous white urban areas were forced into squatter camps or "townships" like sprawling Soweto, outside Johannesburg. After the end of apartheid, the permit system collapsed. Blacks from rural areas seized the opportunity to move with their families to urban areas in order to escape abject poverty.

Yet the housing problem, so long in the making, was not so easy to resolve. After the election of Nelson Mandela in 1994, simmering discontent over housing jeopardized the stability of the country's nascent democratic government. In 1995, George Soros, the Open Society Foundations, and the government of South Africa launched the National Urban Reconstruction and Housing Agency, now known as Nurcha, to provide financial support for the construction of decent housing for low-income people. The Open Society Foundations and the South African government each gave Nurcha $5 million for operating expenses. The Open Society Foundations made $50 million available in the form of loan guarantees and other financial tools that helped newly established, black-owned construction companies build houses for low-income people. In 2003, a $2.5 million investment from the Soros Economic Development Fund, in a partnership with the Soros Charitable Fund and the Overseas Private Investment Corporation, helped establish a $20 million revolving credit facility for Nurcha projects. In 2005, the Soros Economic Development Fund deepened its involvement by issuing Nurcha a direct, ten-year $10 million loan.

During its first fifteen years, Nurcha provided financing that helped almost 1,000 contractors build more than 250,000 homes. Most were modest, detached two-room dwellings with kitchens and washrooms—a great improvement over the traditional huts or wood and corrugated metal shacks that house so many of

South Africa's poor. Built with cinderblock walls, some with stucco, the new houses had roofs solid enough to withstand windstorms, plastered and painted interior walls, running water, and electricity. In 1999, houses built with Nurcha's financing tools cost about $3,370 apiece. This cost was in almost all cases provided by the government in the form of a subsidy paid to the contractor on completion of the house. Some Nurcha client-developers have been highly disadvantaged women who began work on one or two houses and went on to build companies with the capacity to construct several thousand small homes at a time. Nurcha expanded its work to provide financing for the construction of health clinics and other community buildings. It began organizing a nationwide savings effort for home owners.

Nurcha's efforts have been successful, but South Africa's housing problems are not yet over. "Nurcha helped move the market," Stewart Paperin, president of the Soros Economic Development Fund, said. "But the rate houses are being built in South Africa still doesn't keep up with the population's growth. This country desperately needs housing infrastructure."

*   *   *

Sam Lubbe was drowning in red ink and facing a tragic conclusion to a rags-to-riches life story when he approached Nurcha in the late 1990s. Lubbe had been working in construction since childhood. Born in 1959, the youngest child of a bricklayer with three wives and eighteen children, Lubbe lived his earliest years inside a traditional circular hut in an impoverished corner of the mineral-rich Limpopo District. He had not finished the first grade when his mother took him on a train to Johannesburg—250 miles from the family's village—and pleaded with his father's Afrikaner employer to give her son work. The family was going hungry.

Before long, Sam Lubbe began his career as a "tea boy" in the construction company's office. It was there and in the informal settlement where he lived that he learned the language of the building trades. After a few years, he went to work on a construction site as a "toolbox boy." He carried the saws and hammers for a foreman named Harry, who taught him drawing, bricklaying, plastering, and electrical work. Lubbe remained on the job until 1981, when he announced to his boss that he was resigning to form his own company.

"Sam, how much money do you have?" the boss asked.

"A thousand rand," Lubbe answered. It was then about $1,000.

"Where is this money?"

"It is in my camp."

"Bring it tomorrow."

The boss and his wife took Lubbe to a bank, helped him open a savings account, deposited the R1,000, and gave him an additional R800 bonus. With this money, Sam bought the tools to do electrical work. He went to a printer and made a flyer:

Come to Lubbe Construction
Electrical Work
No deposit

"No deposit" in South Africa under apartheid meant trusting people who did not have money to put up a guarantee that they would pay. By doing so, twenty-two-year-old Sam Lubbe was assuming a risk that banks were refusing. With his early earnings, he bought a bicycle and rode from job to job in Soweto carrying his tools and a stepladder. He had his customers pay installments to a lawyer each month. By 1983, the lawyer sent Lubbe a message: "Sam come and collect your money." He had accumulated R48,000, about $37,000. Lubbe deposited the check and went to a savings bank that provided credit for real estate transactions. He told the loan officer that he wanted to start building "garage and two rooms": small two-family houses with one room per family. The loan officer refused. He said Lubbe was too young and lacked the capacity to build houses. Even though Lubbe had a bank balance of R48,000 and each half of a "garage and two rooms" would sell for R14,000, the loan officer refused to give him credit.

The loan officer's supervisor advised Lubbe to find people willing to buy the houses and bring them to the bank for home owner loans. Sam would receive payment from the bank only after he had built the house with his own capital. Essentially, Lubbe was asked to self-finance the construction of houses to sell to the bank. Lubbe found two clients in Soweto and completed the houses. The bank's inspector approved. The purchasers received loans and began repaying them at R300 monthly. The bank paid Lubbe the full amount of the loan.

After the first transaction had gone well, Lubbe returned to the bank and asked for a loan to build more houses. The bank still refused, despite his track record, the solvency of his company, and sufficient cash for collateral. "You bring us buyers," the loan officer said, meaning: Lubbe, you bring us customers. "Then we will loan them the money and pay you." Lubbe returned to the printer:

> Come to Lubbe Construction
> Garage and Two Rooms
> 14,000 Rand
> No Deposit

The flyers found their way into the hands of commuters returning home from work at Soweto's train station. So many interested buyers responded that Lubbe—not the bank—had to hire a secretary to help them complete the loan forms.

This is how Sam Lubbe built houses in and around Soweto before 1990, when Nelson Mandela was freed from Robben Island prison. The government dismantled the apartheid system. International economic sanctions against South Africa were lifted.

As more blacks began migrating to urban areas, Lubbe Construction flourished, building multistory buildings and houses. Yet Lubbe still had trouble obtaining loans from South African banks. They continued to pay him only after the brickwork was laid and the mortar had dried and the space was ready for occupancy.

In the late 1990s, Lubbe discovered Nurcha, and his business expanded when he was able to access credit for the first time. George Soros visited one of his projects south of Johannesburg. But Lubbe's fortunes then took an uncertain turn.

Lubbe took on contracts for building projects involving several million rand. The two companies went into liquidation and were unable to pay him. Lubbe ended up owing money to his suppliers and unable to pay a bank loan that he had received with Nurcha's assistance. The bank's advisers told him he should allow Lubbe Construction to go bankrupt—liquidate a company that had begun with a box of electrical tools, some flyers, and a bicycle. "For me to start over, having not completed the first grade, would have been extremely difficult," Lubbe said. "Who would give me a job? I wanted to try to negotiate with people, to pay the money, to keep the company working."

He approached Nurcha, which sent Lubbe an adviser and mentor who worked with him for almost a year. Nurcha's mentor helped Lubbe manage his creditors ("If you give a small sum of money," Lubbe said, "the supplier keeps quiet.") and keep a tight grip on his cash flow. Workers went three months with no salary. ("We sat them down in the conference room and told them to be patient. When a little money came in, everyone shared.") He struggled but survived. His workers stayed on, and eventually the business flourished, accessing further credit from both Nurcha and the bank. And he continued to rely on the same suppliers. In 2001, the South African parliament presented him with an award for helping ease the country's critical shortage of housing.

In 2009, Lubbe had government contracts to build 2,000 houses in three locations. Nurcha was again a major source of financing. One project was finished, and two were scheduled for completion in 2010. "When we hand them over, the people are very happy. They have lived in shantytowns for a long time. And I feel very happy, because our people are getting better houses now. I am making a difference." Still, payment was a problem. The government housing department had not paid Lubbe for the houses he had built in eight months and notified Lubbe that it could not pay until the next fiscal year. The government had already spent all the money in its 2009 budget. "Now they owe me 25 million rand and cannot pay," Lubbe said. "We are in deep water again." Lubbe Construction was surviving because Nurcha bridge financing was helping to tide the company over, and Nurcha played a crucial role in bringing pressure on the provincial housing department to expedite payments to Lubbe and a large group of other contractors who found themselves in a similar position.

In the meantime, Lubbe is diversifying. He has formed a company to raise poultry to compete with the only poultry company in South Africa. He has worked contracts in Mozambique. In early 2010, he won a contract to build one thousand homes in Sudan.

He has also turned his focus onto his own family. He convinced his eight children—by two wives—to study civil engineering, architecture, accounting, and agriculture, so they can manage aspects of the family business. He has also helped members of his extended family—none of whom has yet succeeded as he has— just as Lubbe's mother once approached his father's boss to make

Sam a tea boy. "If they want 200 or 500 rand, you give it to them," he said. "It is their right in our system." He has provided several dozen nieces and nephews school fees, clothes, and textbooks. He has donated work on schools, and his company has helped re-furbish two houses for abused women.

"We want to list Lubbe Construction on the stock market," he said.

*   *   *

Beyond South Africa. Nurcha's success in South Africa prompted the Soros Economic Development Fund to help launch and support similar financial organizations in dozens of other countries. In Bulgaria, financial support from the Soros Economic Development Fund and the Open Society Founda-tions, in 1999, helped establish Mikrofond, whose mission has been to provide loans to micro-, small-, and medium-size enter-prises, and especially those in low-income and underserved com-munities. By 2008, Mikrofond had disbursed 7,000 loans worth €25 million, financing entrepreneurs in 215 municipalities of Bulgaria; 20 percent of its active clients are Roma or people from other marginalized groups.

The Soros Economic Development Fund's efforts expanded throughout the region as well. In 1999, the fund deposited €750,000 in IK Banka to design and implement Macedonia's first lending program for independent farmers and small- and medium-size agricultural enterprises. In Romania, the Soros Economic Development Fund, in 2001, provided a ten-year, $2 million loan to Centrul pentru Dezvoltare Economica (CDE), a one-year-old nonprofit whose objective was to provide finan-cial services to disadvantaged groups and rural entrepreneurs in economically deteriorating communities. In 2005, the Soros

Economic Development Fund issued a second $700,000 loan, leveraging $7 million in World Bank funding for three rural finance projects through the ministries of labor and finance. By the end of 2009, the CDE had provided more than 13,000 loans totaling over $41 million. In 2006, the Soros Economic Development Fund provided a $500,000 loan to Mikrohitel, a Hungarian financial company whose mission is to finance social welfare projects, particularly those serving the Roma community.

In Panama, the Soros Economic Development Fund purchased a $25,000 equity interest in the holding company of MiBanco, a cooperative bank serving low-income populations, and deposited $1 million in the bank itself. In 2005, the Soros Economic Development Fund made an equity investment in the Global Commercial Microfinance Consortium, an $80.6 million microfinance investment fund managed by the Deutsche Bank Global Social Investments Group and formed by more than two dozen institutional investors and aid agencies. The consortium is a public-private partnership that invests in microfinance institutions that lend to the working poor throughout the developing world. The fund purchased $1 million Class B shares of the consortium, which then provided a total of $80 million in local currency financing to over thirty microfinance institutions worldwide. Since 2001, the Soros Economic Development Fund has guaranteed up to $1 million on $2.3 million in commercial bank loans as well as provided a $1 million direct loan to Haiti's Association pour la Coopération avec la Micro Entreprise, which meets the capital needs of urban entrepreneurs working in the informal sector. Before the earthquake that struck Haiti in January 2010, the association had 24,000 active clients and over $10 million in loans. The Soros Economic Development Fund has also provided support for the Community and Individual Development Association City Campus, a not-for-profit university in South Africa that provides higher education designed to encourage personal, economic, and social development. Since 2003, the Soros Economic Development Fund has guaranteed up to $250,000 in FirstRand Bank Limited loans to disadvantaged students who attend the CIDA City Campus. In 2008, the Soros Economic Development Fund partnered with Omidyar Network and Google.org to launch a $17 million venture capital fund in India, the SONG Growth Company, whose aim is to provide early stage and expansion capital for small and medium enterprises. The fund's investment was $6 million.

Other notable partnerships were with the Besa Foundation in Albania, with Microinvest in Moldova, and with the Tameer Microfinance Bank in Pakistan.

*   *   *

Albania. When Flamur Tema was a boy, his father owned a bakery in a building of time-darkened wood that still stands on a cobblestone street in the mountainside town of Krujë. The building had been in Tema's family for two centuries by 1965 when Albania's Communist rulers evicted Tema's father from the bakery and confiscated the structure. Instead of baking bread, Tema's father went to work for the state. He spent his days issuing driver's licenses. At the time, Krujë had only two trucks, one for delivering milk and one for delivering bread, and three automobiles, one each for the Communist Party chairman, the police chief, and the mayor. Bread shortages were a chronic problem.

Communist rule collapsed in Albania in 1990. By the time Flamur Tema could reclaim his father's store, three rival bakeries had opened in Krujë. Tema operated a struggling café for nine years before losing confidence in the profitability of serving coffee by the cup. He began selling antiques and souvenirs to growing numbers of tourists attracted to Krujë by the nearby castle of Albania's greatest hero, Skanderbeg. Tema needed a minuscule sum of capital to expand his business, but no bank would loan him the money. The country's economy had imploded in 1997, when a pyramid investment scheme collapsed and wiped out the savings of thousands of Albanians. Two years later, financial dealings in Albania were still in a state of turmoil.

In 1999, Tema turned to the Besa Foundation, a nonprofit microfinance organization that the Open Society Foundation for Albania founded that same year with grant funding from the Soros Economic Development Fund and the World Bank. Tema used his first loan to remodel his shop. With a second loan, he filled an entire floor with souvenirs and memorabilia.

By 2007, tourists were arriving in great numbers, buying carved wooden cradles, rusted pistols, grandfather clocks, and marble ashtrays in the shape of the thousands of concrete defense bunkers that dot the countryside like squat toadstools. Carpet weavers and other shop owners along Tema's street likewise received loans from Besa, and their businesses thrived. Today, private cars plying Krujë's busiest streets compete for space with tourist buses, delivery vans, and trucks weighed down with construction materials.

Albania remains one of Europe's poorest countries. Yet by 2007, the Besa Foundation had grown to employ about ninety loan officers working with about 9,500 active clients across Albania. Its largest outstanding loan was the equivalent of $37,000; the smallest loan was $600. Besa's at-risk loans constituted less than 1 percent of its $38 million portfolio, according to Altin Musa, Besa's director of marketing. In addition to antique dealers and carpet weavers in Krujë, Besa provided credit to stonecutters for tools, to shoemakers and seamstresses for machinery, to retailers for purchasing display cases and acquiring inventory, to book publishers and binders for supplies, and to painters for paint, canvas, and other art supplies.

*   *   *

Moldova. As with Besa in Albania, the Soros Economic Development Fund worked with Microinvest in Moldova, a country whose economy dissolved after the Soviet Union collapsed. Thousands of young Moldovans, desperate to survive, sought new lives by emigrating. Thousands of Moldovan young women fell victim to traffickers.

The Soros Economic Development Fund, working with Microinvest, a registered financial institution in Moldova's capital city, Chişinău, is assisting local entrepreneurs, including people who have survived human trafficking, to rebuild their lives. Launched in 2003, with funding from the Soros Economic Development Fund and the Soros Foundation–Moldova, Microinvest made its first loan to a man who wanted to refurbish an old bus and begin transporting passengers between Chişinău and the south of Moldova. Microinvest first broke even in 2006. Two years later, it obtained over €3.3 million in new equity capital from a consortium of investors.

"We market a specific credit product for young entrepreneurs, for members of the age-group that is most exposed to traffickers," said its chief executive officer, Artur Munteanu. "If young people don't have jobs, they will move away. They will risk going abroad illegally to find jobs, lacking information, lacking education, lacking skills." This puts some at the mercy of prostitution rings.

"I remember two women clients who had been trafficked," Munteanu said. "We knew this at the management level, but the loan officers were not informed. They received a loan, the equivalent of $5,000 at that time, to plant a potato crop. It is not an easy job to plant potatoes. I know they paid the loan back."

Moldova's Roma were another group Microinvest was targeting. "Roma face great difficulty obtaining loans anywhere else," Munteanu said. Fiodor Zeleni, a forty-two-year-old Roma blacksmith from the outskirts of Orhei, a town north of Chişinău, obtained his second loan from Microinvest, the equivalent of $3,500, to buy coal and scrap metal for fashioning farm implements. Behind the fine house he built for his wife and four children, Zeleni has set up an anvil and a forge in an open brick shed with a corrugated metal roof and a blow-dryer fan that force-feeds oxygen to the brazier. "My father was a blacksmith," he said. "I have done the same thing since childhood in Soviet times. But I couldn't get a loan. I can sell between eight and twenty horseshoes and hoes in a day at the town market. Without the loan money, I could do nothing."

Belief in the profitability of Moldova's fertile black earth involved a leap of faith for Artur Bobirke and his brother, Gheorghe. The sons of a nurse and an accountant, the brothers Bobirke had no experience in farming before Gheorghe went to work as an intern on a Wisconsin dairy farm. He returned home convinced that Moldova's farmers were mindlessly following obsolete farming methods and that, by applying new ideas, he could make a private farm profitable.

The brothers pooled their savings with money from their sister who was working abroad. They bought a parcel of undeveloped farmland, built five greenhouses for vegetables, and sowed a crop of cabbage in the open fields. They bought a wheezing Soviet-era tanker truck to help them with irrigating the fields during the scorching summer. Using the truck for watering cost about $50 per day. The Bobirkes borrowed the equivalent of $5,000 from Microinvest to build an irrigation pipe to lower the cost and allow them to expand. "This year, we are paying $10 a day for irrigating the fields," Gheorghe Bobirke said. "I can employ three people for a day for what I had been paying."

Over the winter, the brothers built fifteen more greenhouses, each covered by clear plastic and heated by small wood-burning stoves. Inside, they grew sweet peppers, tomatoes, cucumbers, and radishes. They sold the vegetables at a roadside stand and the green market in Chişinău, where they paid a daily wage to two employees.

"I made my choice. I want to be here," said Gheorghe. "I want to be in my country. I am a boss. My brother is a boss. My sister is a boss. And this year, the return will triple our investment and we will have enough of a yield to export to Russia."

*   *   *

Pakistan. In Pakistan, where poverty and a lack of development are fueling lawlessness and Islamic extremism, the Soros Economic Development Fund has partnered with Tameer Microfinance Bank. The mission of Tameer Bank is simple: to provide a full range of financial services to the country's working poor. In Pakistan, large numbers of shopkeepers, seamstresses, artisans, and others are able save the equivalent of $10 to $100 a month but are forced to sock their money away inside mattresses because bank charges are too high. These small savers help create jobs by employing the poorest of the poor in workshops and other modest enterprises.

Pakistan has about 170 million inhabitants, but only 10 million bank accounts, said Shahid Mustafa, Tameer Bank's group executive director for product and risk management. "This means that 94 percent of the people are not saving and borrowing in the formal economy. Fewer than 2 percent of the people borrow from banks. One way to give people access to banking is to make it cheap."

Fulfilling Tameer's mission remains difficult, however, because providing a full range of banking services in Pakistan is expensive. The monthly cost of maintaining each of Tameer's twenty-five branches is the equivalent of about $10,000. If a branch performs 10,000 transactions each month, the cost of each transaction is $1. This is exorbitant, because most of Tameer's depositors have only $100 in their accounts, most of its loan customers borrow only $500 to $1,500, and most transactions total only $2 to $3. Tameer needed to maximize the number of its customers without increasing its investment in new branches.

During 2007, the Soros Economic Development Fund awarded Tameer a grant of $175,000 to solve this problem by developing capacity in "branchless banking." Tameer used the grant money first to give its bankcard holders access to Pakistan's network of automatic teller machines and then to develop infrastructure in which cardholders could withdraw cash, make deposits and loan payments, and purchase goods through point of sale card readers in thousands of retail shops around the country.

"We are making the banking experience the same as buying a pint of milk or bread—buy a dozen eggs and here's my loan payment as well," Mustafa said. "This solution will enable the bank to reach thousands of new borrowers and depositors."

The system came online in late 2007. The number of store counter machines soon grew to thirty. "We are in the process of booking new agents and have issued cards to about six thousand people," Mustafa said. "You can't just go and leave a machine in a store. You have to evaluate the agent. You are putting your name on a third person's place of business."

"Integrating Tameer Microfinance Bank into Pakistan's national payments system, via ATMs and the point of sale network, brings thousands of low-income households into the formal financial system," said Fawzia Naqvi, vice president of the Soros Economic Development Fund. "It helps Tameer Bank take one more step toward breaking down the financial apartheid which exists in countries such as Pakistan."

In 2008, the Norwegian mobile phone company Telenor bought 51 percent of Tameer Microfinance Bank. This partnership has enabled the launch of an innovative mobile phone–based payment product called EasyPaisa, which permits customers to make money transfers and pay utility bills using their mobile phones.

Poverty, huge numbers of refugees, and the hardships presented by natural disasters make Pakistan a daunting challenge to economic development efforts. But Tameer has continued to flourish. By the time of the floods in 2010, it had attracted over 120,000 customers and over 70,000 borrowers countrywide and was continuing to develop innovative ways of improving access to banks for Pakistan's people.

*   *   *

Liberia and Sierra Leone. In 2009, the Open Society Foundations began working to improve the lives of people in Liberia and Sierra Leone, two countries emerging from devastating wars. The Soros Economic Development Fund structured a $15 million investment to enable BRAC, a Bangladesh-based development organization that is one of the world's largest antipoverty groups, to expand an enhanced microfinance development model into Liberia and Sierra Leone. The transaction—which involved a $4 million investment from the Soros Economic Development Fund, as well as investments from the Omidyar Network Fund, the Open Society Initiative for West Africa, and Humanity United—was designed to enable BRAC to provide microcredit, health services, and agricultural support to more than 500,000 people within three years.

Shah Alam oversees the BRAC operation in Sierra Leone. He describes the organization, saying, "We are not just a microfinance institution. We are about bringing social change. Our clients learn about latrines, mosquito nets, schooling, and good nutrition. This can change their lives and those of the next generation." The program began in 2009, and there were over ten thousand borrowers by the end of the year. The average loan was $155. The repayment rate after the first six months was 100 percent.

Fatmata Katta, the mother of a teenage daughter and son, was recuperating from an illness at her father's house in Sierra Leone's capital, Freetown, in January 1999. A week into the new year, the rebels arrived, drunk and armed, looking for loot to steal and girls to rape. They ordered everyone into the street. "I saw them shoot a pregnant woman," Katta recalled, apparently because she did not come from her house quickly enough. They gang-raped a young girl of about ten, who later bled to death. They loaded down an old man with loot from the houses and ordered him to carry it to their camp. He was weak and so they shot him dead. Later in the day, they burned Katta's father and cousins alive inside their house.

A small contingent of British commandos dispersed the rebels, enabling Katta and her husband to start over. Katta earned about $2.50 a day, enough to feed the family, selling firewood, rice pap, and flavored ice. Years passed. Katta's husband began doing farm work and bringing home rice and other staples. Katta spent her earnings on household needs. There wasn't enough profit to reinvest. But Katta was looking for a way to expand. She began saving seriously only after BRAC spread word that it was going to begin making loans. "I knew that with the money from a loan and my savings, I could really do something," Katta said. "BRAC made me believe it would be possible to do bigger business."

In June 2009, she borrowed $150 and used the money to purchase bags of charcoal to sell along with her flavored ice. Each week she made day trips to buy three hundred bags of charcoal to sell in the market for about $3 each, cash and carry, no credit, $1 profit per bag. The number of trips grew to two and three in a week: "It wasn't always easy but now I'm really benefiting. Thanks be to God. My daughter hasn't been well and needs an operation. I know the doctor, so I'm going to negotiate a good price for her, but now I can pay those bills."

Katta has felt the impact of the recent international economic crisis. Fuel prices drove up the cost of transport from $0.75 to $1.00 per bag. The dollar is stronger now too, so prices keep going up. "But my prices have increased too, from $3.00 to $3.50 for a bag. Everybody needs charcoal for cooking, so I still sell the same amount."

"I've suffered a lot, so I don't need to buy many new things. I know how much money matters. For now, I'm putting the money I make back into the business. I'm saving $1.25 a day now and making my loan payments each week. BRAC gives one week's grace before payments begin. I don't have any trouble paying back my loan. Even my husband doesn't know how much money I make. If I tell him he'll want me to give him some to spend but I want to invest. I plan to open my first bank account. I want to buy a small piece of land and build a house, so I won't have to pay house rent anymore."

Salamatu Kamara lost her husband to a gang of rebels who found him sick in bed, dragged him from his house, put a tire around his body, doused him with gasoline, and lit a match. Then they burned the family house.

Kamara was two months pregnant when she was forced to flee to her brother's house in George Brook, a poor neighborhood overlooking Freetown. After the war, she started buying fish from fishermen who brought their catch to a beach near Freetown. "Sometimes I'd buy up to a dozen fish, then bring those to

George Brook market to sell," she said. "It used to take three to four hours to make the trip to buy the fish. If the fishermen didn't get a good catch, there wouldn't be much fish for us to sell. I didn't have any savings so the amount of fish I could buy wasn't steady." On good days, she earned the equivalent of $10.

In June 2009, Kamara received a BRAC loan for $150 in leones, the local currency. She buys her fish each morning now at a dockyard: "I buy cartons of frozen or dried fish. I wrap what I buy in ice and a blanket and take it to the market." She can clear the equivalent of $25 each day now.

"So things are much better for me now. I dress my children in better clothes. They won't go to school in dirty clothes now. And they get to eat lunch every day now. They used to eat only in the morning and evening. I used to worry a lot about money and how my children and I would manage. Now I'm saving $12.50 a month in my bank account. Can you imagine? I'm not too strong financially yet as this is my first business. But it's getting better. I want to provide a foundation for my children by building my own house one day from my savings. I dreamed of it before but I could never imagine actually being able to do it."

Jane Bah is the mother of four girls and runs a hairdressing salon in Freetown. She began learning to cut, curl, color, comb out, braid, and straighten hair after she left school at age thirteen, got married, and had two daughters. Her first husband drove her and her daughters from his house. Bah and her daughters were living with her parents when she met her new husband, by whom she had two more daughters.

Rebels attacked their area in 1991. Bah fled to Freetown and began living with her aunt. For the next eight years, she styled hair in a small kiosk made of wood and metal. Rebels burned it down when they entered Freetown on January 6, 1999: "Rebels were running through the whole area, cutting off people's hands and arms. When the rebels came to our area, we ran away to my brother's house in central Freetown. The tension was so high. The rebels were threatening to burn our houses so we slept outside in the street. It was a Thursday night and the rebels took my eldest daughter away along with many other girls. I was sure they'd kill her, but she escaped and came back."

Three weeks later, after the rebels had fled, Jane Bah started life anew. She had little food and lived jammed together with twenty other people in a small, unfinished house. She bought bundles of lumber, found some metal sheets, rebuilt her kiosk salon, and began cutting, combing, and braiding. "I used to have two or three customers a day," she said. "I didn't have any products to sell, of course. So it was mainly plaiting styles for people."

In 2005, her second husband died. Jane Bah struggled to pay rent on her house, $7.50 a month for a bedroom and a sitting room, as well as school fees for her children. In June 2009, she took a loan equivalent to about $112 from BRAC. She repaid it in $3.50 weekly installments. "I used the money to buy Nigerian hair products to curl and straighten hair. This has made my business more profitable because I can charge more for coloring and straightening." She also bought soap, gel, dye, and products used in traditional medicine.

"I can be very busy during holiday time. But at other times, I can have no hair to do. So with this new business, I make more profits than in hair dressing and I get income every day. Every month, I make a profit on top of what I make from the hair-dressing. It's regular and I buy more goods to sell. I work from seven in the morning until seven in the evening. When I'm not at the salon, my nephew sells for me and takes care of the place.

"I want to see a brighter future," Jane Bah said. "I've bought some land, and I want to put up a house made of dried clay blocks. I'll plaster the walls to make it look nice. I'm planning to build four rooms and a parlor. The toilet will be outdoors. My second daughter and I are building as we go along. We've only just started. The house is for me for when I get old."

When George Soros began his philanthropy, few foundations and nongovernmental organizations were providing financial services to microbusinesses and entrepreneurs. Soros's decision to launch the Soros Economic Development Fund gave impetus to a movement that is improving the lives of many of the most motivated and entrepreneurial people among the world's poor.

*   *   *

GEORGE SOROS

Early in my foundation work, I was averse to social investing because I felt that having a double bottom line confuses issues. It leads to results that are difficult to evaluate because having a social purpose can be an excuse for not having a profit. Whether you are successful in attaining the social purpose is more difficult to evaluate than a profit. Either I am engaged in business where I want to maximize my profit or I am engaged in philanthropy where I am only concerned with the social benefit.

But my foundations did get involved in social investing from time to time. In Bulgaria, for instance, the foundation became the largest book publisher. This raised serious questions about whether by subsidizing publishing we were actually preventing a healthy publishing industry from developing. To satisfy the ever recurring demand for supporting mass media, we set up a special operation, the Media Development Loan Fund. It has been very successful because it is run on business lines. We also got involved in promoting the microcredit industry. Thus, with the passage of time, I gradually came to modify my views about social investing.

Now I recognize that social investing is more difficult than ordinary investment because of the double bottom line, but I do not consider this difficulty to be a deterrent; on the contrary, I treat it as a challenge. Countries we are trying to help need not only aid but also investment, and we are getting increasingly involved in social investing. In many cases, notably Pakistan, Sierra Leone, and Liberia—with the Papua province of Indonesia now under consideration—we bring in BRAC, the Bangladeshi microcredit organization. They are better prepared and better positioned to work in very poor countries than anybody from the developed world.

I recognize that I am not a qualified entrepreneur myself, and I always try to find good managers I can rely on. But I am a good critic of managers. I pride myself on being the most successful, most highly paid critic in the world. That has been the basis of my success in the financial market, so I insist on my role as a critic, not as an actual entrepreneur. When Nurcha was formed, I rejected the first management team that was presented to me. The next one turned out to be highly successful. One of those managers, Cedric de Beer, a South African public health and urban planning official, now plays a key role in the Soros Economic Development Fund.

When I got involved in the problems of economic development, I became a great fan and supporter of Paul Collier, a development economist, We have worked together in a number of countries, including Haiti and most recently Guinea. In his books, such as *The Bottom Billion*, Collier identifies four or five traps, like the resource curse, that are effectively the opposites of financial bubbles. So his theory of traps and my theory of bubbles offer very similar, nonlinear interpretations of economic development.

PART II

Failed States:
Haiti and Burma

Displaced Haitians living in Parc Martissant after the January 2010 earthquake devastated much of the capital city of Port-au-Prince. In the wake of the disaster, George Soros and the Open Society Foundations, long-time supporters of public libraries, community water programs, and poverty alleviation in Haiti, increased their funding for humanitarian aid and economic development. (© Ron Haviv/VII for the Open Society Foundations)

CHAPTER 4

Helping Haiti
Rise from Destruction

Democratic decision making, a functioning free market, transparency and accountability, and respect for civil and human rights: These and all the other building blocks of an open society have no firm foundation to stand upon in countries where legions of people are so lacking in the basic necessities of life that they have little time or energy for anything beyond an immediate, vicious struggle for survival.

Haiti's people—most of them descendants of rebel slaves, many of them energetic, creative, desperate for education, and, to a fault, self-reliant—bear the scars of three centuries of social turmoil and life on the edge of existence. They have been set upon by yellow fever, syphilis, malaria, HIV, and TB, and have watched as their children died of simple diarrhea. They have endured dictatorship, police thuggery, and gang violence as well as foreign (read: United States) invasion, occupation, and economic embargo. Even today, they still endure corruption, drug-trafficking, people-trafficking, kidnapping, brain-addling malnutrition, and stomach-wrenching rates of infant mortality. They have clear-cut their forests, exhausted their fields, and over-fished their waters. Too many suffer from a misplaced faith in divination and other deep-seated superstitions as well as a dependency mentality ingrained by decades of misguided foreign aid.

Electricity lines have yet to stretch far into Haiti's hinterlands, where clean running water and indoor plumbing exist only in tales about the world outside. In hamlets inaccessible even to all-terrain vehicles, villagers, many of them barefoot children, carry everything: sloshing water jugs, sacks of rice and beans and concrete, sheaves of twelve-foot-long steel reinforcement bars, their infants, their sick and injured, and their heavily pregnant women, each patient lying upon a wooden door lifted from its hinges and borne by someone at the corners. Illiteracy is the rule. Information and rumor trickle into minds primarily via radio and gossip.

Education might—only might—be chipping away at widespread ignorance. Nearly all of Haiti's schools are private. Some are run by headmasters and headmistresses who have only a hint of education beyond the eighth grade—and all too many are substandard or outright scams defrauding the unwary.

Haiti and the daunting challenges it faces and presents caught George Soros's attention years before he established his foundations to promote open society. During the 1980s, at the Americas Watch offices in midtown Manhattan, Soros attended talks on Haiti and its ruling regime. He traveled to the country's capital, Port-au-Prince, and once stayed at the Oloffson, the decaying hotel Graham Greene made famous in *The Comedians*. Soros encountered a society atomized and traumatized by decades of repression. Haiti's former dictators, François "Papa Doc" Duvalier and his son, Jean-Claude, had banned unsanctioned gatherings and even unsanctioned discussion of local issues. Their thugs beat and killed people who dared to gripe.

The possibility of an open society arising in Haiti only existed legally from 1987, when the country's constitution was rewritten to grant Haitians the right to express and organize themselves freely. Mired in corruption, infighting, and fecklessness, Haiti's post-dictatorship government effectively abandoned impoverished

Haitians to their own devices. Thousands of them fled the country aboard rafts and fishing boats. Hundreds of thousands more managed to get no farther than the slums in and around Port-au-Prince.

In 1994, three years after remnants of Duvalier's drug-running military overthrew President Jean-Bertrand Aristide, the United States landed 20,000 Marines in Haiti and returned Aristide to power. This was the moment Soros and Aryeh Neier seized to launch an open society foundation in Haiti. It would be called FOKAL, an acronym for Creole words meaning Foundation for Knowledge and Liberty.

As FOKAL's executive director, they named Michèle Pierre-Louis, a woman who, after seeing her family and close friends suffer under Duvalier, went to study in the United States and France and returned to work in a number of private- and public-sector positions before openly denouncing the 1991 military coup. Pierre-Louis recruited Lorraine Mangonès, the daughter of Haiti's most renowned architect, to oversee FOKAL's programs.

The foundation first undertook an analysis of the political, social, and economic situation in Haiti during the early post-Duvalier transition, a violent shift from a thuggish, corrupt dictatorship into a thuggish, corrupt democracy. As the foundation was beginning its work, slum gangs, armed by Aristide and other political leaders, fought pitched battles and began to kidnap and kill in order to extort money from people who managed to find paying jobs and/or start profit-making businesses. "People were crying out for change," Pierre-Louis said. "But how to bring change when people must struggle to survive? How to promote the education of children when their parents are illiterate? How to promote public discussion when so many people have no idea how to participate in a discussion?"

FOKAL's team attacked this problem on two levels. First, the programs set out to lay the groundwork for development of an open society by enhancing the capacity of individuals. On another level, however, the programs worked to expand and strengthen social ties collectively. In its efforts to help develop free-thinking, responsible, and engaged individuals, the foundation initiated debate programs that gave young people an opportunity to sharpen their ability to reason and express themselves. It initiated a program to develop entrepreneurship among adolescents and young adults as well as a scholarship program to give young people a chance to attend universities and technical schools in Haiti.

The centerpiece of FOKAL's early efforts in education was a program to promote the spread of Tipa Tipa, or "Step by Step," a child-centered preschool program that allows children to explore a variety of individual and group activities before they enter mainstream classrooms. The foundation worked for years without success to convince Haiti's education ministry to adopt Tipa Tipa as a component of the national education curriculum, which had no preschool element. After the ministry balked, FOKAL introduced Tipa Tipa in a dozen remote rural areas where community organizations, some of them initiated by Roman Catholic and Protestant clergymen, were working to improve dire living conditions. FOKAL sponsored teacher-training programs, built schools, and, for a time, subsidized Tipa Tipa by providing classroom materials and teacher salaries.

In its efforts on the community level, FOKAL opened free libraries in Port-au-Prince as well as in remote towns and villages. This gave far-flung Haitians unprecedented access to information and ideas from the outside world and provided a space for people to gather and share their own ideas as they discussed issues affecting their lives and communities. The foundation nurtured the growth of community organizations. It sponsored arts and cultural events to bring people together and foster a sense of Haitian community.

FOKAL undertook educational programs and other projects in rural communities outside Port-au-Prince to help staunch the flow of desperately poor country folk into the capital city's slums. "We never went into communities and started from scratch," Pierre-Louis added. "We went into communities that had dynamic leadership and some funding from other sources. We always told them we would not be there forever. We wanted them to be able to continue without us, knowing very well that it would not be easy. It was difficult to find towns and villages with partners who were not clergymen; and in areas where clergymen were the only option, they were many times overbearing, even dictatorial. When you have this situation, you have a problem because the impetus for everything comes from the top down and not from the bottom up."

FOKAL remained well aware of the pitfalls of philanthropy in Haiti. There is a tendency for local people constantly to approach new foreign donors seeking funds to create new hospitals, schools, and other assets—turning on a spigot of operating funds—rather than manage existing assets and projects in ways that make them sustainable. Some foreign donors have inadvertently created incentives for philanthropic pyramid schemes by repeatedly responding to tales of woe, funding new brick-and-mortar and free-aid projects while older projects and nascent for-fee local enterprises fail because the community either neglects them, lacks the means to operate them in a sustainable manner, or will not pay for services when they can be had cost free from another foreign charity.

In an effort to enhance the likelihood that its libraries, preschools, community radio stations, and other projects would endure long enough to make development of an open society possible, FOKAL invested in small-scale, economic-development projects. "What we found was that in poor, remote communities it is impossible to invest only in education projects and expect them to be sustainable based upon local resources," Mangonès said. "We found ourselves investing in environment, health, irrigation projects, food-processing projects, and fishing projects."

In sites like Vallue, a highland village with road access to Haiti's main coastal highway, FOKAL projects appear to have passed the sustainability test. In locations like Sainte Agnès, a hamlet four hours by foot from the nearest road, they have faltered. In sprawling, teeming Port-au-Prince, programs to create a sense of community have survived despite the hurricanes of 2008 and the earthquake of January 2010, and, so far at least, the frustration evident in a sentiment spray-painted on walls across the rubble-strewn capital: *"Bon retour Jean-Claude Duvalier."*

*   *   *

Vallue stands on a swathe of mountainside overlooking a thin stretch of coastal plain. From nearby bluffs, the village's inhabitants can see Haiti's main coastal highway, the pot-holed and earthquake-ripped National Road, just a few miles away. No local road gave Vallue access to the National Road until years after the downfall of Baby Doc Duvalier in 1986. Before then, goods and supplies were transported up and down the mountain on donkey back or human head. The sick were carried down to the hospital. School students walked for hours to get to class and back; too many children dropped out after a few years without acquiring the ability to read. Everyone feared the Duvalier regime's enforcers, the *Tontons Macoutes*.

After Duvalier's fall from power, a group of locally born university graduates—including young men who had completed sociology, project-management, and economic-development degrees at colleges in Canada and France—moved home to Vallue in order to help the area's peasants found a cooperative that would pool their assets and represent their interests. The graduates missed the life and fresh air of their mountain village and sought a peace and quiet that they found missing in larger towns and the capital city's burgeoning slums.

At first, local peasants and civic leaders spread rumors that the new Association of Peasants of Vallue was a Communist organization. These rumors dried up once the rumor-mongers found themselves benefiting from the association's work. The graduates initiated a literacy program in a small reading center, which they used to organize local people. They assembled road crews who, by chipping away at limestone with pick and shovel, began constructing Vallue's first road to the outside world. The association founded a village school. And before local funds ran out, instructors began teaching kids how to play tennis on a court marked out in a parking lot; one student went on to become Haiti's national champion. The association's membership grew into the thousands.

In 1997, one of the association's leaders visited FOKAL and inquired about establishing a library in Vallue. Before it handed off the last of its projects in Vallue eight years later, FOKAL had become the largest of the peasant association's donors and had implemented practically every program it offered. In 1998, FOKAL established a library and trained personnel to staff it. The peasants association utilized the library as a gathering place—a space for local people, many of whom who could not read, to listen to storytellers and discuss local issues. Later, FOKAL introduced Tipa Tipa to the Vallue school and joined a Canadian donor in supporting construction of a new school building. "My wife does not know how to read and write, and I cannot read a letter," said 57-year-old Emile Faustin, a peasant with six children. "But I consider myself a success, because I have sent my children to school."

In Haiti, children with disabilities do not generally receive an education. However, the success of a deaf pupil at the Vallue school demonstrated to parents there and in other areas of the country that children with disabilities can succeed in the classroom as well as enrich school life. "Tipa Tipa's results have allowed the peasants association of Vallue to promote the high-quality education available here," said Yvon Faustin, one of the association's founders. "Our school is considered one of the best in the entire region. It is a school where everyone is involved, and the students participate in cultural activities, reforestation, and cleaning plastic and other litter in the area."

FOKAL also began awarding local high school graduates scholarships to study at universities and technical schools in Port-au-Prince. Some went off to the city to study civil engineering and returned home to build houses and buildings and improve the road; another studied accounting and came home to manage the association's books; yet another was trained in telecommunications.

The peasants association had been involved in economic-development work since its members undertook construction of the road up the mountain. The association launched an enterprise producing jarred peanut butter but had trouble filling orders because they were doing all the milling by hand; FOKAL provided support for an electric milling machine and a generator to power it. The association later received FOKAL's backing to begin production of jam and preserves from locally grown fruit, and at one time the enterprise employed fifty local people.

With FOKAL's support the peasants association obtained seedlings and planted bamboo and fruit trees to slow soil erosion, reduce the risk of catastrophic landslides, and increase production of fruits and vegetables. The association had to urge local people to protect the trees rather than cut them to clear fields for planting and to produce charcoal to sell in local markets.

FOKAL was a partner in a project that helped peasants build decent houses to replace dirt-floor shacks and allowed home owners to rent accommodations as part of an "eco-agro-tourism" enterprise. FOKAL funded a project to pipe spring water to a village and to nearby fields once used only for millet farming; this saved the village's women and children hours of carrying water and enabled the peasants to plant two growing seasons of profitable fruits and vegetables, including tomatoes, lettuce, cabbage, pepper, and papaya.

If any of these projects were going to succeed, however, they needed constant monitoring, Pierre-Louis explained. It took months, for example, for the association to install the peanut milling machine and the generator to power it. The peasants involved in the eco-tourism project had to be informed why guests would be appalled to see the refuse from their meals dumped into an open streambed with the village's other trash. An agronomist from France, who persevered even after he recovered from a bullet wound sustained while riding his motorcycle, spent months overcoming peasant resistance to switching from millet to more profitable, though also more labor-intensive, vegetables and fruits.

FOKAL also funded the start-up of the peasants association's for-profit, self-sustaining, FM radio station. Its signal now reaches three million listeners in seven of Haiti's ten departments, including Port-au-Prince. The station devotes about 60 percent of its air time to local music. The remainder it fills with programs on education, health, environment, agriculture, children, and news.

FOKAL trained the reporters, and they produced, among other things, programs that described for listeners beyond Vallue what the peasants association had undertaken. People descended upon Vallue from all over the country to learn from the association's experience. "Today, when you say you are from Vallue, people everywhere know you are from somewhere," said Benoit Batichon, one of the radio station's staff members.

The announcer and engineer were preparing their evening broadcast at seven minutes to five on January 12, 2010. In a room above the station's studio, Batichon was leaning against a wall as his cell phone was recharging. Then the wall and floor began to shake. *"Tremblement de terre,"* he said to himself. "Earthquake."

Batichon crawled under a table, waited for the initial shock to pass, then walked down the stairs and out into the parking lot where the tennis team had practiced. The quake's epicenter was a few miles north of Vallue, near the seaside town of Léogâne. Like much of nearby Carrefour and districts of Port-au-Prince, it now lay in ruins under clouds of dust.

In the initial shaking and aftershocks, some 230,000 people died, another 300,000 were injured, and a million were rendered homeless. Fifteen people died in Vallue, two of them from the radio station. Some peasants from Vallue were killed while selling vegetables in Port-au-Prince.

Vallue's school building was a total loss. Concrete posts had shattered in classroom corners designated for Tipa Tipa language and math activities. The reinforcement bars did not break, fortunately, which prevented the heavy floors and the roof from pancaking onto people inside.

The earthquake destroyed the building where the jams and preserves were being produced. It ruptured water lines in the irrigation project. In some locations, the hillsides slipped and swallowed people whole. Only the library survived intact inside the building of the radio station.

It took four days to check the integrity of the building, reenter the studio, repair damage, and return to the air. Vallue now had one of only six stations in the entire country able to transmit a signal. The station's team set up its equipment in the open air, in a space beside the parking lot/tennis court, and conveyed information each day in a special program lasting from eight in the morning to two in the afternoon. When there was not enough sunlight to drive solar cells, they fired up a small generator. The team monitored other radio stations and broadcast information from the bulletins it had gathered.

By July 2010, preschoolers in cobalt and crimson uniforms were attending Tipa Tipa sessions in a garage-sized white relief tent at Vallue. The primary school was holding classes in attached wood-and-corrugated-metal booths erected on the parking lot as well as in the room containing the well-worn books of the library FOKAL had provided. The school building was still standing. "Demolition of the school building will be done by work crews of local men using sledge hammers and wheelbarrows," said Eglorie Bernard, a FOKAL scholarship recipient who studied civil engineering. "We are talking about a new school."

The water project, too, was still in want of repair. The peasants had returned to planting millet in areas without water for irrigation. After cleaning out its spoiled inventory and reinstalling its equipment in an undamaged building, the peasants association's jam and preserves enterprise was about to launch operations with a skeleton staff. "Once a gas burner is fixed, we will begin," said Linda René, a university graduate in food processing. "We have the fruit."

The radio station was operating in its studio, broadcasting information on how to build houses that would not collapse in an earthquake. Listeners were calling in from all over Haiti to discuss the integrity of postquake emergency housing, especially in areas exposed to storm surges and heavy rain runoff. "The country has become more fragile," Batichon explained. "And hurricane season is approaching."

*   *   *

Sainte Agnès is a hamlet that extends along the crest of a clear-cut mountain reachable from Port-au-Prince by a five-hour, intestine-twisting SUV drive up a bare-stone track followed by a four-hour hike over ankle-twisting rocks with edges as sharp as broken glass. Local people, including children, routinely ply the path without shoes.

The hamlet's inhabitants age quickly. Too many of them die well before their time. Here, voodoo spirits of the mind warp decision making and mar interpersonal relationships. Here, a white person attracts pleas for dollars during practically every encounter with any locals. Here, people deem it acceptable to take a woman accused of cheating in a marketplace and, without arrest or trial, whip her in public.

Many people seeking better lives migrated from Sainte Agnès to the slums of Port-au-Prince, and many of them fled home after the 2010 earthquake. Returning, they found the daily grind in Sainte Agnès so trying that most returned to the ravaged capital quickly and convinced other people to leave Sainte Agnès to begin life anew amidst the city's rubble.

Before the toppling of Jean-Claude Duvalier in 1986, the people of Sainte Agnès did not dare to gather together to discuss local problems. Neighbors would have overheard and tipped off the authorities. Police thugs would have descended upon the hamlet and beaten and led away people never to be seen again.

Even after Duvalier's fall, the hamlet's inhabitants hunkered down within their own families and faced their hardships by themselves. "Everyone was divided, family by family," said one of the residents, Aline Aritus. In August 1988, however, Aritus and a few local people organized a peasants association to represent the interests of Sainte Agnès and the broader community around the hamlet.

The group's early sessions were small and held in secrecy. In time the number of active members grew to more than five hundred. Their first success came when they helped abolish a tax (read: extortion payments) at a local farmer's market. Then they freed a man whom the authorities had falsely arrested and held in custody. This was precisely the kind of grassroots organization FOKAL was seeking as a partner to collaborate on its projects.

In 1997, representatives of the peasants association made the trek to Port-au-Prince, showed Pierre-Louis a stack of worn paper bills they had scraped together over three years, and asked for help in building a clinic and in sending a local woman to be trained as a nurse so she could administer injections, inoculate the children, take blood-pressure readings, and perform other basic medical services. People of Sainte Agnès were dying, especially malnourished children attacked by waterborne bacteria in the drinking water. The nearest clinic was hours away along the trail of sharp rock.

FOKAL helped the association acquire structural materials, corrugated metal for the roof, and solar panels and car batteries to power a refrigerator for storing vaccines. All of this was carried up the steep trail by foot. Local men built the clinic, fashioning the sun-dried brick, shaping and smoothing the joists and posts, hanging hand-made doors, and installing the metal roof. A village woman completed a nurse-training program. Locally made beds, tables, and chairs appeared, as well as a desk. Vaccines filled the refrigerator.

Next, FOKAL engaged an engineer and paid to install a plastic pipe running from deep inside a spring to reduce the bacterial count in the water Sainte Agnès's peasants rely upon for drinking and cooking. The incidence of diarrhea declined. No longer, it seemed, would healthy people have to carry the sick down the mountain on unhinged doors.

FOKAL introduced Tipa Tipa to Sainte Agnès in 2002, along with a program designed to increase the villagers' disposable income so they could, eventually, pay the teachers and school staff and the clinic's nurse. At first the school, like the clinic, was subsidized. The classrooms filled with ninety preschoolers, including twenty-five who walked two hours in the morning to come to school and two hours to go home. The six teachers, the school's director, and the nurse were paid the equivalent of about $40 each month. Parents were overjoyed. They were paying only a few dollars each year in tuition for each child.

FOKAL's project to help the villagers earn enough disposable income to fund operation of the school and clinic involved, among other things, pig farming. Pigs were distributed around the hamlet. When the females bore litters, the piglets were equally divided, so everyone would share in the cost and profit from their sale. The pigs grew large and fat. The peasants were instructed to sell the bulk of them for profit during October, when prices peaked. The market nearest to Sainte Agnès attracts buyers from the Dominican Republic. Villagers were warned that if the pigs were not sold on time, the pig population would become too large to be fed by the nearby foliage.

During the winter of 2006, after the Open Society Foundations and, subsequently, FOKAL, began withdrawing operational support from education programs, Pierre-Louis visited Sainte Agnès. "I saw that they had not sold the pigs," she said. "The people were complaining that the pigs were becoming smaller and that the prices had dropped." She asked the peasants why they had not sold the pigs in October, when prices were high. "Madame Michèle," one answered, "we will only sell the pigs when we have a problem."

In the highlands of Haiti, a world of chronic hunger and the unexpected onset of disease, people consider livestock an insurance policy against starvation and health emergencies and other unforeseen trials. Since they had not cashed in on the excess pigs, however, the people had less disposable income than they would have accumulated. They chose not to spend what disposable income they had on their clinic or their preschool. The people of Sainte Agnès assumed someone would continue to pay for their clinic and school. They assumed wrong.

In other villages in the region, clinics opened and began providing free medical care and medicines. Rather than pooling their assets to pay the $40 monthly salary of the local nurse and rather than paying for drugs and prescriptions no matter how low their cost, the people of Saint Agnès chose to hike long distances for free medical care. They chose to buy medicines from itinerant pill mongers who wandered up the rocky trail. They chose to entrust their sick and injured to traditional healers. They chose to continue carrying their heavily pregnant women down the mountain on unhinged doors.

The nurse finally quit, because the peasants association owed her back wages. Despite numerous promises, no health official or doctor from the national government ever tried to walk the rocky trail to inspect the clinic in Sainte Agnès, so it never obtained official accreditation to qualify for government-provided generic TB and malaria drugs or for government funding to pay for a half-time nurse. At the village spigot, out in front of the clinic's yard, the flow of water slowed, and no one repaired the system.

The Tipa Tipa school closed in 2008, despite efforts by the peasants association to keep it functioning. Teachers went without pay for two years before giving up. Too few local people were willing to pay tuition for their children to attend the preschool; the tuition had doubled to only $6.25 per child annually and needed to be about $30 for the school to become solvent. Despite parental satisfaction with Tipa Tipa and excellent results shown by children who had completed the program—coupled with less-than-spectacular results shown by children who had not—too many peasants of Sainte Agnès chose to disregard preschool education and send children to church primary schools whose tuition is only slightly less than what the Tipa Tipa preschool would have needed to break even.

By mid-2010, the Sainte Agnès clinic had been closed for at least a year. The solar panels were no longer driving the refrigerator's compressor because the batteries had died. The pupils' desks and chairs and other furnishings were waiting inside the preschool's three deserted classrooms. Spring water was trickling from the white plastic pipe. The village remains a case study in the pitfalls faced by philanthropic efforts in a land where people with few tools and opportunities are trapped in an abject struggle for survival.

*   *   *

Port-au-Prince was once a sleepy, seaside town. Over two centuries, its original cluster of weather-worn, wood-frame gingerbread homes, stores and warehouses, and official buildings became lost in a sprawl of cinderblock and cement, much of it crumbling.

Jean-Jacques Dessalines was the leader of the Haitian forces who, in 1803, thwarted a campaign by Napoleon Bonaparte to reimpose France's rule over its former colony and reenslave 400,000 people whom French revolutionaries had emancipated a decade earlier. Dessalines cautioned his people. He warned them not to invest their hearts in Port-au-Prince and the other towns they had occupied. These places had never belonged to the freed slaves, who had been relegated to hardscrabble villages and hamlets like today's Vallue and Sainte Agnès. The freed slaves had little sense of entitlement to their country's towns. These places had belonged to the slaveholders, the French. Dessalines warned that the French would return to reclaim the land. He warned that it would then be necessary to resist them by burning the towns to the ground. So important was this warning to Dessalines that he enshrined his call to torch the towns—his words were: *"premier coup de canon d'alarme, les villes disparaissent et la nation est debout"*—in the final article of Haiti's first constitution.

As the 1970s passed into the 1980s, hunger forced Haitians to migrate to Port-au-Prince. The city's population, 60,000 in 1947, swelled beyond a million and continued to grow. This migration began before Haitians were free to organize themselves or to criticize their government. The new arrivals had no idea how to live in a crowded urban area. They had little time for community. Slums built on land for which most of the inhabitants still hold no title, ran southward from the city's center. Machetes began to clear-cut hillsides to free tillable land and to produce wood for building homes and making cooking charcoal. During rainstorms, torrents of runoff tore through hillside slums, transporting mud, trash, and garbage through the streets and ravines.

In the 1990s, hundreds of thousands more rural people packed into Port-au-Prince. Desperate men and women cracked open and robbed graves in its cemetery. Families squatted inside emptied tombs. After his return in 1994, Aristide worked to secure his position by dispersing arms to criminal gangs in the Port-au-Prince slums. Violence escalated throughout the country after Aristide won Haiti's presidency for a third time in a tainted election in 2000.

Throughout this turmoil, FOKAL used discretionary funds to create an island of art, music, lectures, drama, and books in the center of Port-au-Prince. The FOKAL library and culture center facilitated discussion and exchanges of ideas; artists and speakers came from abroad; painters and musicians gathered from all around Haiti. The center celebrated creativity and the best minds and talents Haiti has to offer. Its aim was to enhance the pride Haitians feel for their homeland and each other, as it worked to spark the creation of community and dampen the overwhelming sense that Haitians were in an abject struggle for survival in which they could rely only upon themselves. Only by combating this dread might a truly open society take shape.

In October 2003, street demonstrations began against Aristide. Gangs of his supporters attacked radio stations critical of the government, including stations FOKAL had supported. Students marched through the streets of Port-au-Prince, deriding the president and demanding change. The police turned away as pro-Aristide gang members overran the university and smashed the knees of the dean with an iron bar.

By February 2004, passions in Port-au-Prince were approaching the combustion point. Rumors spread that former members of the military had crossed over from the Dominican Republic and were on the way to remove Aristide. On February 14, Aristide's police surrounded the FOKAL cultural center and offices in central Port-au-Prince. The lawlessness grew worse. Gangs fought new gun battles in the slums, including those on the hillsides glowering down into the city's last patch of virgin tropical forest. Criminals began kidnapping people rich and poor and receiving ransoms large and small. People in the slums "gathered intelligence" and then set upon neighbors who had received wages or obtained money from relatives abroad. Roads from the center of Port-au-Prince became a gauntlet of men with guns.

Aristide came under severe pressure to step down. Wild rumors circulated through the capital. People said that if Aristide were forced to leave Haiti, his gangs would burn the city, just as Dessalines had advised his followers to do two centuries earlier. It took another day before the United States withdrew its support from Aristide and got him out of the country. The violence spiked and dipped and waned only slowly. The social fabric of the slums was in shreds. Residents of one neighborhood refused to walk through another. Women feared being raped. Businesses paid for protection. Kidnappings continued.

Such was the chaos when FOKAL launched an effort to help instill a sense of community in the slums on the city's southern edge. The project began as a neighborhood-outreach effort for the capital's first public park, Le Parc Naturel de Martissant, which occupies the city's last patch of virgin tropical forest. The property had become the possession of the state, and the government, which lacked the capacity to do the job, handed over temporary management of the park to a FOKAL project team.

How, in creating a park, can you help build a community from a mass of individuals who are literally at each other's throats? "Talk with them, and give them a place to talk with each other," answered Cécile Marotte, a French psychologist and professor of philosophy who had worked on victim-relief efforts in Haiti and Rwanda and was hired by FOKAL to oversee the outreach effort. "Here in Haiti, nobody explains anything to anybody. Everything is done by force. You are dealing with people on the margins. So to begin, you have to sell the idea of the park to the neighbors, to instill in them all a sense that they have ownership of the park, a sense of pride in the park and respect for its riches."

In the park's offices, Marotte created a meeting room where people from the slums could gather in organized groups to share their experiences, concerns, and aspirations. Marotte's assistants identified potential community leaders in the neighborhoods around the park, people who had demonstrated a willingness to help improve living conditions. Some were university students. Some couldn't read. Some were traditional healers, some voodoo priests and priestesses. Some were victims of violence, including rape, and some former gang members who had surrendered or stashed their firearms. Some ran legitimate local organizations—

political, environmental, youth, religious, social, and cultural; and some ran organizations that existed only on paper. Marotte sent each of them a written invitation to visit the park's office, to learn about Parc Martissant, and to provide their vision of how the park might best benefit the community. Perhaps none of them had ever been asked to speak openly about who they are, what they think, what they have experienced and suffered, what challenges they are facing, and how they envision the future.

After individual meetings, Marotte asked each of the potential local leaders to join her in a series of group discussions about the park. Marotte called these group sessions Espace de Parole, "Discussion Space." She structured the discussions to be an instrument for establishing lines of communication between people from neighborhoods whose gangs had been at war with one another for over a decade and whose inhabitants were terrified to speak with one another, had no opportunity to develop empathy for one another, and assumed each other to be killers, rapists, and thieves.

Since mid-2008, the discussions have taken place twice each week, noon to three on Tuesdays and Thursdays, for three weeks at a time. A new group of local participants arrives each month. Verbal abuse is not tolerated. No free meals are offered. No soft drinks or juices are served.

Marotte trained the discussions on core values she wanted the meetings, and the park itself, to promote: health, security, and citizenship. She asked, for example: What is physical hygiene? The participants would talk it over. She asked: How does a person respect the environment? How does one respect others and feel attachment to a neighborhood and community and a land? What is security? What does freedom of movement mean when people in one neighborhood are afraid to walk through another? What are the consequences of violence? What is rape? What is freedom of expression, the right to protection, and respect for the rights of

others? And what is citizenship? What are the rights and responsibilities of a citizen? What are human rights and respect for the law?

The participants' answers spoke of ambition, hope, and
despair. Paulette Ligonde, the owner and director of a primary
school for about fifty students, described finding dead bodies in
the streets near her house. "My kids don't know what it is like in a
place with trees and flowers."

Maurice Rozin walked to Espace de Parole from beyond the
eastern edge of the park, where a local gang leader had won
popularity and power after his armed men became vigilantes and
stopped armed men from adjoining neighborhoods from raping
local women. Later, the vigilantes began shaking down residents
who came into money. "I saw people killed all the time in my
neighborhood," he said. "The gangs from up above came down
to kill people. When you live in a neighborhood, you have to
keep this from happening again. The police were powerless. And
you cannot fight with stones."

"I don't know what a park is," said Rozin, who was supporting a
wife and two children repairing cars, working as a plumber, and
assembling windows. "I've seen parks on television. A park in the
neighborhood means many things. We have to make a lot of effort
to protect the park. We feel special because of it. We would like
Martissant to become the place it used to be, where you could
listen to birds singing. When employers know these people are
not criminals, they will come and invest in these people. This is
our dream." Maurice Rozin's dream died a few months later, when
he was gunned down near a construction site. People in the neighborhood said he died because he was forcing workers to pay him
kickbacks and a rival gang leader wanted the kickbacks for himself.

Andre Wiguens, age twenty-three, went to a Catholic school
and belonged to an organization that was working in conflict resolution and organizing summer outings for young people in an area

that has no electricity, no flush toilets, no easily accessible drinking water, no nearby road, no health clinic, and no school. "We teach them how to live in a city," he said. "We teach them not to throw trash. We let them know about rights and responsibilities and what it is to be a citizen. A person is a full citizen only after he understands his civic and political rights. We organize workshops on how to deal with conflict. We invite organizations fighting against each other, organizations that were involved in the conflict. We allowed them to meet. They talked and discussed conflicts going on in their neighborhoods. This contributed to maintaining peace.

"We would like people to be allowed to visit the park soon. Once people can visit the park, they will know there is something in this area promoting peace and dialog in the community. We would like the park to have a library, because there are many people who want to know more. We would like our organization to have access to the park for children to attend camp. We would like to organize conferences for people from the neighborhood. The park can bring the world here."

Pierre-Louis Alwich, thirty, was living in a family whose home stands about a football field's length away from the park. Alwich said his parents and Christian upbringing gave structure to his life. He had studied computer science and literature and went on to earn a degree in social work. The organization he and two other friends founded had thirty-five volunteers who were using drama to teach children from the area not to despair or turn to alcohol and drugs. "They take drugs and lose control of themselves and become violent," he said. "They find it acceptable to be aggressive with any young woman passing by. Now this violence is diminishing. We think that one day the issue will be eliminated. The park won't solve the problems that exist in the neighborhoods around it. And things that cause insecurity in the neighborhood are impunity and extreme misery. Food in the morning becomes a luxury. The fact that the insecurity has decreased does not mean there are no guns. Guns are silent but they are still there." If change is to come to Haiti, he said, Haitians should lead. "This is the first time that members of the community have an opportunity to sit down with other civil society organizations to talk and see what can be done to bring change."

The earthquake of January 2010 altered the life equation of everyone that lived in the slums and neighborhoods around the park. About four hundred residents died in the disaster. Others disappeared. Many more lost legs and arms.

All of the park's landmark buildings were destroyed. The European Union and an urban development organization from France undertook projects to improve the neighborhood, but the job of community building became arguably more difficult. Gang members escaped from Port-au-Prince's jail and returned to the nearby slums. Young people seeking ways to find food were burglarizing and robbing homes. With the approach of each election season, people feared eruptions of political violence. FOKAL pressed on with its neighborhood outreach. Whether Cécile Marotte's efforts would have a lasting effect remained an open question.

*   *   *

The earthquake of January 12, 2010, did more than kill and maim. It left a million people homeless. It destroyed schools, workshops, stores, warehouses, offices, and houses of worship; it brought down the seat of Haiti's government; and it exposed the fecklessness of the country's political elite. Between mid-October 2010 and the earthquake's first anniversary, a cholera epidemic claimed about three thousand lives; and enraged villagers went on a vengeance-killing spree that left more than forty voodoo priests dead. Massive fraud during national elections at the end of

2010 exhausted what was left of the Haitians' confidence in their political leadership and triggered street riots that shut down Port-au-Prince. The uncertainty did not abate with the surprise return of Jean-Claude Duvalier, or his quick arrest.

The Open Society Foundations do not provide emergency relief in response to natural disasters. But during 2010, George Soros, the Open Society Foundations, and FOKAL adjusted their activities in light of the earthquake, the cholera epidemic, and the long-term need for economic growth that will alleviate the abject poverty that has undermined Haitian society for too long.

In addition to FOKAL's microdevelopment efforts to enhance the sustainability of its projects, the Soros Economic Development Fund has provided loans and loan guarantees to foster economic growth in Haiti. Before the earthquake of 2010, the development fund had guaranteed up to $1 million on $2.3 million in commercial bank loans. After the disaster, the development fund provided a $3 million loan to CODEVI, Haiti's only fully operational free trade zone, which is wholly owned by Grupo M, a privately held manufacturer producing knits and woven products for the U.S. market. "The apparel manufacturing lines located at CODEVI are best positioned to take advantage of the HOPE II Act, which expands trade preferences to Haiti's textile industry while creating jobs in a city outside of the capital," said Neal DeLaurentis, the fund's vice president. This garment manufacturing investment was expected to create 1,400 new jobs for low-income Haitians in 2011. The fund also provided a combined debt and equity investment of $2.3 million that enabled JMB, one of Haiti's largest exporters of the Madame Francis variety of mango, to export frozen mango chunks; this investment is designed to increase the incomes of small-scale farmers, because mangos that would have been rejected as fresh produce can now be frozen and exported.

FOKAL undertook efforts to provide public and professional input into the government's planning for the reconstruction of Port-au-Prince, Léogâne, and the other earthquake-damaged areas. While waiting, and waiting, for the government to decide what it would do, however, FOKAL launched a program to stimulate restoration of some of the city's most precious historical landmarks, its array of colorful, wood-frame gingerbread houses, by helping to organize the owners of these structures and by working with the Ministry of Culture to have a neighborhood of these houses listed on an international watch list of world monuments. Together with the World Monuments Fund, the Prince Klaus Foundation of The Netherlands, and other foundations, FOKAL completed an inventory of the gingerbread houses and worked to establish a loan mechanism to help their owners rehabilitate them. The project included a school for artisans, so local skilled craftsmen, and not foreigners, can do the restoration work and undertake gingerbread house construction elsewhere.

FOKAL also sought to play a role in the coordination of the participation of foreign institutions of higher education in postearthquake Haiti in four areas: distance learning, technical support in university administration, the building of laboratories, including computer labs, and student and teacher exchanges.

The Open Society Foundations also invested more than $2 million and partnered with one of the world's most innovative schools of agronomy, EARTH University in Costa Rica, in an attempt to make a significant contribution to helping Haiti feed itself in a sustainable way in the future. The Foundations and EARTH joined forces to provide full scholarships and travel and living expenses for young Haitians—as well as students from three other hard-pressed countries, Sierra Leone, Liberia, and

Mozambique. In early 2011, as increasing food prices were contributing to social unrest around the Arab world, ten Haitians were studying at EARTH's modern campus on a former banana plantation carved out of a rainforest. The students, who must, as part of their studies, perform community service with poverty-stricken peasants, prepare entrepreneurial projects, and undertake internships and study abroad, were learning how to use simple techniques to produce cooking fuel from animal manure, to raise fresh vegetables in urban gardens, and to prevent soil exhaustion and depletion, all of which can help Haiti overcome decades of clear-cutting forests, soil erosion, and counterproductive farming methods, that have blighted huge swathes of the country. EARTH provides its four hundred students, almost half of them women, with tutoring support, close professor-student contact, Spanish- and English-language training, and an extraordinary degree of practical, hands-on instruction, including work in the fields. A significant percentage of its graduates return to their countries of origin. Almost 96 percent of the university's graduates are employed or pursuing advanced degrees, 10 percent have their own business, and another 7 percent are working for family enterprises.

One of the Haitian scholarship winners at EARTH, Carena Théodore, lost a sister in the collapse of a building during the earthquake. Théodore grew interested in agriculture during visits to the small farm of her grandmother, who grows sugar cane, mangos, avocados, yams, bananas, and plantains. "My grandmother lives in poverty," Théodore said. "Not extreme poverty, but basic poverty. The soil is depleted.

"I will go back and train my grandmother in how not just to take out, but to add natural fertilizers. I expect she will be able to train all the farmers in her village. There are sufficient animal waste and materials for compost to improve the soil. But the people are not taking advantage of them. The people need someone to guide them to take advantage of these techniques.

"Haiti is my country. It is my land. I won't change my story for this new place. Everything for me is in my country."

*   *   *

GEORGE SOROS

If you look at where we are spending most of our money—Liberia, Sierra Leone, Haiti, the Congo, and, more recently, Guinea—they are failed states, dysfunctional countries, and countries emerging from civil war. Perhaps my attraction to insolvable problems has led us to work with failed states.

In Haiti, we established a foundation for the benefit of the people after the United States sent troops to the country in 1994 to restore constitutional rule. We found Michèle Pierre-Louis to lead the foundation. She has been an island of honesty and reliability and good administration in a dysfunctional country. I often wondered whether we should continue working in Haiti because the situation wasn't getting better. I only stuck it out because of the people who were devoting their lives to improving conditions—and also risking and sometimes losing their lives. I felt that as long as they see some hope, I can't abandon them, and that's really why we have stayed there.

There was one real moment of hope. Michèle became prime minister in 2008. The United States passed legislation that gave Haiti preferential access to the U.S. market. Former President Clinton invested time and energy in helping Haiti. Paul Collier prepared a promising economic plan, and we were willing to invest in projects through the Soros Economic Development Fund. All the stars were aligned. Then, in the fall of 2009, President Préval pulled the rug out from under the whole effort by sacking Michèle because she was too honest and refused to go along with the corrupt practices of Préval's party. Shortly after that the earthquake happened.

I first went to Haiti some forty years ago. I went back once or twice to visit the foundation, and I went with Hillary Clinton when she visited Haiti in the mid-1990s. Each time the country had deteriorated further. The last time I went was after the hurricane when Michèle became prime minister. We flew around in a helicopter and saw the most fertile land under water as a result of the hurricane. I thought you can't go any further in terms of destruction, and then came the earthquake. It's just incredible how far conditions can deteriorate in the absence of good government. We have still not given up, although I must confess I found the sacking of Michèle Pierre-Louis profoundly discouraging.

Liberia was another hopeless case we got involved in. Ellen Johnson Sirleaf, the former chair of our West African foundation, became president of Liberia. We knew she was very capable and honest, so we went out of our way to help her succeed. I figured that since the country was relatively small and now had a capable leader, it should be possible to make a big impact and bring about real change.

This turned out to be a false concept because everything had been destroyed, the human capital as well as the infrastructure. It was extremely difficult to get anything done. Our first effort was a capacity-building fund, which enabled her to bring back a few qualified people to form the core of a cabinet. We also invested large amounts of money to help get the education system started.

It remains very questionable whether these investments will actually pay off. The situation may be irreversible. Former child soldiers roam the streets, and though calm prevails while the UN peacekeepers are there, they are not going to be there forever. If development doesn't reach the point where the former child soldiers are gainfully occupied, you could have a new wave of civil war. According to Paul Collier, the most reliable predictor of civil war is a civil war in the past.

I feel a great sense of urgency to make progress now. We have put a lot of effort into making Ellen Johnson Sirleaf successful, but we cannot be involved in helping her to get reelected; that would violate our principle of allowing democracy to take its course.

The Open Society Foundations are engaged in Sierra Leone as well. The human capital in Sierra Leone had been better preserved than in Liberia. The ruling class in Liberia had connections to the United States. When Charles Taylor pushed them out, most of them went to the U.S., leaving very few educated people in Liberia. In Sierra Leone, by contrast, the people had nowhere to go, so they were still there when democratic elections were held and a decent president was elected. He could quickly appoint a cabinet and make the country functional: In my view, this is why Sierra Leone has developed much faster than Liberia.

Our latest engagement is in Guinea. This country has never seen a democratic government. The recent elections were preceded by a massacre in which several hundred civilians were killed by mercenaries recruited from former child soldiers in Liberia and Sierra Leone. The new president is Alpha Condé, an émigré returning from Paris. Although the elections were controversial, he checks out well. He is determined to break the stranglehold of corruption, and I intend to pull out all the stops to help him succeed. We can benefit from our past experience and do better this time. Guinea is rich in natural resources and the Revenue Watch Institute is well situated to help the new administration to renegotiate the contracts that had been obtained through bribery. Guinea, Liberia, and Sierra Leone are contiguous. The three countries, together with other democratic states, could transform ECOWAS, the Economic Community of West African States, into a region of good governance.

Protesters marching in 2007 during widespread demonstrations in Burma initiated by Buddhist monks. The Open Society Foundations' Burma Project supports advocates for democratic change in Burma and works to lay the groundwork for a transition to an open society. (© Christian Holst/Edit/ Getty Images)

CHAPTER 5

Laying the Groundwork
for an Open Society in Burma

Burma was once one of Southeast Asia's richest countries. Its paddies produced more rice for export than any on earth. Its over-arching jungles yielded three-quarters of the world's teak. Its jade, pearls, rubies, and sapphires won fame around the globe. Most of Burma's people were literate. Rangoon's faculties of science, medicine, and literature drew students from all over Southeast Asia.[1]

For the first twelve years after Burma gained its independence in 1948, the country's economy grew, and most of its numerous ethnic groups participated in a democracy that was representative, though weak.[2] But rivalries among members of the ruling elite and the national army's clashes with Communist partisans and ethnic militias destabilized the country. The army's commanders grumbled that the Rangoon government was binding its hands in the struggle against the Communists and the separatists threatening the country's territorial integrity.

In 1962, the army seized control of the government. A military junta proceeded to steer Burma into a precipitous decline. A country that was once the envy of the region became a dystopia of violence, government repression, poverty, disease, and heinous abuse of women and children: the polar opposite of an open society.[3]

Burma's military regime has for decades taken pains to justify its existence and excesses by asserting that it has defended the country from Communists and foreign threats while resisting armed campaigns by ethnic militias to break the country apart. Members of the junta have enriched themselves by plundering the country's abundant natural wealth and by helping drug lords deliver heroin to the world. Arbitrary decisions by a judiciary dependent on the junta pose as the rule of law. The military regime censors all publications and doles out prison sentences to critics and activists as well as journalists and labor organizers.

By 2010, Burma's jails were holding over two thousand political prisoners—many with sentences ranging from sixty to over one hundred years—all of whom suffered beatings, torture, hunger, and a lack of water and medical care. The junta had forcibly displaced hundreds of thousands of people. About two million refugees and economic migrants from Burma were living in Thailand. Another 700,000 or so undocumented migrants from Burma were in Malaysia. Nearly a hundred thousand people belonging to Burma's Chin minority had fled to India; fighting between Burma's army and members of the ethnic Kokang militia had forced tens of thousands of people into China; tens of thousands of women from Burma, including women sold into sex slavery for a few dollars, were working in bordellos in Thailand, India, and China. Hundreds of thousands of Muslim Rohingya, perhaps the world's most oppressed minority, had fled into neighboring Bangladesh, where the authorities were attempting to force many back across the border into Burma to suffer more forced labor, more starvation, and more restrictions on their freedom of religion, mobility, and right to marry. Moreover, the Rohingya were not alone in this persecution: The junta's soldiers had killed civilians and raped young girls and women from the Shan, Mon, Karen, Palaung, Chin, and other ethnic groups.

The regime was spending less than 1 percent of the country's gross domestic product on health care and education, half of what it was spending on defense. One in every ten babies born in Burma was dying in infancy. One in every four of Burma's people lacked access to safe drinking water, and one in three of its children was chronically malnourished.

Billions of dollars that Burma was receiving in annual revenues from the export of oil and natural gas were disappearing somewhere into the junta. Transparency International ranked Burma among the three most corrupt countries on the planet. It would have been naive to suppose that subsequent years would bring anything different if the military dictatorship remained in control.

The United Nations special rapporteur on human rights in Burma, Tomás Ojea Quintana, issued a special report in early 2010:

> Given the gross and systematic nature of human rights violations in [Burma] over a period of many years, and the lack of accountability, there is an indication that those human rights violations are the result of a state policy that involves authorities in the executive, military and judiciary at all levels. According to consistent reports, the possibility exists that some of these human rights violations may entail categories of crimes against humanity or war crimes under the terms of the Statute of the International Criminal Court. Given this lack of accountability, UN institutions may consider the possibility to establish a commission of inquiry with a specific fact finding mandate to address the question of international crimes.[4]

By the time Quintana had issued this call for a commission of inquiry to explore the possibility of bringing indictments against officials in Burma for violations of international criminal law, the military regime had already taken care to amend the country's constitution by adding provisions that provided its members impunity, under the country's national law, from prosecution for "any act done in the execution of their respective duties."[5]

George Soros's efforts to promote the development of an open society in Burma began after widespread prodemocracy demonstrations in 1988 prodded the military regime to hold elections that produced a landslide victory by the National League for Democracy, an opposition political party led by Nobel laureate Daw Aung San Suu Kyi. Soros, working through his daughter, Andrea Soros, a student of Tibet, met Michael Aris, a Tibet scholar who was, until his untimely death in 1999, the husband of Aung San Suu Kyi.

Soros began his engagement by supporting work on Burma by Human Rights Watch/Asia. After joining the Open Society Foundations in 1993, Aryeh Neier oversaw the creation of the Foundations' Burma Project to support efforts to document the junta's human rights abuses and other misdeeds and to lay the groundwork for a transition from a dystopian present to a postjunta open society. Between 1993 and 2009, George Soros spent more than $33 million to support the establishment of an open society in Burma.

*   *   *

Groundwork for an Open Society. Since the day it seized power, Burma's ruling junta has jealously guarded its monopoly on political and economic power. The lack of free speech and expression, freedom of assembly, and other basic rights as well as the jailing and executions of political opponents, the use of mass rape as a weapon, the herding of people into forced-labor brigades, and other human rights violations have not only destroyed whatever vestiges of an open society had existed in Burma before the junta's ascendancy, they have stunted the development of cadres of people capable of building an open society.

Burma is a country in desperate need of qualified leaders and managers. It requires women and men who have not only an understanding of how open societies work but also the ability to make tough, selfless decisions that would keep Burma from succumbing again to greed, interethnic rivalries and violence, and military dictatorship. Supporting these men and women is one of the Open Society Foundations' primary goals in Burma.

After the crackdown against Burma's prodemocracy uprising in 1988, thousands of young people—many of them university students, some of them just high school kids—fled through the jungle to escape to Thailand, India, and China. One of the Open Society Foundations' first efforts related to Burma was the funding of educational programs for students from Burma, and especially scholarships to foreign universities for those students whose education, such as it was after years of government neglect of schools and universities, had been interrupted by the crackdown. The Open Society Foundations' scholarship programs have provided funding for students from Burma to attend schools and universities in Australia, the United Kingdom, Canada, India, the Philippines, Thailand, and the United States. The program also funded internships for young people from Burma to gain experience working for nongovernmental organizations in Southeast Asia and Europe. It provided support for academic counseling services and university courses for refugee students in Thailand and students coming from inside Burma. From 1997 to 2010, the Open Society Foundations awarded $7.7 million in scholarships and extra assistance to 2,548 recipients.

*   *   *

Groundwork for Ethnic Comity. Ethnic violence, some of it exacerbated by a winner-take-all struggle for control of lucrative natural resource and heroin exports, has been the bane of Burma's existence since the country gained independence.

Burma's fifty-four million people form a complex ethnic mosaic that spreads out over a territory the size of Texas. The broad, rice-rich basin of the Irrawaddy River occupies the country's heartland, which is bisected by the famous China Road stretching northward from Rangoon. Surrounding much of this basin are the highland homelands of a farrago of peoples. About 60 percent of Burma's people are ethnic Burmans—the group that dominates the central Irrawaddy basin as well as the army, the agencies of government, and the military regime. The Karen and Shan each make up about 10 percent of the population; the remaining pieces of the ethnic mosaic include the Akha, Chin, Chinese, Danu, Indian, Kachin, Karenni, Kayan, Kokang, Lahu, Mon, Naga, Palaaung, Pao, Rakhine, Rohingya, Tavoyan, and Wa peoples.

During World War II, many Burmans fought with the Japanese invaders in a bid to end British colonial rule, while many members of the larger ethnic minorities fought with the British against the Japanese in an effort to thwart Burman domination of the country. Against a backdrop of interethnic violence between 1945 and 1947, General Aung San, one of the architects of Burma's independence and the father of Aung San Suu Kyi, convinced leaders of the Kachin, Shan, and Chin to join a new, multiethnic union of Burma. Aung San was assassinated in 1947. Successive governments never fully honored the constitutional guarantees the Kachin, Shan, and Chin had received.

By 2010, most of Burma's ethnic minorities still lacked cultural autonomy for their home regions and a significant voice in the country's affairs. Armed ethnic militias have controlled varying amounts of Burma's territory over the years. The military regime has exploited divisions within and among ethnic groups to secure its control of the country. The regime—by 2010 it was calling itself the "State Peace and Development Council"—had negotiated cease-fires with most of the country's armed ethnic militias and undertaken military operations to defeat the others. The regime and armed groups from the Wa, Kokang, and other minorities had entered into agreements that allowed these groups to cultivate poppies, refine opium into heroin, and export it from Burma with apparent government collusion.

Members of Burma's democratic opposition undertook efforts to lay a foundation for addressing the crucial problem of ethnic animosities and violence. In 2001, a group of political leaders in exile revived a coalition of non-Burman political parties, the United Nationalities League for Democracy, which originally formed in the wake of the 1988 uprising and captured sixty-five seats in the 1990 elections. Working abroad, the revived United Nationalities League for Democracy passed a draft national constitution and elected members of a shadow government. Another coalition of ethnic groups, the National Democratic Front, also set to work promoting positions shared by the country's ethnic minorities.

The Open Society Foundations provided grants for a variety of activities designed to draw attention to the plight of Burma's ethnic groups and promote interethnic comity. The Foundations backed groups working inside and outside of Burma to document human rights abuses by the junta against members of the country's various ethnic minorities, including human rights abuses linked with exploitation of natural resources. Grants supported capacity-building for the training of community health workers, doctors, and teachers as well as training in community and political organizing, human rights monitoring, leadership enhancement, environmental issues, community development, political empowerment, information technology development, HIV and AIDS awareness, peace building, and nonviolent resistance. The Foundations also supported media organizations producing news in English, Burmese, and languages of Burma's ethnic minorities for audiences inside and outside of Burma. These media organizations, including news agencies dedicated to collecting and disseminating news and information about specific ethnic groups and sharing their output with agencies from other ethnic groups, used a wide variety of methods to deliver their product, including DVDs, CDs, newspapers and magazines, the World Wide Web, community radio broadcasts, and satellite television broadcasts.

The nonprofit Kaladan Press Network, one of the media organizations supported by the Open Society Foundations, was the first news agency ever to serve the Rohingya, a Muslim ethnic group that has resided for centuries in what is now the Arakan state of western Burma. The junta has for decades refused to recognize the Rohingya as citizens or legal residents of Burma. Rangoon has kept Arakan, which is adjacent to both Bangladesh and the Bay of Bengal, off-limits to foreign journalists and human rights investigators, making Kaladan a crucial source of information.

The Kaladan Press Network's executive editor, Tin Soe, first got into trouble with the junta in 1979, when he began documenting the suffering of some 200,000 Rohingya refugees who had been rousted from their homes and driven into Bangladesh or border-area refugee camps a year earlier during a government sweep called Operation Dragon King. This was a combined effort by Burma's police, the army, and the immigration authorities to expel "illegal aliens." Operation Dragon

King targeted civilians and was marred by widespread killing and rape, the razing of mosques, and other forms of religious persecution.

Tin Soe delivered his photographs of the Rohingya refugees to political figures and opponents of the junta in Rangoon as documentary evidence of the effects of the operation. When any police officer or soldier questioned Tin Soe about what he was doing in the area of the Rohingya camps, he would tell them that he was a student doing research. Before long, the police caught on.

Tin Soe fled Burma to Bangladesh in 1982, after learning from friends that the police were tailing him. He reported on the plight of hundreds of thousands of Rohingya refugees in Saudi Arabia and on their behalf worked to obtain labor permits, health care coverage, and access to schools. During 1991 and 1992, another 250,000 Rohingya fled to Bangladesh from Burma with accounts of the army forcing them to work, practically as slaves, on road construction sites and military bases as well as descriptions of summary executions, torture and rape, land grabs, destruction of homes, extortion, and other abuses.

In 2004, Tin Soe joined the Kaladan Press Network in Chittagong, Bangladesh. "We have twenty-one journalists working in Arakan, watching the border and reporting from the interior," Tin Soe said. The reporters send their news reports by means of cell phones in signal areas covered by the Bangladesh mobile network. Kaladan edits the material and presents it in a monthly print magazine and a daily news report on a website. "I warn the reporters not to carry their mobile telephones with them when they leave their homes, but to keep the phones in their houses in case they are stopped by the police," Tin Soe said. The police have arrested several Kaladan journalists over the years, mostly on suspicion of being in Burma illegally.

Working through intermediaries, Tin Soe has had to bribe police officials to free some Kaladan journalists.

"We support the existence of Burma," Tin Soe said. "We send our information all over Burma, to all of the country's minority groups, as well as out into the world, so people can see what is happening to the Rohingya." Kaladan became a founding member of the Soros-supported Burma News International, a skill- and information-sharing network through which news agencies of eleven of Burma's ethnic groups share their output. "Through Burma News International, we cooperate to support ethnic peace," Tin Soe said. "We include the Burmans, and meet twice each year, in India or Thailand. The goal is to make it clear to each group what the others are suffering under the Rangoon regime."

From 2005, Kaladan reported on efforts by the authorities in Bangladesh to force Rohingya refugees back into Burma. The government of Bangladesh recognized the refugee status of only 28,000 of the Rohingya who had fled there from Burma; the remaining 200,000 to 300,000 Rohingya in Bangladesh were struggling to survive without official refugee status.

In January 2010, Bangladesh began a new campaign to drive the Rohingya back into Burma. Kaladan reported on how the main United Nations refugee-relief organization, the United Nations High Commissioner for Refugees, was assisting the repatriation effort. "The UNHCR is sending Rohingya back, and I don't understand it," Tin Soe said. "They say it is the policy of the Bangladesh government." By the summer of 2010, there were as many as a thousand Rohingya in jail inside Bangladesh, Tin Soe said. "People don't want to return to Burma and they are taken to the border at gunpoint. They would rather face the Bangladesh police than Burma's police. There are about 500,000 Rohingya living in Arakan along the border with Bangladesh. The Bangladesh authorities are afraid all of the

Rohingya will come from Arakan if the UNHCR designates the Rohingya in Bangladesh as refugees."

*   *   *

Groundwork for Economic Development. Burma lies at a crossroads. Since ancient times, it has been traversed by caravan routes linking China and Tibet with India and the lands of Southeast Asia. China, Singapore, and Thailand still rank as Burma's chief trading partners, along with far-off Japan. In 2010, Burma was deriving revenues by exporting natural resources, including natural gas, precious and semiprecious stones, and exotic hardwoods. The country's poppy fields are as fabled as its rice paddies.

Between 1962 and 1988, the junta restricted the access of private businesses to outside markets. The junta interfered with the workings of the country's internal market and gave full rein to corruption. Meanwhile the economy failed to produce enough wealth to fulfill official promises of "socialist" welfare.

Most of Burma's people are peasants who till small plots and work rice paddies. Decades of forcing peasants to sell a significant portion of their rice output to the state at below-market prices contributed to a collapse in rice yields. The military regime, directly or indirectly, controlled almost every significant company involved in trade and natural resource production. State enterprises, especially those controlled by the military, sucked up most investment capital. The Union of Myanmar Economic Holdings Company, run by the Defense Ministry's Directorate of Procurement, was a participant in almost every joint venture involving foreign partners. Spending for an ever-expanding military—one that had no foreign enemies—was consuming a fifth of all government expenditures.

By 1988, Burma was bankrupt. The junta, hungry for new inflows of hard currency, cast aside its "socialist" pretensions, though it continued to set prices, wages, and currency exchange rates, and opened the country to foreign partners to assist in extracting the country's natural resources.

Broad swathes of Burma's rain forest were cut for quick profits. Up-front, hard-currency payments allowed foreign commercial fishing companies unregulated access to Burma's coastal waters, which had a devastating impact on fish stocks and, consequently, the livelihoods of local fishermen. The country's low wage structure left its people to suffer the predations of foreign factory owners. Massive human rights abuses led to boycotts by Western consumers, the drying up of international financing opportunities, and a ban by the United States on all new investment in Burma.

Meanwhile, the junta carried on with business as usual, expelling thousands of families to make way for infrastructure projects, including construction of a gas pipeline. The junta continued to press-gang laborers to toil on road, rail, pipeline, and other construction sites as well as at tourist facilities. Heroin and other narcotics still ranked among the country's leading exports, and local investment in new hotels and other real estate ventures was linked to families of heroin traders. The junta siphoned off revenues from natural gas extraction, mining, and exports of sapphires, pearls, jade, and rubies.

The Open Society Foundations' Burma Project sponsored workshops for activists from Burma to discuss ways to ease the transition of their country's economy from one monopolized by the military's top brass to one with a freer market that would include transparency and accountability in government management of revenues derived from extraction of natural resources. The Burma Project helped fund a workshop and a report describing how Burma's people might develop national strategies and mechanisms to manage relations with the International Monetary Fund, the World Bank, the Asian Development Bank, and other international financial institutions. The report warned that Burma's lack of a comprehensive strategic social and economic policy framework as well as the country's commodity-dominated trade with China and other nearby countries were yielding only short-term gains that tended to benefit mostly foreign interests and people associated with the military.

The Burma Project also provided funding for EarthRights International, a U.S.- and Thailand-based nongovernmental organization that was part of a team that won a multimillion-dollar settlement in a lawsuit filed in the United States on behalf of victims of human rights abuses committed by the military forces the junta had sent in to secure the construction of a gas pipeline across Burma to Thailand.

One of EarthRights International's founders, a Karen human rights activist, Ka Hsaw Wa, helped lead the student demonstrations in Rangoon during 1988 and, after the junta's crackdown, suffered imprisonment and torture at the hands of government troops. Ka Hsaw Wa subsequently fled Burma but secretly re-entered the country in order to participate in a lengthy campaign to document severe human rights abuses, including the destruction and relocation of entire villages during the construction and operation of the gas pipeline. The lawsuit named as a defendant Unocal, one of the partners in the gas pipeline joint venture. The plaintiffs sued under the U.S. Alien Tort Statute of 1789, arguing that the statute allowed foreign plaintiffs to bring complaints in U.S. federal court against U.S.-based corporations for abuses committed abroad. Unocal agreed to settle out of court and pay compensation to fifteen anonymous villagers who claimed to have suffered human rights abuses, including forced labor, rape, torture, and the killings of family members.

"At the beginning, we had no money even to prepare a report and distribute it to the international community," said Ka Hsaw Wa. "We were able to do this because of the Open Society Foundations. We lived and slept in the office to focus on our work and our mission. We did not get a salary until the end of 1997. Earth-Rights gathered information itself and, in Thailand, trained people to go back into Burma to conduct interviews.

"I went into Burma a lot, into the pipeline region and to other places where I met with villagers who had fled the pipeline region. Altogether we interviewed about a thousand people."

EarthRights used the information as the basis of a report, *Total Denial*, on the human rights violations linked with the pipeline project and turned these interviews into supporting evidence for its litigation against Unocal. "After we received the Open Society Foundations' money, we expanded human rights documentation and launched an international campaign, writing and publishing reports. The Soros funding also gave us credibility with other donors."

*   *   *

Groundwork for Democracy. During the years after 1988, the junta continued to restrict the movement and activities of Daw Aung San Suu Kyi as well as other key opposition political figures. It continued to gag the press and arrest and abuse dissenters, and its jails still held hundreds of political prisoners in miserable conditions. In 1996, it crushed new student protests. In 2007, it put down a series of widespread demonstrations across the country led by Buddhist monks.

By early 2010, the junta's reclusive seventy-eight-year-old leader, General Than Shwe, had named no successor. He began making decisions suggesting that he sought to prevent the emergence of a new predominant leader who might, as Than Shwe had done to his predecessor, retaliate against his family and wrest from them whatever wealth he had accumulated since taking power in 1992. The junta began preparing for elections, although legitimate opposition parties were still either banned or boycotting the balloting.

The Open Society Foundations' Burma Project worked to promote the establishment of a democratic government based on the rule of law. The Burma Project also called on Burma's military regime to lift restrictions on the movement of aid organizations in the wake of Cyclone Nargis in 2008, the worst natural disaster to befall Burma in modern times. The Burma Project committed funds to funnel much-needed assistance to the storm's victims.

Another recipient of funding was the Human Rights Education Institute of Burma. The institute worked to identify committed young activists from urban and rural areas in Burma and provide them training, outside of Burma, in human rights, women's rights, community organizing, and democratic leadership concepts. These youth activists have been high school teachers and college instructors who have close relationships with their students and, after their return to Burma, have passed on what they have learned. The trainers placed particular emphasis on how to integrate human rights into their formal teaching without using the explicit terminology of human rights, which is dangerous in Burma.

The prerequisite for a democratic government is a free flow of information, and the prerequisite for free-flowing information is a free press. The Burma Project has supported broadcasters whose radio and television signals reach deep into the country with information in the local languages. Among these is the Oslo, Norway–based Democratic Voice of Burma, which organized about a hundred undercover freelance journalists and secret couriers inside Burma. The journalists used hand-held video cameras to capture images of popular protests against the junta as well as acts of brutality the junta used to quell them. The couriers carried mini-tapes, hard disk drives, and memory sticks with digital images out of the country.

Both the journalists and couriers assumed significant risk. As of mid-2010, a total of seventeen Democratic Voice of Burma journalists were serving prison terms from thirteen to sixty-five years in various prisons across the country. The Democratic Voice of Burma does not usually reveal the identities of the journalists who have been arrested for fear that the regime will subject them to further torture. One journalist whose name has been publicized, however, is a twenty-five-year old woman named Hla Hla Win, who was given a twenty-year jail term after she visited a Buddhist monastery in 2009.

"We started with Norwegian support alone in 1992, when no one knew the Democratic Voice of Burma," said Khin Maung Win, one of the four founding members of the organization. "Soros joined the following year. Without them we would not be able to do what we do."

Khin Maung Win spent eight months in Oslo during 1992– 1993 when the Democratic Voice of Burma began taking shape. He later set up studios along the Thai-Burma border and in India as well as an office in China near the border with Burma, where three or four journalists work. "Operating inside Burma must be secret. None of us can go back to the country, because we are too easily recognized. So we created a network of new people in Burma. Our journalists can take pictures and record audio and video. They can send text and audio by mobile phone and by the Internet. But video files are too large. In normal situations, for video, we use our own secret courier system to transport tapes, memory sticks, or discs. Sometimes we even get hard copy classified documents from inside the government. Not all government offices are happy about some things. And they leak information to us."

One leak involved a report about the aspirations of Burma's junta to acquire a nuclear weapon. The Democratic Voice of Burma produced a documentary film on the nuclear weapon story, which Al Jazeera's English service broadcast to the world in June 2010. "This was an investigative documentary," Khin Maung Win said. "We have a very good source in the government. The Burmese government never gives out such information officially."

For breaking news, the Democratic Voice of Burma cannot wait for couriers to transport its video images out of the country. "We need to send quickly," Khin Maung Win said. "For such situations, we have our own satellite system. The regime knows we have this advanced technology, but they cannot trace it."

The Democratic Voice of Burma broadcasts three or four hours of new programming each day around the clock from Norway on satellite radio and satellite television. The signal's footprint covers about half of the globe, including Africa, the Middle East, and Asia. "People in Burma receive the signal through the satellite," Khin Maung Win said. "There are dishes everywhere. You can even watch our signal in hotels even though the government is unhappy about it. We know our nuclear weapons documentary ran in tea shops inside Burma."

During the Saffron Revolution of 2007, when demonstrating Buddhists monks took to Rangoon's streets, the Democratic Voice of Burma's reporters were on balconies and in windows recording video images. "We had about thirty people there," said Khin Maung Win. "The international mainstream media had no one, and suddenly we became a major news source for them."

A journalist with the Democratic Voice of Burma, who goes by the pseudonym Joshua to protect his identity, was arrested in Rangoon at the time of the demonstrations. "We carry the camera in a bag with a hole for a lens and are trained to operate the camera from outside the bag, without looking at the viewfinder. Sometimes we can zoom in and out. Sometimes we make a mistake and don't get the image we want. Mostly, we capture pictures of the police beating up street vendors or people bribing other people."

Joshua was arrested while documenting a demonstration by a single protester in a marketplace. "I filmed it and was placed under arrest for a brief period. They questioned me and took my identification and then sent me out, but they got my camera and the tape. I told them that I had hired the camera from a friend for a trip to a tourist resort and that I saw a crowd of people and filmed it. They said they didn't believe it but that they were busy and let me go. I didn't leave the country immediately. We knew there would be bigger demos."

During the Saffron Revolution, troops killed one Japanese reporter. "We had journalists with cameras on him," said Khin Maung Win. "Within two hours, we had two minutes of footage of the killing. That footage was sent out of Burma within a few hours via satellite linkup inside Burma. We distributed it through Reuters and the Associated Press."

*   *   *

Groundwork for Women's Rights. There is a saying in Burma: *Thaa goh thakhin, liin goh phaya.* The words mean: "Respect the son as a master, and respect the husband as a god."[6] The junta for years used sayings like this to promote "traditional values" in Burma, values that assume women to be of limited worth and keep them relegated to a subordinate position in the family and society. For the junta and for too many members of the opposition to the junta, the "good woman" is modest in appearance and behavior. She is obedient in serving her husband and parents. She is subject to two Buddhist concepts: *hiri*, moral shame, and *ottapa*, fear of repercussions. And she is expected to remain silent.

This attitude—one that is official but also reflected by many of Burma's ethnic groups—leaves the country's women and girls to suffer all the problems that their fathers, sons, brothers, and husbands must endure under the junta, in addition to all the problems that fathers, sons, brothers, husbands, sweatshop managers, and militia men who come in the night foist upon women directly, as well as indirectly through their children.

Women, needless to say, hold no significant decision-making positions in Burma's junta. Despite the international celebrity of the leader of Burma's opposition, Aung San Suu Kyi, a living, breathing refutation of the notion that Burma's women are not equal to the men, and despite the risks so many of the country's women have taken to participate in demonstrations and other activities to end the junta's rule, women were holding few critical positions in the opposition. The education of sons was still given priority over the education of daughters. Vast legions of girls were abandoning school to do housework. Mothers and children were bearing the brunt of the lack of health care, especially in conflict areas where almost a quarter of the children die before reaching the age of five and one in twelve women die in pregnancy or childbirth. As many as 40,000 women from Burma, most of them members of minority groups, were believed to be working in the brothels of Thailand. Others were trafficked into China, India, and Pakistan. Some had been abducted. Some were sold by their parents. Some were being lured into traps with false promises of legitimate employment. Many were contracting HIV and other devastating diseases. Instead of addressing the root causes of trafficking, the junta introduced laws that restricted the movement of women and girls; these laws gave local authorities the opportunity to extort money from the families by arresting the victims.

The Open Society Foundations funded efforts to help establish women's rights in Burma. The Burma Project supported vocational training programs as well as efforts by the Burmese Women's Union to promote women's rights and gender equality and mount international pressure on the junta by reporting violence against women by government troops. The Women's League of Burma, an umbrella group of twelve women's organizations representing a broad range of Burma's ethnic groups, received Burma Project funding for a number of its programs. The project has backed activities that support peace-building, a women's empowerment program, internships, and organizational development initiatives. All of these activities endeavor to train young women to play leadership roles in a future democratic Burma. The Burma Project also provides direct support to many member organizations of the Women's League of Burma to conduct capacity-building training and the documentation of rights abuses targeting women in their communities.

One of the women whose efforts have enjoyed Burma Project support is Khin Ohmar. Born to parents of Mon, Shan, and Burman backgrounds, Khin Ohmar was an unassuming, twenty-year-old student of chemistry at a Rangoon university when the prodemocracy uprisings began in 1988. Within days, she had undergone a personal transformation. She stood up in front of a crowd of demonstrators, began to speak, and never sat down again. "I was just a regular girl. I got teased the first time I gave the speech," she said. "Whenever I went back home, my mom cried hard looking at me and tried to convince me to stop."

Khin Ohmar rose to leadership positions in two pivotal organizations of the student protests. When the government crackdown came, she was one of the thousands of students who fled to Thailand. In a jungle camp, she grew angry that, even in the opposition movement, women were expected to take an inferior position: "I started to see how gender really plays a role in the larger context in society. I was frustrated. In the camp, we were set aside when it came to leadership and decision making. Some men started to say things like, 'You women are a burden to the revolution. You should never have come to the jungle.'"

Khin Ohmar was granted refugee status in the United States, won a scholarship, and earned a degree in natural science. After completing an internship at Human Rights Watch/Asia and the AFL-CIO, she began advocacy and research work in support of halting foreign investment in Burma and promoting a consumer boycott of companies that had invested there. From 1995, she was the coordinator of the Open Society Foundations–funded Public Education Project for Burma at Refugees International in Washington. She traveled across North America seeking support for Burma.

Khin Ohmar eventually moved back to the Thailand–Burma border area. She won leadership positions in the Network for Democracy and Development, the Burmese Women's Union, and the Forum for Democracy in Burma—an umbrella organization of Burmese political groups in exile. She helped found the Women's League of Burma. She became the women's affairs coordinator for the opposition's government in exile, the National Coalition Government of the Union of Burma, and head of the Burma Partnership, a network of organizations throughout the Asia-Pacific region advocating for democracy and human rights in Burma. During debate on a United Nations resolution on Burma, her efforts contributed to the addition of language on widespread rape by Burma's military against women of ethnic minorities.

Yet again, however, Khin Ohmar was taken aback by the paucity of women in the opposition. "The voices of women are not heard," she said. "The women's movement had no access to the political leadership and policymaking of the democracy movement." She and other women set about building this capacity. Their first accomplishment was to secure funding for the Burmese Women's Union and contribute to the establishment of the Women's League of Burma.

The challenge Khin Ohmar faced, after almost a decade abroad, was identifying with women from Burma who had spent those same years fleeing Burma's army and dealing with other hardships of life in refugee camps, all the while tolerating the domination of men. "I am one of them, but I'm not perceived as one of them," Khin Ohmar said. "It was sometimes difficult for me when I expressed my ideas. I came back with a certain experience, but I had to make sure that I respected them and their experiences and that I didn't have an attitude towards them that made it seem that I knew anything better than they did. I made sure, and make sure, I don't treat them that way."

A significant aspect of Khin Ohmar's work links the effort to establish women's rights in general in Burma with the effort to end military rule and the ethnic conflicts that have exacerbated the misery of Burma's people for over half a century:

> There is also a common ground to what women of Burma, no matter what ethnic, religious, or social background we come from, have experienced in their lives. But at the same time, it is painful because of this barrier, of

these ethnic issues. The result of the decades-long conflict is mistrust, and no confidence in each other.

I see how women can be a catalyst to a bridge between divided communities. Gender violence is not only by the state. It is within our families, within our community. How are we going to ensure that, even with a federal democratic government, women will be safe in their own homes?

The Women's League of Burma is bringing women from different ethnic and religious groups and creating a space for them where it is safe to exchange ideas and experiences and to learn from each other. In the first training session on peace-building, we as facilitators came to see that the participants think that if a man from their same ethnic group tries to sleep with them and marry them without having their consent it is not seen as rape. Whereas if a Burmese army soldier acts the same way, then it is a rape. Then we were like oh, okay, and thought, what should we do now?

With that we realize that, in our culture, peace is misinterpreted. Peace for many women means to keep silent. Peace means keeping the family together no matter what kind of domestic violence, keeping silent about abuse. The mother or sister cannot make a decision for the family, in other institutions, in areas like education. The women's world is so confined by the cultural, social traditional norms.

Peace-building work is vital for women. The first step is breaking the silence. It takes a lot of courage for individual women to break the silence of what is happening to them, what injustice, what violence or abuse or the way that they've been treated either by their family or by the community, the state, by culture, tradition. To achieve the goal, which is of course getting rid of the military regime, is the tip of the iceberg really. What I really see is the transformation of the society. I mean, if we can remove the military regime there can still be another military regime again and again forever in Burmese society unless we transform these deep-rooted norms and practices of discrimination, abuse, and violence against minorities.

*   *   *

GEORGE SOROS

It is difficult to resist the development of repressive regimes from the outside. The chances of helping democratic regime change—when a well-intentioned government is elected but lacks the capacity to deliver on its promises—are much better. In cases of repression, the sooner the international community intervenes, the better its chance of success. Crisis prevention cannot start early enough. I tried to prevent crises by helping to build open societies, and we must have had some success, which has manifested itself in the absence of crises in certain countries or in the ability of other countries to cope with crises.

There appears to be a tipping point beyond which a repressive regime becomes practically impervious to outside pressure. If you want to be a ruthless dictator, history teaches you not to be half-hearted about it. Burma, North Korea, Zimbabwe, and Uzbekistan are cases in point.

I have found our Burma Project extremely frustrating. I was constantly tempted to cut it. We have religiously supported the international sanctions against the military junta, but the regime went from bad to worse: It turned into a one-man dictatorship. Burma has a lot of natural gas and other natural resources; now that the pipelines have been completed, the military are assured of a regular flow of funds. After they killed Buddhist monks and lost whatever respect they still enjoyed from people, they withdrew to a mountain stronghold where they are protected from any popular uprising. Fortunately they began to realize that their policies produced the opposite result from what they intended. They were fiercely nationalistic and jealous of their independence; yet they became extremely dependent on the Chinese. They wanted to restore some measure of legitimacy and introduced a constitution. The elections were thoroughly rigged in their favor; still, they are becoming more susceptible to international influence. They finally released democracy leader Aung San Suu Kyi.

This opens a new chapter. It is liable to prove as frustrating as the previous one but in a different way. At least there will be some forward movement, only justice will not be served. Aung San Suu Kyi will not be allowed to reenter politics; but she is unlikely to be prevented from running a foundation. Eventually the military will have to recognize her and enter into a dialogue. The groundwork that our Burma project has been laying may serve a useful purpose, after all.

PART III

Public Health:
TB and Mental Disability

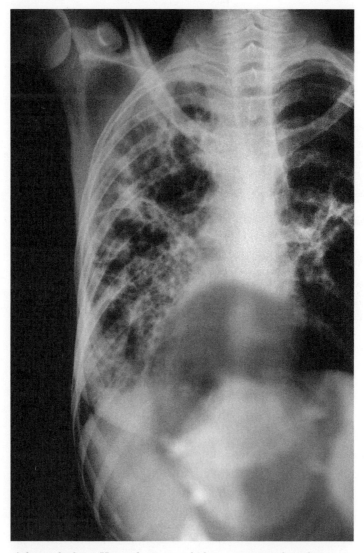

A doctor checks an X-ray showing multidrug-resistant tuberculosis (MDR-TB) at the Maseru clinic in Lesotho. Through the Open Society Public Health Program, George Soros has helped draw critical attention to the scope of the TB problem, the looming consequences of multidrug-resistant TB, and the lethal force of dual TB-HIV infection.
(© Open Society Foundations, photograph by Pep Bonet)

6

CHAPTER

Tackling TB

By the late 1980s, political leaders and public health policy-makers in many parts of the world had been lulled into believing that because tuberculosis was a curable disease it was therefore a conquered disease. But in the gulags of Siberia, the lowland villages of Bangladesh, the barrios of Latin America, the diamond mines of South Africa, and many other places far from the daily cares of people in developed countries, TB was still a wholesale killer.

Ravaging men, women, and children who could neither find nor afford effective treatment, the disease continued to thrive not because of some innate physical vulnerability of the people it victimized, but because of social conditions largely beyond their control. These conditions combined to give tuberculosis opportunities to propagate and spread and, sometimes, to mutate into more lethal and less curable forms.

In 1998 alone, the microscopic rod-shaped bacilli struck down an estimated two million people, many of them infected with HIV. By then, this dual scourge—TB and HIV—had reached epidemic proportions across swathes of southern Africa. Untold numbers of households were losing their breadwinners and homemakers; uncounted children were losing parents and caregivers.

Even more frightening was the rise of multidrug-resistant TB. Haphazard TB treatment in southern Africa, Russia, and other areas was nurturing the development of forms of tuberculosis resistant to the best drugs available to treat the disease. Evidence had emerged that strains were spreading from Siberian prison cells, South African mining camps, and other hot spots to urban areas with daily flights bound for the world's most densely populated areas.

The propagation of multidrug-resistant strains of tuberculosis in southern Africa, Russia, and other regions began to pose a threat to people in New York, London, Paris, and Tokyo. This potential grew for years without attracting the attention it deserved. In 2006, reported cases of drug-resistant tuberculosis rose to a record 490,000, but barely 20,000 of the people infected were finding their way into treatment regimens approved by the World Health Organization.[1]

George Soros invested his time and personal credibility with policymakers and, working through the Open Society Public Health Program, helped draw critical attention to the scope of the TB problem, to the lethal force of dual TB-HIV infection, and to the looming threat of drug-resistant TB. With his backing, Soros's collaborators, including public health specialists in Geneva, New York, Washington, and Harvard Medical School, as well as doctors caring for patients in Russia and southern Africa, helped realign the international campaign to reverse the disease's progress and ensure that human rights would be respected along the way.

When the Open Society Foundations began working on TB, there was little awareness of the threat posed by drug-resistant TB and no global action plan to defeat TB. There was no tried and tested public health treatment model to combat multidrug-resistant TB in countries where the disease was most likely to develop into the gravest threat: countries where victims were spread over inaccessible areas with little access to health care services. Countries whose people were beset by poverty and ravaged by AIDS. Countries like Russia.

In 1991, the Soviet Union disintegrated. The engines driving Russia's economy had sputtered and seized up. Miners, oil riggers, doctors, and nurses stopped receiving their wages. Store shelves went empty. By the late 1990s, about half of Russia's people had sunk below the poverty line, millions of them physically weakened by malnutrition, alcoholism, and drug addiction. Petty crime escalated. The existing criminal justice and penal systems were unable to cope with the numbers of persons being arrested, many for minor offenses and possession of inconsequential quantities of drugs. Detainees languished behind bars for months and even years because the legal system did not provide for release on bail or speedy trials. Living conditions in Russia's prisons and jails were squalid. In some institutions, dozens of inmates crowded into each cell and shared the few available beds by sleeping in three shifts. Toilet facilities amounted to a hole in a corner of the floor. Windows were sealed against the bitter cold, and heavy shutters blocked the sunlight. Cigarette smoke poisoned the air. At mealtime, attendants ladled out an unidentifiable soup and gave each prisoner a chunk of black bread. There was no milk, no meat, no fruit or vegetables— luxuries even on the outside.[2]

Blind to guilt and innocence, TB consumed the arriving wave of prisoners and detainees. By the mid-1990s, Russia's prisons held about a million people, 29 percent of them under twenty-five years of age.[3] About 10 percent of all prison inmates and persons awaiting trial had active, infectious TB.[4] If they were treated at all, prisoners either received inappropriate drugs or obtained the appropriate drugs in insufficient doses or over an insufficient period to be effective.[5] More than anything else, this fostered the development of multidrug-resistant TB strains that spread through the prison population.

Mortality rates rose. Bodies of the dead were stacked in one Siberian prison. Guards and other penal workers meanwhile succumbed to the disease as well. Those who came and went from the prison facilities carried the bacilli to the world outside, where TB treatment was almost equally haphazard due to a lack of appropriate drugs. Doctors exacerbated the drug resistance problem by prescribing patients whatever medicines happened to be available.[6]

Russia won admission to the Council of Europe in 1997, after Moscow had agreed, among other things, to improve conditions in its prisons and detention facilities. The Russian government transferred responsibility for administering the entire penal and detention system to the justice minister, who sought to tackle the prison TB epidemic.

In the autumn of 1997, Soros made a substantial commitment to invest in social reform efforts in Russia, including public health and education. Soros and Aryeh Neier were also keen on supporting efforts to reform Russia's criminal justice system, including its teeming pretrial detention centers, jails, and prisons. Moscow's interest in solving the prisoner TB problem provided Soros and Neier with an opportunity not only to combat TB but also to help promote work on reforming these institutions, which had once been off-limits to practically all foreigners except foreign prisoners.

Soros donated $12.3 million in 1997 to launch a program to treat Russia's prisoners and detainees. The aim of this program was to introduce the Directly Observed Treatment Short Course (DOTS), a medically effective and cost-efficient treatment option recommended by the World Health Organization, though previously shunned by Russian public health authorities.

Soon it was discovered that the DOTS treatment method was failing to cure a significant portion of the prisoners infected with active TB. Research would eventually show that, due to the failings of Russia's treatment efforts, about 20 percent of the active TB cases in the Russian penal system—and in some facilities over 50 percent—involved strains of the disease that were resistant to the DOTS drugs.[7] A member of the project's advisory committee, Dr. Paul Farmer of the Harvard Medical School and a founder of Partners In Health, a nongovernmental organization that provides health care services and undertakes research and advocacy work on behalf of sick people living in poverty, realized that the anti-TB efforts in Russia's prisons were not providing meaningful treatment for inmates suffering multidrug-resistant TB. Farmer was concerned that the DOTS treatment was doing more harm than good.

After a debate between Farmer and the director of Soros anti-TB efforts in Russia at the time, Alex Goldfarb, at the Open Society Foundations' headquarters in New York, Soros altered the direction of the program so it would counter multidrug-resistant TB. The Open Society Foundations also helped bring the problem to the attention of other donors, including the European Union and the World Bank.

The support from Soros and the Open Society Foundations helped tip an international debate over how to allocate TB resources—whether to invest solely in DOTS and strengthen the infrastructure for treating TB or to focus on treating all patients, including those with multidrug-resistant strains. Despite initial opposition from within the World Health Organization, Soros and the Open Society Foundations urged international organizations, donors, and national health ministries around the world to develop and implement programs to also combat multidrug-resistant TB. In 1999, Harvard Medical School and the Open

Society Foundations published *The Global Impact of Drug-Resistant Tuberculosis*, a groundbreaking report that drew attention to the growing threat.

With the increasing recognition of the TB problem, Soros and the Open Society Foundations received numerous requests to fund undertakings to solve it. Soros followed his businessman's instincts and challenged the international community to develop a well-engineered action plan to wage its struggle against TB more effectively. The Open Society Public Health Program, then led by Nina Schwalbe, provided funding and other support for an effort by the Stop TB Partnership to develop an action plan to combat the disease and to rally a consensus in support of the plan. The Public Health Program organized meetings and workshops, performed advocacy work, and provided funding.

About 150 doctors, public health specialists, scientists, donors, representatives of nongovernmental organizations, and, most crucially, representatives of countries most affected by TB participated in formulating the Global Plan to Stop TB. It achieved consensus support in 2001. The Global Plan called for investing $9.1 billion over five years and projected the line-item costs of what was needed to defeat TB, to mitigate the effects of TB-HIV coinfection, and to thwart the development of drug-resistant TB strains. The effort to create the Global Plan demonstrated that public-private partnerships to solve world public health problems can achieve an international consensus.

George Soros, James Wolfensohn, president of the World Bank, and Gro Brundtland, director general of the World Health Organization, launched the Global Plan on World TB Day in 2001. The plan became the blueprint for the Global Stop TB Partnership, a network of national governments, international organizations, nongovernmental organizations, public- and private-sector donors, as well as individuals whose aim is to eliminate TB as a public health problem. The Open Society Foundations won representation on the partnership's board.

In 2001, the heads of the G8 nations met in Genoa, Italy, and determined to back the establishment of the Global Fund to Fight AIDS, Tuberculosis, and Malaria, an international institution whose purpose was to increase significantly financial support for intervention against the three targeted diseases. Since its launch in 2002, the Global Fund has gone on to provide 20 percent of all international funding to combat HIV and AIDS and has become the world's largest international funder of programs to combat malaria and tuberculosis. The Open Society Foundations continue to support the Global Fund by advocating before governments on the fund's behalf.

The impact of these efforts has primarily been felt in the United States and in Europe. At the time, the Open Society Foundations also gave one Japanese nongovernmental organization—Friends of the Global Fund Japan—a first grant of $99,000 to assemble a blue-ribbon committee of Japanese political leaders and business executives to advocate for the fund. Japan's government subsequently announced a donation of $500 million over two years, going on to substantially increase its contribution to the fund in the ensuing years.

During this same period, representatives of United Nations member states and some two dozen international organizations were also finalizing a concerted international strategy aimed at overcoming the most severe developmental problems on earth: extreme poverty, woeful maternal health and high infant mortality, the lack of even primary education for vast numbers of children, diseases that hobble large swathes of entire populations, and disregard for environmental sustainability. This international strategy was elaborated in the Millennium Development Goals, which called for their achievement in the first decade and a half of the twenty-first century. The Open Society Foundations and their partners played key roles in the advocacy effort that eventually succeeded in having tuberculosis included with HIV and AIDS and malaria among the targets for action by the Millennium Development Goals.

In 2005 and 2006, world health officials registered the first declines in the incidence of tuberculosis. The worldwide death rate from TB fell by 2.6 percent in 2006, to 1.7 million people. The number of persons with multidrug-resistant TB, however, grew to 490,000. In September 2006, the World Health Organization announced that a new, practically incurable strain of drug-resistant tuberculosis had been detected in Tugela Ferry, a rural town in the South African province of KwaZulu-Natal. Of 544 TB patients examined in the province during 2005, 221 were infected with a multidrug-resistant form of the disease; and 53 of these 221 victims had acquired the incurable new strain; all but one of the 53 died. The reaction of the South African government was to detain individuals suspected of having drug-resistant TB, often in appalling conditions and without proper infection control measures or adequate treatment. Staff at the Public Health Program sought to fund alternatives to this panic-induced approach.

Tegula Ferry is close to the eastern border of Lesotho. At least 25 percent of Lesotho's people are HIV positive, and TB had by then infected about 90 percent of them. In just a decade, life expectancy had plummeted from only fifty years to just thirty-five.

Lesotho's government sought outside help. It won support from the World Health Organization and other United Nations agencies to obtain medicines to treat cases of drug-resistant TB. It also approached Partners In Health and another organization, the Foundation for Innovative New Diagnostics (FIND), which have expertise in setting up medical laboratories.

With help from FIND, Partners In Health launched a multi-faceted program to treat the disease's victims, with a view to demonstrate that detention of multidrug-resistant TB patients was unnecessary, and that, with the right support, they could be treated effectively, safely, and much more cheaply in the community. In April 2007, FIND began upgrading Lesotho's main TB laboratory to make it capable of detecting drug-resistant strains of the disease. At the same time, Partners In Health trained a network of doctors, nurses, and community health workers to treat patients around the country. For critically ill patients from remote areas and their caretakers, it rented several tiny houses in Lesotho's capital, Maseru, so the victims could be monitored while they were receiving treatment on an outpatient basis. For the most severe cases, Partners In Health and the Lesotho government applied a $3 million donation from the Open Society Foundations to transform an underutilized leprosy clinic into the twenty-bed Botsabelo Hospital. Both Partners In Health and the Open Society Foundations saw Lesotho as a proving ground for an unprecedented treatment model for multidrug-resistant tuberculosis, a model that respected human rights and would, if effective, inform standards set by the World Health Organization as well as policies and programs developed by government health ministries across southern Africa and beyond.

One of the first patients to arrive at the Botsabelo Hospital in Maseru was a woman named Mabafokeng. Her story could be the story of any of the thousands of women and men who have contracted tuberculosis in Lesotho. She was the youngest daughter of a large family living in a village on the upper flanks of Echo Rock, a brown and yellow outcropping of sandstone in northwestern Lesotho. Her father spent most of the year across the border in South Africa working in a diamond mine. Her mother managed the family homestead, including a vegetable plot and a cow. Over the years, with her father's earnings from the diamond mine, they had constructed two small houses of stone and mud brick and were now building a third.

Her father, Albert, would make the six-hour journey home from South Africa every month or so. It was at the diamond mine, probably in some crowded dormitory or amid the foul air of an underground chamber, where Albert first inhaled the tuberculosis bacilli. And it was along the asphalt road that crossed South Africa into Lesotho that his lungs, like those of thousands of migrant miners from his country, carried the bacilli home.

Mabafokeng remembers watching her father struggle with constant bouts of coughing and chest pains over the years. A clinic at the diamond mine treated Albert's first infection during the late 1980s, just as the apartheid regime in South Africa was beginning to come apart. In 2003, Albert suffered a second TB infection, which required another six-month treatment program. At that time he stopped digging diamonds, moved home permanently, and began collecting payments from the mining company.

After Albert moved home, Mabafokeng was determined to earn money to help her family survive. She took a job sewing T-shirts and track suits in a poorly ventilated garment factory, exposing herself to the bacilli that tuberculosis-infected workers were discharging in their sneezing and coughing. The commute to work in a closed bus consumed more than a third of Mabafokeng's wages, stole more hours from the long days she toiled, and increased her exposure to infected, coughing people. Yet she remained on the job, just as her father had remained in the mines. After all, the family depended on her wages.

In February 2005, Mabafokeng discovered that she had contracted tuberculosis and underwent treatment. But the disease struck her again in 2006. Mabafokeng began, and insists that she completed, a second medical treatment program. At the same time, her father regained the familiar cough and pains that had plagued him for more than two decades. But he refused to submit to another TB test or undergo a new course of treatment.

In July 2007, tuberculosis bacilli took hold in Mabafokeng's lungs for a third time. She began, as before, to take drugs to fight back the disease's most common strains. This time, a former midwife, a woman whom the Partners In Health program had trained to be a treatment supporter and to watch for possible cases of drug-resistant tuberculosis, monitored Mabafokeng's progress. When the telltale fatigue, weight loss, coughing, and chest pain worsened, the treatment supporter urged Mabafokeng to have more testing. The results came back positive for a multidrug-resistant strain of the disease. Defeating it would require a harsh and lengthy treatment with injected drugs. Almost immediately, Mabafokeng started vomiting and suffering other side effects. On August 8, the program transferred her and her mother to one of the small houses Partners In Health had rented in Maseru. Mabafokeng simmered with anger at her father. She suspected that Albert had infected her. Perhaps he was refusing to take further tests because he, like so many other people infected with disease, feared learning the results. Perhaps he feared the drugs and the toll they would exact.

Vomiting, stomach pain, and fatigue continued to torture Mabafokeng after each new injection, and finally she abandoned the treatment. Her decision allowed the bacilli within her body to flourish and possibly develop a resistance to more drugs. Telling no one, Mabafokeng and her mother boarded a bus and began the trip home.

Bikhapha is a community coordinator for the Botsabelo Hospital for patients with multidrug-resistant tuberculosis. It is her job to locate people infected with the disease and to track down persons with whom they have had contact. When Bikhapha caught up with Mabafokeng, she told her what would happen if she stopped the treatment, how she would die slowly and suffer terribly, vomiting blood and breathing with difficulty. "She would risk infecting everyone she loved and the other people in her village," Bikhapha said. "The community would shun her family." But Mabafokeng did not comply until her brother, Lempe, who was a traditional healer and had assumed the role of the head of household in place of his ailing father, demanded that Mabafokeng return to treatment. Before departing her home, Mabafokeng urged Albert one last time to take a tuberculosis test. Again, her father refused.

The Botsabelo Special Hospital for patients with multidrug-resistant tuberculosis is a single-story brick building above Maseru. Its only corridor leads from a nurse's station to a common room with a few chairs and a television set. Along one side of the corridor are patient rooms, each with six beds. Along the opposite side are the isolation rooms for patients who are critically ill, still contagious, or suffering incurable forms of the disease. All is new and meticulously sterile.

Mabafokeng was assigned to Room 5, Bed 13, and began receiving daily injections. During hours of tedium, surrounded by white walls, the hiss of the ventilation system, the occasional cough, and gospel music coming over a transistor radio, Mabafokeng chatted with the other women in the room. She learned that one of them, Maretsepile, was thirty-four years old and HIV positive. She was the widow of a man who had succumbed to tuberculosis in 1999 and the mother of two boys, one sixteen, one twelve. Before coming to Botsabelo, Maretsepile went to a traditional healer who said she was under a spell. He made cuts on her body, put a black ointment on the cuts, and made her drink some herbs mixed into milk. "I have never vomited so much in my life," she said. "After that, I never went back to him again."

Mabafokeng's father finally decided to go to the hospital for tests, and his family made plans to take him on the morning of Monday, November 5. The distance from the house to the main road was too great for Albert to walk. Mabafokeng's brother arranged pillows and a blanket in a wheelbarrow and prepared to push him to the crossroads. While his son made the preparations, Albert began to cough and gasp for breath. It took only a few moments for him to die.

In Lesotho, tradition dictates that funerals are held on Saturdays. Albert's funeral took twelve days to prepare. By Friday, November 16, the drugs were beating back Mabafokeng's tuberculosis. She was no longer vomiting. Her energy was returning. The pain and other side effects had waned. Her vital signs were stable. The hospital's doctors agreed to release her so she could bid her father farewell, so long as she agreed to show up each day for her injection and to wear a surgical mask around other people while she was still infectious.

In the car returning her home that Friday, masks covered the mouths and noses of everyone breathing the closed air. Mabafokeng said she would not return to the garment factory or any other job that risked a new tuberculosis infection. "I will finish my injections in February," she said. "I'll decide then what to do. The family needs income, so I will have to get a job. The nearest one I can find. Housekeeping probably, anywhere an opportunity arises."

The Botsabelo Hospital and patients like Mabafokeng have helped inform the work of Partners In Health and others struggling against tuberculosis. In May 2006, Partners In Health released new guidelines for community-based treatment of multidrug-resistant TB in resource-poor settings. The program in Lesotho went on to provide training for medical professionals from Ethiopia, South Africa, Swaziland, and Tanzania to show them how to address multidrug-resistant TB without routinely detaining patients. In 2009, Partners In Health and the World Health Organization jointly issued *Management of MDR-TB: A Field Guide*, a groundbreaking reference manual for health workers in poor countries.

By that time, the Open Society Public Health Program was working in more than sixty countries in Central and Eastern Europe, the former Soviet Union, Central Asia, Southeast Asia, Africa, and China to develop the capacity of community groups to press government, health care institutions, and health programs to be accountable to the people they were designed to serve. The program was sponsoring programs and seminars that enabled civil society representatives, policymakers, funders, government, and business leaders to debate and discuss crucial policy issues and, where possible, to forge partnerships on emerging health and human rights concerns.

By 2010, George Soros had donated more than $300 million to advance human rights in the field of health and promote public health worldwide. During the course of its development, the Open Society Public Health Program has supported efforts ensuring access to essential medicines, promoting transparency of public funding and increasing the effectiveness, equity, and impact of health expenditures. The program has also worked to enhance the ability of the mass media to raise awareness about the health care issues of marginalized populations; to reduce the harm related to injecting drug use, including HIV infection; to protect the human rights of drug users; and to increase public awareness and educate health care professionals about palliative care. The program's activities in the policy realm have included promoting legal action to advance public health policies that respect human rights, holding governments to their commitments in international public health agreements, and ensuring human rights protections and access to health care for people who are stigmatized because of sexual practices, sexual orientation, or gender identity.

Soros and the Open Society Foundations continue to support and advocate for health policies and practices that are based on inclusion, human rights, justice, and evidence. At the root of the Open Society Foundations' efforts to combat TB has been a focus on the rights of patients. Working with the Stop TB Partnership, UNAIDS, and the World Health Organization, in 2010 the Open Society Foundations helped launch a global taskforce to assist national governments in developing human rights–based approaches to TB care, such as the pilot project in Lesotho.

Coordinated efforts like these have helped turn the tide against TB. Conditions are much more promising today than they were in the 1990s. All regions of the world are on track to meet the Millennium Development Goal established in 2000 to cut TB prevalence and deaths in half by 2015. But the fight is far from over. TB remains the second biggest infectious killer of adults worldwide. Rates of decline in TB prevalence are slow, and in many countries multidrug-resistant TB is still a very real threat.

Božidar and Milica Čičić have built new lives together in their community after spending decades locked in an institution for the mentally disabled in Croatia. Through the Open Society Foundations' work in Eastern Europe and elsewhere, George Soros has supported organizations that help people with mental disabilities move from institutions to suitable housing in their community. (© Open Society Foundations, photograph by Damir Fabijanić)

7

Liberating People
with Mental Disabilities

M., a woman about thirty years old, was conceived and raised in one of the several thousand state institutions in Eastern Europe where people with mental disabilities spend their lives in confinement. The Demir Kapiya Special Institution is the name of the place where M. was confined. It is located in southern Macedonia, near a crack in a chain of mountains that allows the Vardar River to press southward into Greece.

At the moment of M.'s conception, her father was able to propel himself around the ward in a wheelchair, and her mother could drag herself along the floor from room to room. Six months passed before attendants on the ward realized that M.'s mother was pregnant. When her due date approached, a social worker drove her to a maternity hospital. Infant M. resided in an orphanage for three years before its staff reported signs of an intellectual disability and relegated her to the special institution. She was assigned to the children's ward but placed in a bed close by her parents.

M. learned to talk among people who slurred their words and strained to form coherent sentences. One of the attendants became a kind of godmother. Someone brought her a pink bike. But no physical therapist or speech therapist ever called. No one bundled her off to school. No one taught M. to read and write or add and subtract. No one registered her birth. No one informed her that she was not indigent. No one told her that she had an uncle in the world outside. No one introduced them when he came to visit her father. On visiting days, Demir Kapiya's staff hid M. away.

To be admitted to the Demir Kapiya Special Institution, prospective residents are supposed to be diagnosed as severely disabled. The bedridden children M. has seen lying in metal cribs in the main building spend their days staring at the walls. They shake and rock to an internal rhythm. They respond to a touch with a grimace that might be a smile. Their coos, grrrs, and ahhs are attempts at speech.

M.'s mother and father, their limbs bent, their utterances indecipherable except to M., are severely disabled, as are the main building's other adults, including the bedridden consigned to the highest floor, which is closed to visitors. An official commission—doctors, social workers, and other professionals—determines whether persons meet the criteria for "severely disabled" and then relegates them to lifelong confinement in the institution.

In some cases, such as M.'s, the commission's members have disregarded those standards. M. speaks and sings simply and coherently, even though she slurs her words. She dances the Macedonian circle dance, the *oro*, without breaking step. Another resident, her friend B., a polio victim, taught M. how to thread the spindles, needles, and bobbins of a sewing machine and to make articles of clothing. Perhaps none of the staff members actually believed that M. or B. rightfully belonged in the special institution. Perhaps none of the staff thought that, after almost thirty years, M. would seek to leave. Perhaps none imagined that anyone outside the institution would discover that M. even existed, or that she and B. and many other residents were not severely disabled. And perhaps none of the staff ever imagined that M. and the others, the severely disabled and not so challenged, would end up someplace other than the lonely, weed-choked corner of the local graveyard where the special institution's deceased residents are buried and forgotten, separated even in death from the rest of the community.

*   *   *

For much of human history, families in all cultures have tended to reject children unable to walk or talk or think as quickly or effortlessly as others. This was not necessarily intentional. Many parents lacked the means to provide their disabled children with adequate protection and care, and some loving, protective parents and caregivers died before they could find someone to adopt their disabled dependents. But some parents mistreated them, and beyond the family home, disabled people suffered mockery, homelessness, deprivation, and violence. Some were castigated as vessels of demons or condemned souls. In *Notre Dame de Paris*, for instance, Victor Hugo's Parisians threatened to burn Quasimodo alive when he was abandoned in a sack at age four.

In the past century, there have been both progress and tragic setbacks for the disabled. In the late nineteenth century, social reformers took steps to protect people with disabilities by concentrating them in institutions where they were sheltered, fed, and clothed. The Nazis gassed residents of these institutions in Germany even before the Holocaust.

After World War II, governments in the developed West as well as Eastern Europe's Communist countries launched efforts to institutionalize and educate the disabled so they might re-emerge and take their rightful place in society. But these institutions, among them the Demir Kapiya Special Institution, became warehouses for human beings. In the Communist East, residents were provided no meaningful education or training. Hardly any returned to live in the broader community.

Institutions for disabled people had also become problematic in the developed countries of the West. Several decades ago, the governments of some Western countries began to move disabled persons from institutions to apartments and homes with organized support according to their individual needs. Assistants helped the disabled purchase their own food, cook their own meals, wash their own dishes and laundry, attend classes, hold down jobs, deposit their earnings in bank accounts, and walk to the movies.

Twenty years before George Soros chose Aryeh Neier to direct his Open Society Foundations, Neier—as executive director of the American Civil Liberties Union—had helped found an organization called the Mental Health Law Project, which was later renamed the Judge David L. Bazelon Center for Mental Health Law. This organization became the leading legal advocate in the United States for people with mental disabilities and pursued precedent-setting litigation that outlawed institutional abuse and created protections against arbitrary confinement. The center advocated effectively for enabling people with mental disabilities to leave the institutions in which they were confined and take their place in community life.

No such organization could work in Eastern Europe until the Berlin Wall had fallen. The horrid conditions suffered by disabled people in the region attracted widespread media attention after journalists gained access to institutions in Macedonia, Romania, Serbia, and other countries. For example, inside an institution in Plătărești, a town just east of Bucharest, not-so-disabled children bundled in winter coats and boots struggled to keep warm on Christmas Eve 1990 by lying on scraps of cardboard spread over iron radiators that dispersed a rumor of heat. Disabled kids, hardly dressed, wallowed on the floor in their own excrement. Three, four, even five infants were confined to a single metal crib that resembled a cage for circus animals.

Attendants in overcoats herded other residents of the institution into a corner of a room, covered them with blankets, and kept watch as they sat idly on the floor, the cacophony unbroken by a toy or a televised talking head or a song from a radio.

Horrified workers for aid agencies and humanitarian organizations arrived from abroad. Individuals and organizations sent donations. In some institutions, heat began to rise from radiators. Wheelchairs and new beds and bedding appeared. Walls were painted in bright blues and yellows. Toys occupied shelves. But the physical improvements to some institutions and the release of some nondisabled residents did nothing to alter the fundamental fact of life for the hundreds of thousands of disabled people still locked inside: They were still segregated from society, still confined by walls and fences and gatehouses. Moreover, in too many institutions, even basic living conditions had not improved.

In 2009, human rights investigators working in Bulgaria, a European Union member state, discovered a caged area with shacks next to a newly renovated institution. Thirty mentally disabled women were living in the shacks. The staff did not permit them to eat with the other residents. The investigators saw one woman eating bread she had dipped into a puddle next to an outdoor toilet. Flies were crawling over another woman. Investigators have reported that many residents of institutions in Bulgaria and other countries are being improperly administered medication for the convenience of staff members.[1]

Soon after Neier joined Soros at the Open Society Foundations, an organization founded by a former Bazelon Center lawyer, Eric Rosenthal, received the Foundations' backing to investigate and publish reports on human rights abuses in institutions for people with mental disabilities in Eastern Europe and elsewhere around the world. After Rosenthal's new organization, Mental Disability Rights International, undertook a fact-finding trip to Hungary, the Open Society Foundations launched a project aimed at fostering the development of grassroots organizations that would advocate on behalf of people with mental disabilities and press for their transfer from institutions to suitable, supported housing in the community.

The project's initial target countries were Croatia, Hungary, and Romania. By 1998, the project, the Open Society Mental Health Initiative, was also at work in Armenia, Azerbaijan, Bulgaria, Georgia, Kazakhstan, Kyrgyzstan, and other republics of the former Yugoslavia. "In these countries, people with mental disabilities comprise one of the most marginalized and neglected segments of the population," said Judith Klein, the initiative's director. "These people are given almost no opportunities to advocate on their own behalf, and this, in part, prolongs the history of institutionalization, which is a massive violation of human rights and of the principles of an open society."

Liberating people with mental disabilities from institutions requires altering the attitudes of parents, political leaders, professionals, and members of the government bureaucracy, as well as the general public, which foots the bill without paying any heed to its effects or demanding transparency and accountability. In Croatia, Klein found a partner in Borka Teodorović, a professor at Zagreb University who now manages the Association for Promoting Inclusion, a nongovernmental organization that advocates closing the country's institutions and replacing them with community-based services. "We are about thirty years behind," Teodorović said of Croatia, which has about 4,500 people with intellectual disabilities institutionalized countrywide. "The ministry here has not come to the conclusion that it has to change things. Political leaders and bureaucrats give lip service to moving people with intellectual disabilities from institutions to communities. But they create barriers. We believe that it doesn't matter whether an institution is new and spotless. These institutions are still places of confinement. None of these people should be locked away. The community can and should bear the costs, because the alternative deprives these people of their human rights."

Still, Croatia has perhaps done more than other Eastern European countries to free people with intellectual disabilities from institutions. Zdenka Petrović, one of the first persons freed from an institution in Croatia, knows the pain of rejection, segregation, and confinement. She was abandoned at birth in 1965 and lived in an orphanage and in a foster family until the age of nine, when she was confined in an institution in the Bosnian town of Višegrad. "When I was small, the other residents took care of me," she said. "I wanted to go to school but was never given the chance.

"Whenever visitors came to inspect the institution, we would be locked up in the buildings so we wouldn't speak to them. They beat us. They would tie us up. They would cut our hair to punish us. When clothing donations arrived, the nurses and workers took everything for themselves. We got nothing. We weren't allowed to use the phone and had to do it secretly. Everything everyone told me in the institution was a lie. I didn't trust anyone. I was afraid of everything. I was afraid people would yell at me. I was afraid to learn to cook. Even when I was small, I wanted to get away. I wanted to have my friends. I wanted to have a boyfriend."

The war in Bosnia led to Petrović being transferred to an institution on Croatia's Dalmatian coast. "We were locked up there, too," she said. "The sea was right in front of our eyes." In 1998, Borka Teodorović asked Petrović if she would like to attempt to live outside the institution. She agreed. In the eleven years after she left the institution, Petrović learned to cook, to read, and to do arithmetic. She finished elementary school and found work as a kitchen assistant in a hotel. She found her own apartment and paid her own rent without state assistance. "I buy what I want," she said. "I pay my own rent. I can work and earn money on my own. In the institution they said I was incapable of working. They said we were of no use to anyone else."

Petrović became president of the region's first nongovernmental organization run by people with mental disabilities for people with mental disabilities. She lobbied the government to stop institutionalizing the disabled and demanded respect for their human rights. On July 13, 2005, Petrović appeared as a witness before the Croatian parliament's Committee on Human Rights. She wore a business suit and enunciated her words clearly, slowly, and with resolve. "My friends who are still in the institution today would also like to come out," Petrović testified. "They want our help. They want to live independently. And I would recommend that a decision be taken to close down all these institutions and give these people the opportunity and support to live independently and work."

At the time, Petrović was preparing for the day she would go into Croatia's institutions and approach residents one at a time and explain to them the possibilities of life on the outside. This is what she said she would do:

> I'll ask them whether they want to go outside. If they say no, I'll ask why.
>
> If they say they don't want to leave, I'll ask them why it is fine in the institution. If they say it is fine because they have something to eat and a place to sleep, I'll ask whether they would like to have a place to sleep and something to eat outside.
>
> If they say they can't leave, I'll ask them why they can't leave. I'll ask them whether they would like to work and be paid for it. I'll ask them if they want friends, men and women friends.

If they say they already have friends, I'll ask them whether their friends are from inside the institution or outside. And when they answer only inside, I'll ask them whether they'd like different friends, friends from outside the institution.

If they say the staff won't let them, I'll explain that, once they're outside, they'll have their own friends, they'll decide what to do, what to eat, when to wake up, when to go to bed.

People are afraid of what they do not know.

In each country where the Open Society Mental Health Initiative has been active, the stiffest resistance to moving people with mental disabilities from institutions to supported housing has come from government ministries and employees of existing institutions, whose livelihoods depend on maintaining the status quo. "Too many members of the general public see people with mental disabilities as a subhuman species that is not worthy of basic rights," Klein said. "But the biggest problem is posed by government officials, institution administrators, and professionals. Some administrators say there is no money to provide support for persons with disabilities living in the broader community. But money isn't the problem. The cost works out to about the same. The problem, beyond protecting self-interest, is a paternalistic attitude and reluctance to change. People assume that the disabled will be left in communities without support and protection. But they fail to see that the disabled are not receiving sufficient support and protection in the institutions, and never will."

In Hungary, civil society organizations focusing on the rights of disabled people are still few, and the number of people freed from a life of confinement in institutions is small, because the

Hungarian authorities opted to transfer them to smaller institutions. (A nun in one institution in Hungary assured Klein that "fresh air is enough for them.")

Across the border in Romania, the Open Society Foundations' effort had, by 2009, helped to develop an effective program in the city of Timişoara, and negotiations were under way to close three institutions with four hundred residents in one county and develop supported accommodations in the community. Living conditions for hundreds of disabled persons in Romania, however, remain miserable. In some institutions, investigators from Mental Disability Rights International, who were working with the Open Society Foundations' support, saw children tied to cribs and wrapped in sheets to restrain them from moving. Some residents had open wounds and bedsores. Many were grossly malnourished, including teenagers so emaciated that they appeared to be less than five years old. A staff member in one institution informed Mental Disability Rights International investigators that children with little or no disability could easily be adopted but remained institutionalized because they lacked identification papers.[2]

In Serbia, the Mental Health Initiative's effort to assist in the transition of disabled persons from institutions to 120 houses in local communities collapsed after an election campaign, when the government reneged on its pledge to provide matching funds. The initiative supported the development of a community living program in Belgrade where twenty-three disabled people were placed in eight apartments. By 2009, these people were at risk of being returned to a wretched institution because local and federal officials disagreed over who was responsible for their support.

With the Open Society Foundations' backing, Mental Disability Rights International published a report in 2007 that exposed deplorable conditions in Serbian institutions. The report documented the routine use of physical restraints and seclusion, inadequate staffing, and horrendous living conditions—filthy quarters, contagious diseases, a lack of medical care and rehabilitation, and a lack of supervision—that were putting the residents' lives at risk.[3] As in Romania, the investigators found children and adults tied to their beds. Some residents were kept in cribs for years at a time. Serbian officials told the investigators that physicians were still encouraging parents to institutionalize infants born with disabilities. One newspaper in Serbia subsequently published an anti-Semitic diatribe against George Soros for the Open Society Foundations' efforts to press the country's government to bring people with mental disabilities from state institutions and place them in decent, well-supported housing in the wider community.[4]

In Georgia, the Open Society Mental Health Initiative began an effort to keep disabled infants and small children out of institutions and have them remain with their own families or have them placed in housing arrangements with a family atmosphere. Moldova's government joined with the Open Society Mental Health Initiative in a project to close an institution for boys and develop services to support them in the community. In Azerbaijan, George Soros committed $1.5 million, and the Mental Health Initiative joined with the United Nations Children's Fund and local partners to assist the government in implementing a program to move children from institutions to the community. Soros drafted letters to Azerbaijan's president, Ilham Aliyev, to press for his backing. In 2009, he sent Macedonia's prime minister, Nikola Gruevski, a letter urging him to honor a written commitment the Macedonian government had made in September 2008 to see to the release of almost two hundred residents from Demir Kapiya. If it had been up to most of Demir Kapiya Special Institution's administrators and staff members, M. and other inmates of the institution would remain confined. Local political leaders were by then publicly lamenting the "loss of jobs" if Demir Kapiya were to close down.

*   *   *

By the time M. was born, the Demir Kapiya Special Institution had existed for over two decades and had become the town of Demir Kapiya's largest employer. One attendant honored the new mother with a sampler of chocolates. His colleagues thought the gift an odd gesture and joked that he must have fathered her child. Back then, about 160 staff members were providing care for the special institution's 640 or so residents. During the 1980s, however, Communist Yugoslavia's economy collapsed, destroying the special institution's financial underpinnings.

Conditions on the wards deteriorated. When M. was a child, there were problems heating the facility in the wintertime. Lunch and dinner became a monotony of potato and cabbage soup. After Yugoslavia's disintegration in the 1990s, residents of the special institution who had been referred from Kosovo, Montenegro, and Serbia found themselves transferred to similar facilities across new international borders. Though Demir Kapiya's resident population declined by half, the size of the staff did not decline proportionately.

Living conditions in the special institution improved with assistance, mostly from abroad. Workers remodeled some wards, including the rooms for severely disabled children. An "independent living" dormitory was constructed. (The living was still done in confinement.) Staff members giving tours to visitors have shown off its outdoor play area and an immaculately clean arts and crafts room in the basement. Toys perch in rows on shelves. Pencil holders are filled. Staff members admit that the good order exists because residents are rarely allowed to use the room.

Over time, Demir Kapiya developed a third component: a set of barracks to house residents who were not severely disabled. It is called the Dependence, and it is situated about three kilometers from the main compound. M. had moved to the Dependence by the time she became a teenager. There, in the sewing room, B. taught M. and other residents to work the sewing machines.

"At Demir Kapiya," one staff member said, "residents with severe disabilities are the fewest in number. Most of the residents have been transferred in from other institutions, and some have even finished high school. The authorities didn't have a place to put them, so the commission simply labeled them as severely disabled. In two hours you can see they are not. Some of these residents are social welfare cases. And they have been here for thirty or forty years."

One woman was deposited in the special institution because the state authorities did not know where else to put her, the staff member said, adding that this woman had earned a high school diploma and had suffered a failed marriage: "She was abused. She fell into depression. They put her in a room somewhere in Skopje. A social worker was supposed to look in on her. But she needed someone to work with her. They eventually decided that she needed round-the-clock supervision. There was no appropriate facility. So they placed her in Demir Kapiya."

"I was a seamstress in Demir Kapiya," M. said. "We made pants for other residents. A friend and I sewed our own clothes." But M. could not endure the yelling and shouting. "I could not stand the hitting," she said. "People beat themselves. People beat each other. I feel sorry that they did this. I couldn't look at them. No one would listen. They didn't trust me there. The attendant didn't trust me. I was allowed to walk outside on Saturdays and Sundays. I would put on makeup and pick out nice clothes. I wanted to go out more often. But they said no."

As her youth passed in the Dependence, M. would walk or catch rides back to the main building to visit her mother and her father. She bathed them. She prepared them meals and fed them. She laundered and mended their clothes, and sewed them pajamas. And, like caregivers for disabled persons everywhere, she felt the weight of her parents' demands. She talked of feeling incapable of dealing with them each day, each month, and each year for decades.

*   *   *

Macedonia's government had adopted a policy to stop admitting new residents to Demir Kapiya eight years before it signed the September 2008 agreement with the Open Society Mental Health Initiative to move almost two hundred residents, including M., from the Demir Kapiya Special Institution, place them in housing units in the community, and provide them with the support they need. A few weeks later, Gordana Trajkovska, the head of a tiny nongovernmental organization, was asked to organize and manage independent living apartments and houses for people with intellectual disabilities in and around Negotino, her home town. Trajkovksa is a mechanical engineer and the mother of a developmentally disabled daughter. Doctors had advised Trajkovska to place her daughter in Demir Kapiya when she was born. She refused. "The place stank," she said, "and it still stinks of water and disinfectant on the floors, which seem never to dry. My daughter would never have learned to speak a word if we had placed her there. She would never have learned to walk. No one would have worked with her. She would have ended up on the ward with M.'s mother and father, where they are crawling on the floor with the cats that come in to snatch food."

In November 2008, Trajkovska toured the community living program in Croatia and grasped what might yet be possible. "I saw normal life," Trajkovska said. "I knew it would work for us." She understood that a community living program would be a boon for people with disabilities in Macedonia. It took her no time to find the first suitable apartment in Negotino and hire and train assistants who would work twenty-four-hour shifts in turns. The government refused, however, to release any of the residents during a federal election campaign. M. and other residents were at their wits' end waiting to leave. "I was having arguments with the staff because they would not let me out," M. said. "One of my friends didn't want me to leave. He wanted to hit me in order to keep me from leaving."

After the December 2008 elections, the first four residents, including M. and B., moved to an apartment in Skopje. In the following months, a dozen more residents departed the special institution and moved into two apartments in Negotino and one apartment in the town of Demir Kapiya.

Winter had set in and the residents arrived with practically nothing. Several were without jackets. The clothes of some were so tattered that their attendants threw them into the trash and, using money made available by the Open Society Foundations, ran off to a store to purchase new ones. "They did not want to let go of one woman who had worked for them for practically no pay inside the institution," said a staff member. "They did not allow her to bring out anything she had bought with the money she saved, a few euros a month. They say her things are under lock and key. Perhaps they are. But it is so low."

By early May 2009, Macedonia's government had relocated only eighteen of the sixty residents it was supposed to have moved into the community six months earlier. Officials said a second local election had interfered. Inside Demir Kapiya, administrators and employees had concluded that the departure of the special institution's residents would erode their job security, though staff members had rejected offers to work with the clients in the community living program. Moreover, local political leaders, desperate for votes, had pressured the management of Demir Kapiya to pad the workforce by hiring scores of part-time workers, which was enough to turn the outcome of the balloting. "These aren't workers, they are party soldiers," a staff member said. "They can't get rid of them, and many are less qualified than residents who have spent twenty or thirty years in the institution. The only thing they do is vote for the mayor." The special institution also continued to accept new residents, violating government policy. "We would have moved many more residents to the community if it had not been for the administration," Trajkovska said.

The expectations and frustrations of residents at the Demir Kapiya Special Institution soared. Another ten were supposed to be brought out in April, right after the local election. Attendants had been trained. Apartments had been rented. Bedding, food, toiletries, and new clothes had been readied. With so few residents, the system that the Open Society Mental Health Initiative and its local partners had created was not efficient or cost-effective because it was not running at capacity. (At capacity, the cost for a person in the community living program works out to be about the same as the cost for a person in the institution, but provides a significantly better quality of life.) The Mental Health Initiative paid for the training of assistants and was paying all costs incurred during a one-year transitional period. When it expired, the Macedonian government was to fund the entire operation by reallocating funds that would otherwise have gone to the special institution.

On April 25, the day the release of the next ten residents was scheduled to take place, officials from the government ministry responsible for social policy gathered at the special institution. Present, too, were directors and deputy directors and social workers of social welfare centers from various Macedonian districts that had placed these ten residents in the special institution and bore legal responsibility for them. In all, thirteen officials had come to hand over a pair of documents for each departing resident. All of these documents were dated April 25. All required the signature and stamp of the director or some other legally authorized official of the special institution. The institution's management had been informed of the transfer date long in advance. Staff members had the ten residents ready to leave.

None of the institution's officials showed up at work to sign the papers. Absent was the special institution's director—who, a few months later, took off for four weeks in a special institution car to participate in a bicycle marathon to the Vatican to lobby the pope to hold the canonization ceremony for Mother Teresa in Macedonia. Absent, too, was his deputy. Every other person legally authorized to sign the documents on behalf of the institution was simply missing. Their mobile phones rang and rang unanswered.

Trajkovska had come with a van because eight of the residents were going to be moved to Negotino. Two others were to move in with M. and her housemates in Skopje. A staff person called the ministry. "What should we do?"

"Better to just go," a voice on the line said. "We'll set a new date in a week."

"We kissed the door and left," a staff member said.

"We as nongovernmental organizations are used to this kind of treatment from public institutions," Trajkovska recalled. "But the people from the social welfare centers were not. They were appalled. It was the ministry's own people who were responsible."

Trajkovska visited Demir Kapiya to meet the residents who had been left behind. A woman who had informally "adopted" a son pleaded for them to be let go. Another woman attempted to stow away in the back of Trajkovska's van. One of the attendants shouted behind her back: "Everything was fine here until you came along. These people have had everything."

Two more months passed before the transfer finally took place. In the end, it required intervention from the country's prime minister, which was only obtained after the personal letter from George Soros.

*   *   *

Six months had come and gone since M. had passed through the gate of the Demir Kapiya Special Institution and found a new life in an apartment in Skopje. At twenty-eight, she was beginning to learn numbers and the Cyrillic alphabet. She was to sign her name. Her speech was less slurred. A speech therapist was a possibility.

"I like the city," she said. "I like the house. I like the fact that I can go out. I like my clothes. I like the city center and the shopping. But most of all, I like it that here people listen."

M., like other former Demir Kapiya residents, wanted to work on an office building cleaning crew. She wanted to save money to buy a sewing machine so she could make her own clothes. She worked for months as an unpaid understudy for a cleaning company. She could not be hired, for a time anyway. Officially, in the eyes of Macedonia's government, M. did not exist. In a quarter of a century, no one on the staff of the Demir Kapiya Special Institution had ever bothered to register her with the authorities. She had no official last name. She had no identification card or identification number. She did, however, find her uncle. As the months passed, he became more involved in her life. M. also learned that she was not indigent, and had the right to receive a pension through her grandfather.

By the summer of 2009, M.'s goal was to bring her parents out of Demir Kapiya together, because, she said, "They are still in love." "I don't want to live with my parents in the same apartment," she said. "I don't want to be with them nonstop. It is difficult. I used to feed and bathe them. I want them here, nearby, but I would rather have them in another apartment."

Yet the Demir Kapiya Special Institution continued to defy its orders. As late as the spring of 2009, it was continuing to accept new residents. The latest to arrive was a young man with an intellectual disability. His mother had died. Before his father went to work in the morning, he would tie the boy up to a tree, like a dog or a goat, to keep him from running off. Local television stations showed video of the boy on a leash. "I can't do anything," the father told the camera. He could not cope. In order to have his son institutionalized, the father reported that the boy was dangerous even though he was not. He later contacted a staff member at the institution and admitted his son had never posed a danger to anyone. The staff member mentioned the possibility of transferring his son to a special, supported home, a place in the community, where the boy would not be locked up. Then she told Trajkovska about him.

"I'll get him out," Trajkovska said.

*   *   *

In its first fifteen years, the Open Society Mental Health Initiative helped hundreds of people with mental disabilities escape a life of isolation in wretched institutions like those in Croatia, Macedonia, Romania, Serbia, and other countries of Eastern Europe and the former Soviet Union. It has helped them to find jobs and build lives for themselves in the greater community and to obtain the health care, schooling, and other social support that are their right. (Some couples have been married by Catholic priests. Other couples live together even though the civil authorities consider them incompetent to qualify for marriage licenses.) The numbers of the disabled removed from institutions are still relatively small. But the Mental Health Initiative effort has been instrumental in initiating a change in how people view the institutionalization and segregation of people with disabilities.

Significant challenges continue. Another woman in Demir Kapiya gave birth in early 2010. The Mental Health Initiative and its partners in Macedonia insisted that the mother and baby be placed in the community housing program. But the management of Demir Kapiya intended to take the baby away from the mother and to ship the mother back to the special institution as if nothing had happened. In Romania, in one of the institutions the Mental Health Initiative is working to close, a client recently died. An autopsy report requested by a human rights nongovernmental organization showed that the cause of death was abuse. Yet members of the staff dismissed for their possible involvement in the abuse were reinstated when a court found the autopsy findings irrelevant to the employees' case, alleging wrongful dismissal.

With the Open Society Mental Health Initiative expanding its geographical scope to Kenya, it is clear that while some issues are context dependent, others are of global relevance. Social exclusion, discrimination, and stigma against people with mental disabilities are present everywhere, and the Open Society Foundations' work in supporting the development of grassroots advocates to address and eliminate these problems is just as important today as it was when the work began fifteen years ago.

*   *   *

GEORGE SOROS

Tuberculosis. You could say that I got sucked into most of my philanthropic efforts. It started with the success of my first foundation in Hungary, which worked so well that it gave me the appetite for setting up foundations in other countries. Our engagement in public health was no exception.

We got involved in tuberculosis work in Russia in the late 1990s because we wanted to get access to the prison system. TB was particularly rampant in Russian prisons, and it threatened the guards as well as the prisoners. For that reason the prison authorities were very receptive to help in dealing with tuberculosis. Our involvement was meant to eliminate or mitigate the tuberculosis threat and, at the same time, open up the prison system to reform.

Alex Goldfarb, who had previously proven himself as the manager of the International Science Foundation, proposed a treatment based on the World Health Organization's DOTS protocol that would have a major impact for an expenditure of not much more than $10 million. Goldfarb also wanted to use the tuberculosis program to shake up the Russian medical establishment, which was still treating tuberculosis in sanatoriums that were very expensive and available only to the privileged few.

The program ran into unexpected difficulties with multidrug-resistant tuberculosis. Though this strain didn't respond to the treatment protocol, Goldfarb was undeterred. He was ready to carry out his plan and accept that we would get 50 percent success instead of the hoped-for 100 percent.

We were worried, however, that if the DOTS treatment cured only half of the tuberculosis cases, then the other half would take over, and multidrug-resistant tuberculosis would become even more prevalent. So we brought in Paul Farmer, an expert in infectious diseases, to overcome Goldfarb's resistance. Farmer prevailed and the WHO modified its procedure for multidrug-resistant tuberculosis and called it DOTS-Plus.

This meant that a program we had expected to cost about $10 million now required several hundred million dollars. This would be beyond our resources, so we had to get the major authorities like the World Bank and WHO involved.

When the Global Fund to Fight AIDS, Tuberculosis and Malaria was formed, AIDS received overwhelming attention, malaria had its own champions, and we ended up as the champions of the fight against TB. What started in Russian prisons grew into a global effort. As I said, we got sucked into both the formation of the Global Fund and fighting TB worldwide.

I consider the Global Fund the best-designed international institution. It allocates funds on the basis of merit, not national quotas, and it allows for the participation of civil society as well as governments. We have been great supporters of the Global Fund ever since, agitating for greater funding worldwide. I am currently working toward setting up a fund for rainforests modeled on the Global Fund.

Today, our public health program is one of our largest and best-functioning network programs; it has a subboard composed of world-class experts. In recent years, my role has largely been ceremonial. It did allow me to get to know BRAC, the Bangladeshi microfinance company, as well as Paul Farmer, both of whom have excelled in community-based treatment of infectious diseases.

I cannot conclude without mentioning another initiative that sucked us in: the training of doctors from less developed countries at the Open Medical Institute in Salzburg. It was the organizing energy of Wolfgang Aulitzky and the enthusiasm of the American doctors who participated in the project that attracted and sustained my support.

Mental disability. While I have visited our projects and approve of our advocacy for people with mental disabilities, I have not had a lot of direct involvement in our efforts to improve their situation. But mental disability remains an important issue for the Open Society Foundations.

On a range of issues, we have helped the disadvantaged to make up for their disadvantage and to deal with the constraints that the disadvantage imposes on them. We generally help people who are disadvantaged to advocate for themselves. But in the case of the mentally disabled, they are often not in a position to advocate for themselves, so we have to advocate for them.

To the extent that the mentally disabled can look after themselves, they are better off than if they are the objects of treatment. If they can act on their own, they are closer to living a normal life than if they are purely passive recipients of treatment. I think that is a fairly sound principle. Our objective has been to bring the mentally disabled into situations that are more community based, to give them more autonomy than they would have in a mental institution.

We are spreading the American doctrine of deinstitutionalization to Eastern Europe, but I hope we don't go overboard. In the United States, it has been a pretty revolutionary change to close down institutions and release people, but many of them wind up living on the streets. They need support and assistance to live in the community.

Of course, mental illness is also often a false metaphor, a clear case of mistreatment. It is easy for autocratic regimes to treat deviants and political opponents as mentally ill. It is obviously an area where there is much room for intervention and a need for protection.

PART IV

Minority Empowerment:
The Roma

Finalists for an Open Society Foundations' Roma health scholarship listen to a Roma elder in Vânători, Romania, describe the hardships he and other Roma have endured. (© Open Society Foundations/Pamela Chen)

8

Asserting the Rights of the Roma

Europeans have reviled the Roma people as gypsies, thieves, pickpockets, and beggars ever since the first Roma immigrated from the Indian subcontinent during the Middle Ages. Over the centuries, Europeans have enslaved Roma women, men, and children, beaten them up, burned them out, and bludgeoned them off to the periphery of the next town, and the next, and the next. The Ottoman and Habsburg authorities tried and failed to halt the nomadic migrations of the Roma across Europe. The Nazis and their nationalist allies in Eastern Europe deemed the Roma to be a "criminal and antisocial element," herded them into camps, and shipped them in cattle cars to the gas chambers at Auschwitz.

After World War II, Communist bloc governments tried to assimilate the Roma into the general populations of their countries. During these efforts, many Roma obtained state jobs requiring the dirtiest, most hazardous work. Some Roma also got state apartments and an education, but the vast majority remained mired in poverty and ignorance, inhabiting burgeoning shantytowns, or *màhale* in the Roma language, situated on the outskirts of cities and towns. At a time when the Roma birthrate was outstripping that of the majority populations in the countries where they lived, some doctors even sterilized Roma women without their knowledge or consent. The practice of coercive sterilization persisted even after the fall of Communism in democratic countries such as the Czech Republic and Slovakia.

The fall of Communism had a sharp impact on the Roma of Eastern Europe and the states that emerged from the former Soviet Union. It removed the social safety net on which so many impoverished Roma relied for job opportunities, public welfare, health care, education (such as it was), and other state benefits. According to *The Economist*, at the beginning of the new millennium, Europe's Roma were suffering the continent's highest level of unemployment, lowest level of education, highest degree of welfare dependence, highest rate of imprisonment, and worst segregation.[1] Hunger and malnutrition, bad hygiene and health practices born of deprivation, squalid housing in communities without plumbing or sanitation, substandard health care, substance abuse, and other factors kept their infant mortality high and reduced their life expectancy to Europe's shortest.

Even before the economic downturn of 2008, right-wing political leaders in Eastern Europe were fomenting hatred of the Roma in order to win popular support on the cheap. Their messages of intolerance resonated widely. Some people in Hungary, the Czech Republic, Romania, and other countries were willing to carry out acts of violence. Six Roma were murdered in Hungary during a spree of nine attacks over fourteen months that ended in November 2009. The killers invaded the home of an impoverished Roma widow, shot her to death, and wounded her thirteen-year-old daughter. They gunned down a Roma factory worker as he was walking to his job. They set fire to the house of a twenty-seven-year-old Roma man and his five-year-old son and shot them to death. (Hungarian police mounted an unprecedented manhunt, and in late August arrested four suspects, including men adorned with swastika tattoos.) In April 2009, in a town near the city of Ostrava in the Czech Republic, neo-Nazis tossed firebombs into a house where nine Roma were living; two received minor injuries, but a two-year-old girl suffered burns over 80 percent of her body. During November 2009, two medical students in Romania killed and dismembered a sixty-five-year-old Roma man and left his remains in the trunk of a car.

George Soros's network of foundations has spearheaded an unprecedented effort to organize Europe's Roma and assist them in a campaign to secure their rightful position in European society.

To achieve this goal, the Soros-backed effort has exploited opportunities created by Eastern Europe's transition from Communism. New guarantees of freedom of association and freedom of speech in the former Eastern bloc states for the first time gave Roma the legal right to organize themselves independently and to demand respect for their civil liberties as well as access to all of the social benefits provided by their home countries. The eastward expansion of the European Union moreover gave many Roma the freedom to migrate across international frontiers in search of employment and better opportunities and to demand the protections guaranteed in European Union documents defining and elaborating human and civil rights.

The Open Society Foundations helped establish Roma organizations that work to defend the civil liberties of the Roma people vis-à-vis both their national governments and the European Union authorities. In 1995, Aryeh Neier, a number of Roma leaders, and several lawyers experienced in Roma issues met in Prague and founded the European Roma Rights Centre, an international public interest organization that assists the

Roma with strategic litigation, international advocacy, research and policy development, and training of Roma activists. From 2003, the Open Society Foundations and the World Bank became major backers of the Decade of Roma Inclusion 2005–2015, an unprecedented international initiative that committed its signatory states to combat discrimination against the Roma, to halt exclusion of the Roma from society, to break the cycle of poverty that has trapped them, and to close the gap in welfare and living conditions between the Roma and the overall population.

By 2010, the Decade of Roma Inclusion had been endorsed by twelve European countries and focused on four main issues: education, health, housing, and employment.

*   *   *

Education. About 25 percent of all Roma people and 33 percent of Roma women are illiterate. Lack of education is one of the factors most responsible for the abject poverty suffered by many of Europe's eight to twelve million Roma. A survey by the United Nations indicated that about 40 percent of Roma children never attend school, and about 66 percent do not complete the primary grades. Roma children who attend school do so, on average, for less than half as long as children from the majority populations of the countries in which the Roma live. Moreover, the schools most Roma children attend are segregated and inferior. Some Roma parents do not recognize the value of education. Some parents cannot afford basic school supplies or appropriate clothing for their children. Some fear that their children will become victims of violence and bullying.

George Soros and the Open Society Foundations have worked to overcome this chronic education problem through their commitment to the Roma Education Fund, which works to bring increasing numbers of Roma to school as students, teachers, and teaching assistants. The fund's programs provide scholarships for Roma students, lunches to overcome the "hunger barrier" to school attendance for children from households on the brink of penury, academic support to help poor children catch up with their peers, and teacher training to create better schools for all children. To act as positive role models for Roma children, the fund promotes Roma teachers; Roma community and political leaders; Roma lawyers, doctors, and other professionals; as well as Roma young people who have succeeded in school. By late 2009, the fund had assisted about 156,000 Roma children and young adults.

School Segregation: Czech Republic. Julius Mika remembers his first day of third grade well. It was September 1997. There was a bus ride with his parents, eight stops through his hometown, the city of Ostrava in the Czech Republic. Their destination was not the regular primary school where Mika had finished second grade, but a special school for children with developmental disabilities. There were only seven children in Mika's class in the special school, a big change from the thirty-four kids in his second grade classroom. Five of the second graders had been Roma kids, like Mika; he was one of three sent to the special school; the two others were transferred to another class. This, even to eight-year-old Mika, did not seem right. He asked his parents why he and his friends were not going to the regular school anymore.

"The teacher didn't like Roma," Mika said during an interview twelve years later. "She took it upon herself to have me transferred to the special school. Other children were rewarded with a stamp, a piggy or a doggy, for good behavior. She told me

I would never get one." Mika completed four grades in the special school. "Two years were for nothing," he said. "I was studying things I had already learned in the first and second grades. The subjects were all taught at a slower pace. There was no depth. I was doing homework for my cousin in the ninth grade at the special school. I was bored." Mika's mother and father complained to school officials. Soon even the special school's principal said Mika did not belong in a program for children with special needs, including children with intellectual disabilities.

For years, over half of all Roma children in Ostrava's public schools were barred from regular classes and relegated to such special schools, where they comprised over half of the student body. Most Roma children who remained in the regular program were enrolled in segregated Roma schools. These facts amounted to compelling evidence of systematic illegal discrimination and segregation in Ostrava. This pattern was evident in other areas of the Czech Republic as well.

In 1999, Julius Mika became one of eighteen Roma plaintiffs from Ostrava who filed a lawsuit in a domestic court seeking remedy from the government of the Czech Republic for unlawful discrimination. James Goldston, then legal director of the European Roma Rights Centre, conceived the case and represented the plaintiffs. Antidiscrimination legislation barely existed at that time in the countries of Eastern Europe, and the Czech Republic's constitutional court ruled in the government's favor. In 2000, with the support of the European Roma Rights Centre, the plaintiffs appealed the ruling to the European Court of Human Rights in Strasbourg. The Czech Republic, as part of the European Union, found itself bound to uphold European Union antidiscrimination laws. Goldston, who became executive director of the Open Society Justice Initiative in 2002, continued to represent the plaintiffs, appearing before the court twice.

The European Roma Rights Centre also undertook research to reveal the pattern of school discrimination. "I knew how to approach the Roma to get accurate information from them," said Ivan Ivanov, the organization's researcher. "They were reluctant. Few of them believed we could succeed. I had to persuade them that the case would have an impact for thousands of Roma children forced to attend special schools."

In 2007, the court delivered a landmark ruling that segregating Roma students in special schools is a form of unlawful discrimination. During the two years after the ruling, however, the Czech Republic authorities made little or no meaningful effort to correct segregation in education. School officials in Ostrava and other cities and towns were still sending inordinate numbers of Roma children to special schools.

By the time the court handed down its ruling, Mika had finished his education. He had been returned to a regular school, but too late for him to catch up to his peers in math. He ended up completing occupational courses in pastry making and house painting. In 2009, married and a father, he was working from time to time on construction sites and filling his down days by collecting scrap metal. Still, he said, the lawsuit was worth it because it promises to help Roma kids in the future.

Outreach to Roma Parents: Macedonia. In many communities, enrolling Roma children in good schools demands something more than persuading government leaders and school officials to allow them to enter. It requires convincing many Roma parents that education is worth the effort involved in enrolling their children, ensuring that they attend class each day, and making sacrifices—some as basic as obtaining hand-me-down clothing and, despite the lack of running water at home, making sure the children have bathed—so schoolmates do not subject the Roma pupils to ridicule or worse.

Ristem Muslievski, thirty-three, was a journalist before he became an outreach worker for the National Roma Centrum, a Roma organization and Open Society Foundations grantee in Kumanovo, Macedonia. In 2007, Kumanovo school officials opened the town's best schools to Roma students for the first time. Muslievski began moving through Kumanovo's Roma *mahala* and urging parents to enroll their children and to keep sending them to school.

Many parents were reluctant. Some told Muslievski that they did not know where the assigned school was located—even though it was only a few blocks away—and they feared that their children might get lost on the way or run afoul of bullies. "We take the most vulnerable kids—the poorest kids, the kids who don't know the Macedonian language, the kids whose parents are less enthusiastic—and drive them to school in a van, about eighty of them," Muslievski said. "Maybe four of the eighty would attend classes if we didn't do this. We have to keep talking to the families. We warn them that there is a fine if they do not send their children to school." One first grader, for instance, a tiny girl named Violeta with big, piercing eyes, disappeared from her classroom in mid-October. Muslievski later learned that she was traveling during the weekdays to the town of Tetovo, where she was living in a tent and waiting beside her mother as she begged on the street. "We went to the parents many times," Muslievski said. "We explained to them what education means." It was mid-December before Violeta's parents allowed her to return to school. By February, she had caught up with her classmates.

Desegregation and Teaching Assistants: Bulgaria. The twin doors to the Prince Alexander Elementary School in Plovdiv, Bulgaria, are cut from heavy wood and tower far over the heads of its first graders. By 2007, three years had passed since they opened to the first Roma children taking part in a desegregation program implemented in dozens of schools in nine Bulgarian cities. The program involved some three thousand pupils, about one in every eleven of Bulgaria's school-age Roma children. "People once thought the Roma were incapable of being educated and did not want to be educated," said Donka Panayotova, then a forty-nine-year-old schoolteacher from the town of Vidin who initiated the desegregation process in 2000 with the Open Society Foundations' support. "We have proven that Roma children can be educated in the mainstream and that their results are much higher than those of the Roma kids who are in segregated schools."

In 2007, thirty-two-year-old Asen Karagyozov was working at the Association of Roma Youth in Plovdiv's *mahala*, Stolipinovo, a drab array of prefabricated concrete apartment blocks surrounded by shops, garages, and streets neglected by the city's road crews and garbage collectors. Karagyozov and his father, Anton, founder of one of Bulgaria's first Roma nongovernmental organizations, were helping to operate a program to bus Roma children accompanied by Roma teaching assistants from Stolipinovo to Prince Alexander and other elementary schools in the city's center. About two hundred Roma children were participating in the desegregation program. Another 3,300 were attending a segregated school in the *mahala*. "No Bulgarian would come here to Stolipinovo to go to school," Karagyozov said. Zhivka Boshnakova, the mother of a Roma second grader in the desegregation program, knew why. "I went to the *mahala* school," she said. "I know my son reads, writes, and knows math better than children who are still going there."

English Scholarships: Bulgaria. The three of them were in their
early twenties in 2007. Each had felt the slap of discrimination
and the sting of personal loss. Each was the living antithesis of
a stereotype. Zina Tenekedzieva, a speaker of French, German,
Bulgarian, Turkish, and Romany, the language of the Roma,
had earned degrees in medicine and social work. Her mother had
died of kidney failure after a long struggle that sapped her
family's assets; her father was an ailing former steelworker and
professional accordionist. Bulgaria's former national champion
in women's judo, Raina Becheva had graduated from the national
sports academy before a devastating injury cost her an Olympic
dream. Rosen Asenov had languished in a segregated Roma
school until a Bulgarian teacher helped his father, who works in a
car battery factory, and his mother, a teacher, obtain his transfer
to a Bulgarian school.

Tenekedzieva, Becheva, and Asenov were recipients of Open
Society Foundations scholarships designed to foster the development of prospective Roma leaders by giving them the
opportunity to study English in an eight-month postgraduate
language course at the American University in Bulgaria.
Mastering English enables young Roma to advocate at the
EU level and compete for Open Society Foundations–funded
internships with the European Commission, OSCE, and
Council of Europe.

The life experiences of Tenekedzieva, Becheva, and Asenov
have tempered their ambitions. "I've seen how some people from
government institutions mistreat Roma people," Tenekedzieva
said. "I was discriminated against by a college professor who
did not like the Roma part of me. My sister lost her job because
the other workers said she was a gypsy and refused to work with
her." Despite the setbacks and barriers, Tenekedzieva is
committed to helping her people and contributing to Bulgaria's

larger society. "I want a job in some institution, in a municipality or ministry," she said. "I want to work with our people, especially our women, because they need someone to protect them from discrimination."

For Becheva, judo meant freedom and achievement: "Roma girls need to break free. They withdraw into themselves. The environment of the *mahala* closes in around them. They have choices, but they don't know them. They don't know the possibilities. They get married very young. They have many children very young. They don't go to school. They remain illiterate. Sports are a way to break free. Judo gives you a sense of strength, a way to defend yourself, and something useful to do with your time. So I want to establish a judo club for girls."

Asenov was preparing to attend the Central European University in Budapest and to work in a Roma organization or in the European Union in some capacity helping Roma community development. "When I see the children begging on the streets, I see the politics, I see that they are not educated, I see that they have no options. Organized crime selects kids like this," he said. "It is time for us to obtain positions in the government. It is time for us to define our interests and our rights. It is time to improve our position in the broader community. We learn fast. And we will destroy these stereotypes forever."

*   *   *

Health. There is a paucity of reliable data on the health problems Europe's Roma suffer. Many Roma know little about good hygiene and health. Too many navigate the world of health leaflets and hospital forms through the fog of illiteracy and poor language proficiency. Often they lack health insurance and the money to pay the informal "gratuity" doctors in some Eastern

European countries depend on to augment their low salaries. In some countries, the average life expectancy for the Roma is ten years shorter than the average for the majority population, and the infant mortality rates for Roma are twice as high. Throughout the region, Roma suffer disproportionate rates of tuberculosis, HIV and AIDS, viral hepatitis, type 2 diabetes, heart disease, adult obesity, malnutrition, anemia, dystrophy, and childhood rickets. Human rights groups have documented instances of ambulance services refusing to respond to calls for help from Roma *màhale*. In *Ambulance Not on the Way: The Disgrace of Health Care for Roma in Europe*, for example, the European Roma Rights Centre reported that the practice of not sending ambulances to Roma neighborhoods was common in some parts of Bulgaria and Hungary, endangering the health and lives of Roma in need of emergency services.

The crucial component of the Open Society Foundations' effort to help break down barriers that keep the Roma from accessing quality health care services is the Roma Health Project, a subset of the Public Health Program. By collaborating with other programs and grantees of the Foundations, the Roma Health Project is fostering the development of sound public health policies across Central and Eastern Europe—and especially in six priority countries: Bulgaria, Macedonia, Romania, Serbia, Slovakia, and Ukraine. It has initiated programs to respond to the challenges of HIV and sexually transmitted diseases, tuberculosis, and drug addiction. The Roma Health Project also supported an advocacy campaign aimed at obtaining justice and compensation for Roma women who were victims of coerced sterilization.

Health Mediators: Romania. The Open Society Foundations and its partners have supported the work of health mediators, most of them Roma women, who liaise between the Roma community and the health care system in Romania, Ukraine, and other Eastern European countries. The health mediators inform Roma of their rights and help document cases of discrimination in health care settings. They help Roma obtain the documents required to gain access to state health care services. They calm tempers when disagreements arise between Roma and medical professionals.

It took Carmen Andrei, a health mediator in Romania, longer than expected to gain the trust of a community of about 250 Roma living beside Vânători, a town in the eastern foothills of the Carpathian Mountains. Andrei made visits to Vânători's Roma community for over a year in an effort to convince them to participate in a vaccination program. Yet they ignored her appeals. Though Andrei was herself a Roma, Vânători's Roma considered her a *gadjo*, someone from outside the Roma community. The only person who could help Andrei was the community's elder or *bulibasha*.

Lacatus Codrea had gathered many insights tempered by adversity during his years as *bulibasha*. He saw a mob torch Vânători's Roma community, chase his people into a forest, and raze every structure the flames had spared. Fifteen years passed as Codrea pleaded with local officials to issue the Roma building permits so they could improve the dirt-floored shanties they had clapped together to shelter themselves and their children. "We were not allowed to rebuild our homes," he said.

For decades, Codrea watched as neighbors succumbed to violence and alcohol abuse. He saw children grow to adulthood without being vaccinated or properly nourished. He saw pregnant Roma women go without medical support. Codrea's thirteen-year-old granddaughter, Adina, once lay partially paralyzed for hours after touching a live power cable; he had erupted in anger at doctors and nurses who refused to examine and treat her. "The first time Andrei came, she started talking and didn't stop for half an hour," Codrea said. "Back then, when someone tried to give me advice that was good for me, I would ask myself, 'Why is he giving me this advice?' I had no trust."

Codrea said the change came when Andrei learned to listen. Andrei said that a measles outbreak finally convinced Vânători's Roma to seek vaccination for themselves and their children. Whatever the reason, Codrea persuaded the Roma of Vânători to listen to Andrei. "Now, if she speaks," Codrea said, "it is impossible for people not to listen to her. Now the local general practitioner knows all of us. The women go to the doctor. The children are vaccinated."

Yet there is still more work to be done. "The problem now lies with the hospital," said Codrea. "The doctors in nearby hospitals expect to be paid a tip, *baksheesh*, to provide care." A tip for medical services is a commonplace form of payment in Eastern Europe for Roma and non-Roma alike. "If you don't have the money, you die outside." This is another reason why it is important to address the paucity of Roma working in medicine.

Medical School Scholarships. In the autumn semester of 2008, the Open Society Foundations began funding scholarships for Roma students to pursue degrees in medicine, nursing, pharmacology, and related disciplines at accredited schools and universities in Romania. By the beginning of 2010, the program had sixty-three scholars in Romania and twenty-three in Bulgaria, with more to come in Serbia and Macedonia. The main goal of the scholarship program for Roma medical students is to increase significantly the presence of Roma doctors in hospitals, not just to provide patient care but also to deter discrimination and other abuses. For this reason, the recipients of the first Roma health scholarships in Romania were selected not only based upon academic merit and professional motivation but upon leadership skills. The applicants attended Open Society Foundations–supported training programs to help them become effective advocates for Roma rights in health care settings.

On a September morning in 2008, Carmen Andrei brought applicants for the Roma health scholarships to Vânători to meet and take counsel from Codrea and other members of his community. With few exceptions, the scholarship applicants were Roma who had schooling and jobs and resided in integrated neighborhoods in towns and cities. The students had to learn firsthand about the hardships endured by less fortunate Roma who huddled in substandard housing on the fringes of society.

The scholarship applicants and their mentors—Romanians who were nearing completion of medical school—crowded into the sitting room to hear the *bulibasha*. Most of them had never visited a Roma settlement like Vânători. The students and mentors listened in silence as the *bulibasha* told of Andrei's communication problem, of the lack of vaccinations, and of how, two years earlier, he had come upon his granddaughter Adina lying still on the ground next to the power cable. Codrea took her in a horse cart to a nearby clinic. In the clinic's car they went to a hospital, then to a pediatric center, and then back to the hospital. "The first doctor didn't want to touch me," said Adina. "I was sick to my stomach and my feet and hands were paralyzed. He did not want to touch me."

Codrea argued with a doctor and finally took Adina into a room and put her on a table. "The doctor was unhappy," he said. "He was threatening. And I think I spoke badly, but the child was worse and worse, and I had waited for two hours." Adina spent several weeks in the hospital recovering from the electric shock she had received.

Codrea advised the students and mentors how to speak when dealing with Roma. "This is a group that gets angry easily. When they speak loudly, it doesn't mean that they are bad. They think this is the way to get action. You have to be patient. You have to listen. If you don't, the person will conclude that you have something against them."

After several hours, the students and mentors left. "I have heard of places like this," said Corina Stanciu, a medical student from the city of Ploieşti. "I have seen Roma begging on the streets, but I haven't seen Roma like these. Where I live, Roma have houses, not like this. I could not want to be a doctor any more than I want to be one now."

*   *   *

Helping the Roma Stand Up and Be Counted. Beyond the areas of education and health care, the Open Society Foundations have helped Roma organizations in Eastern Europe to assert the presence of the Roma in the broader community in a number of ways: by working for an accurate accounting of their numbers, which can yield a fairer share of state benefits and political power; by documenting their past, which has largely been ignored; and by pressing their governments to honor the commitments made in the Decade of Roma Inclusion. The Roma population is notoriously understated in official statistics. On census forms and other official documents, many Roma have refused to identify themselves as Roma, and thousands of Roma are not registered with the authorities at all. In Europe's popular memory, the Roma and their culture barely exist beyond stereotypical characterizations, and certainly not as victims of Nazi genocide. In the halls of power of the countries where the Roma live, their needs have been ignored for too long.

Obtaining Identity Documents. In her twenty-four years, Roziana Zakiri never learned to read or write. She did not know how to tell time. And until early autumn 2007, Zakiri did not officially exist in the land of her birth, Macedonia, or anywhere else on the planet for that matter. A house fire consumed the only official paper she had with her name on it: a copy of a form her mother got from the hospital on the day Zakiri was born.

Zakiri's mother never obtained an official birth certificate or a personal identification card for her daughter. So Zakiri went through life without health insurance and social benefits. No school record indicated she ever attended a single day of class. No certificate vouches for her marriage to a man, Safet, who was also not recorded on official registers. None of their five children had birth certificates. When Zakiri was in labor with her twins in early 2006, the local hospital sent her away because she had no national health card. Zakiri gave birth to a boy and a girl in a crumbling one-room brick house to which she and Safet hold no title. The house sits on a plot of land about twenty feet by fifteen for which they hold no deed.

In the fall of 2007, for tending a farmer's livestock, Safet was bringing home the equivalent of about $50 a month and occasionally some milk and cheese. Zakiri said that she brought in the equivalent of about $4 a day begging on the streets of Kumanovo, a few miles from Macedonia's border with Serbia. "We would often start in front of the post office," Zakiri said. "The children would sit beside me while I begged. We'd walk back and forth to the center of town. When the twins were really small, I would have slings for them, one in the front, one in back."

Two years earlier, in 2005, Asmet Elezovski, founder and manager of the Open Society Foundations–supported National Roma Centrum, spotted Roziana and her children begging in front of a store. "She was a new face, so I knew she was not from Kumanovo. After that, I sent a team to check things out. We appealed to her several times to come to us for help. One morning in the winter of 2005–2006, she showed up at the office very early. Her mother-in-law was seriously ill. Roziana was pregnant with her twins. She was seeking help. We began by trying to get her emergency aid and a doctor's examination. Then we asked about her documents, and we found she had none and had no money to obtain them."

The field workers at the National Roma Centrum had seen many complicated registration problems before. But even the officials at the government offices did not know where to begin with Zakiri. It took until September 2007 to obtain Zakiri's personal identification card. Her five children obtained birth certificates by October, and her eldest daughter, eight-year-old Serdjana, entered the first grade. The authorities assigned a social worker to Zakiri's case and obtained welfare benefits for her. But health cards had still not arrived by the New Year. With the health cards, Zakiri could obtain additional security and protection for her children: She could get them vaccinated.

Media Mentors. Years ago, Serbia's Roma might have accepted without protest a government decision to terminate a school program that was benefiting their children; and even if the Roma had protested, no radio or television station would have reported it. Until recently, Roma in Romania would never have seen a documentary film about killings of vast numbers of their people during the *Porrajmos*, the Great Devouring, the Roma term for the Holocaust.

To rectify this situation, since the mid-1990s, the Open Society Media Program has assisted Roma organizations across the region to enhance their use of the mass media. One of the Media Program's components provides mentors to Roma organizations who help develop the skills of broadcast professionals and filmmakers. Their work is crucial to bridging the gap between the Roma people and the societies from which they have been alienated for so many centuries.

When the 2007–2008 academic year began in the sprawling city of Niš, Serbia, the school authorities announced the cancellation of a program that had placed Roma monitors in primary schools with significant numbers of Roma children. By all accounts, this program had been a success. The monitors were providing assistance to teachers and parents and were instilling confidence in Roma schoolchildren at ethnically mixed schools, especially Roma pupils who needed help with the Serbian language. Dropout rates for Roma students fell. The performance of the Roma children improved. The decision to eliminate the monitors was made without input from parents or teachers and effected without an official explanation.

Serbia's first Roma broadcast outlets, Nišava Radio and Television in Niš, took up the elimination of the school monitors for an episode of a television magazine that deals with local Roma issues. "If Roma children don't know the Serbian language well and finish poorly on a placement test, they are sent to a special school for slow or retarded children," said Goran Jovanović, program manager. "So the monitors were having a direct, beneficial effect on the lives of the children."

Nišava Radio and Television had produced effective reportage before. One radio program focused for five days in a row on a neglected, rutted mud track to a Roma neighborhood; on the sixth day, the Niš authorities sent out a paving crew. The station's reporters had pressed managers of the local electrical utility to explain why a Roma settlement had no power. They had confronted the local health authorities about problems Roma women were having obtaining cancer treatment. They reported on murders, small thefts, and begging. The station had publicized a microcredit program, and dozens of Roma, many of them illiterate, had come for help to learn more about the program and fill out forms. But the broadcasters themselves considered Nišava's television reporting uneven and knew that, in spite of their efforts, it was failing to enhance either the Romas' self-image or the image Serbs have of the Roma.

In an effort to sharpen their productions, the Roma broadcasters began receiving advice from a freelance broadcast media trainer, Radmila Dulović Rastovac, who had become the station's mentor under the Open Society Foundations' program. "They call on me night and day," Dulović Rastovac said. "I taught them to define what they want to present and why. Their goal was to show the Serbian audience their problems, so the broader community can better understand them." After consulting Dulović Rastovac, the Roma broadcasters decided to produce a television magazine with each segment focusing on a pressing issue related to health care, housing, education, and jobs.

To capture the Serbian audience, however, they had to go further. "I taught them to ask pointed questions of the appropriate authorities," Dulović Rastovac said. "I also told them that without a story in each episode of their magazine about successful Roma, about positive examples of individuals in the Roma community, Serbs would not watch. There had to be a mix."

"Radmila changed my whole view of television," said Damir Barčić, editor of the television magazine. "She showed us how to produce a segment based only on facts." The station put this new orientation to work on the school monitors story.

Initially the broadcasters received word that, within several months, the Roma school monitors would resume their work funded by the school system's budget, and not through a donor. But nothing happened. "We went to the school authorities and asked why they did not go forward," Barčić said. "They would not even give a statement. They avoided all contact. So we asked Radmila what to do, and she said do a stand-up in front of the building and explain that the authorities were refusing to speak with us."

Months later the Roma of Serbia had still not received an answer. But the school authorities knew that the Roma broadcasters, and through them the Roma of Niš, were not going to stop asking.

Current events are not the only focus of the media project. So many Roma suffer illiteracy that the past tends to fade away after two or three generations. Even memories of an event as devastating as the Holocaust become murky if they are not recorded. Cristinela Ionescu tried to change this. A Roma woman from a village near the Romanian mining town of Petroşani, she was active in a Roma nongovernmental organization before she began producing documentary films. *The Judge*, a documentary about a Holocaust survivor who became a traditional conflict mediator in the local Roma community, was the first film Ionescu produced with the help of a mentor, Nenad Puhovski of Croatia. "We were already producing films, but they were not so well developed," Ionescu said. "Puhovski worked closely with us and greatly improved the quality." Puhovski in particular helped with the editing and the rough cut. He urged Ionescu's crew to improve sound quality and provided advice on camera work and on shooting special scenes.

He assisted in promoting *The Judge* and arranged an invitation for the film to be shown at the documentary film festival in Zagreb, Croatia's capital city.

The judge, Marin Constantin, the avuncular, graying man Ionescu's film crew followed, was twelve years old when Romania's pro-Nazi wartime regime forcibly deported him and thousands of other Roma across the Bug River to Transnistria, now Moldova, where thousands were killed or died of disease, malnutrition, and exposure.

Constantin managed to survive and after the war began rebuilding his life in Romania. He worked as a waiter and a police officer. When he was thirty-six, the Roma community chose him to be a conflict mediator and enforcer of traditional Roma laws, a function that was valued even by the ruling Ceauşescu regime, because it maintained peace within the Roma community and minimized input from the Communist authorities. Today, a younger generation of Roma, including lawyers and police officers, come to Constantin for assistance.

The Judge made headlines across Romania and galvanized about 250,000 viewers, including its Roma audience, with their first glimpse of the genocide against the Roma during the wartime years. On televisions and viewing screens in auditoriums, meeting halls, and movie houses, the film reignited memories few written words had ever recorded. It opened up discussion of the horrors and accountability and stimulated a hunger to know more.

Monitoring Compliance with the Decade of Roma Inclusion. Young Roma activists are organizing efforts to monitor how well the governments of the countries that have signed on to the Decade of Roma Inclusion 2005–2015 are meeting their commitments in the areas of education, employment, health, and housing.

Nadir Redžepi was executive director of the Roma Democratic Development Association until January 2010, when he joined the Open Society Foundations' Local Government and Public Service Reform Initiative as project manager. Among other activities, the association joined with Decade Watch, an organization created by the Open Society Foundations and the World Bank to support local efforts to press governments to meet their commitments. "For the first time in history, Roma from nine countries worked toward the same goal, and we learned by doing," Redžepi said. "At first we thought that, since the state had adopted official policies, changes would come automatically. But changes did not come. So we decided to research what government institutions, international organizations, and Roma nongovernmental organizations were doing. We confirmed that in Macedonia and elsewhere state support was weak. Implementation and official policies on the Roma needed instruments and structures."

Redžepi was present in Sofia, Bulgaria, on June 11, 2007, when George Soros launched Decade Watch's assessment report. "We went to the government with the findings and said we needed implementation immediately," Redžepi said. "We've already seen results in budget lines. We've seen structures put in place. Now they are developing an action plan on Roma women and working on a human rights action plan."

With the support of the Open Society Foundations, a group of young Roma activists, including Toni Tashev, a Roma lawyer who knows firsthand what education is like in a segregated school, formed a nongovernmental organization in Bulgaria, the Regional Policy Development Center, which promotes legislation and government policies to overcome discrimination and also participated in Decade Watch's monitoring project.

For Tashev, the key revelation from the Decade Watch report was that in all the participating countries there is a significant lack of relevant data to assess government compliance with the commitments made in the initiative. "At the moment, we can only assess the inputs made by national authorities, and not the outcomes," Tashev said. "In employment, for example, there are no clear data on how many Roma are covered." In health and housing, improvements are coming only slowly, Tashev added, but in education much more has been achieved.

*   *   *

The Open Society Foundations helped the Decade for Roma Inclusion, in its first five years, achieve significant progress at the European Union level. The Decade has moved the issue of Roma inclusion from the margins to the center of policy agendas, providing a working template for the European Union to adapt in designing a comprehensive EU Roma policy.

Since its earliest work on Roma issues in the 1990s, the Open Society Foundations pioneered and piloted successful approaches that show in practical terms how integration can and does work. As the Decade of Roma Inclusion moved into its second five-year period, the Open Society Foundations planned to continue to support programs that integrate Roma and improve their lives. Even so, progress in the communities where Roma live has turned out to be slower than expected.

According to Bernard Rorke, the international research and advocacy director for the Open Society Roma Initiatives, advancing the rights and well-being of Roma children remains a priority. In a region characterized by aging populations and falling birthrates, the Roma are the youngest and fastest growing demographic. Another priority is challenging negative stereotypes and public hostility through support for public information campaigns and the work of Roma film directors and journalists. Roma media organizations needed to be strengthened, and alliances between Roma and non-Roma media organizations established. Following up on public campaigns challenging racism, the Open Society Foundations in 2010 launched a national "Read with Us" campaign targeting children and young people in Hungary to promote integration. The Open Society Foundations were also working to duplicate a successful voter registration drive in Serbia, which registered more than 45,000 Roma, including internally displaced persons, so that Roma in other communities would begin to participate in electoral decisions and gain political power proportionate to their numbers. "If we are to avert a deepening crisis," Rorke said, "there is an urgent need for a comprehensive European Union Roma policy to combat poverty and discrimination, overcome anti-Roma prejudice, and bring an end to segregation."

*   *   *

GEORGE SOROS

Of all the activities in which my foundations are engaged, addressing the problems facing the Roma is the one with which I have been the most personally involved. The Hungary foundation, established in 1984, drew my attention to the Roma by making them a priority from its inception. The foundation's primary concern was with the preservation of Roma cultural traditions, mainly in music. Education and combating discrimination were other important concerns. The Hungary foundation's main achievement—later replicated by my other foundations in the region—was to provide mentors and other kinds of support to educate a small, new Roma elite who were conscious of their identity and proud to identify themselves as Roma. There were other Roma who had obtained an education and made their way in the world, but they had ceased to be Roma. They could disappear among the general population because they did not fit the negative stereotype, yet the stereotype would remain. The new elite we had educated held out the prospect of challenging and breaking the stereotype. I have since met many of these new Roma leaders and I have found them impressive and inspiring. They are articulate and motivated, having overcome great odds to become educated.

After the collapse of Communism, the social position of the Roma deteriorated, both in absolute and relative terms. Many Roma had been working in the heavy industries, which were shut down. The unemployment rate jumped as high as 80 to 90 percent in some areas. Also, in Communist times, people had houses or lodgings allocated to them at very low rents. When rents were liberalized, the Roma were forced to leave.

That is when the Roma became a priority program area for my foundations. The character of our programs reflects my personal influence: They are diffuse, diversified, and well funded. They make an impact, but they could be better organized, and we are in the process of dealing with this deficiency.

The Decade of Roma Inclusion and the Roma Education Fund were my creations. They constitute perhaps the first instance where I could achieve something by getting others involved rather than doing things entirely on my own. I cannot consider them an unqualified success: They are moving forward, but only because we keep pushing. Altogether we can be proud of our achievements, but we cannot be content with the results because in absolute numbers the growth of the Roma population is greater than the growth of our programs.

In 2010, the Roma problem finally penetrated the European public's consciousness because of President Sarkozy's antics in expelling Roma from France. Berlusconi has done worse in Italy, but it did not get as much attention. I regarded this event as an opportunity to get the European Union to pay more attention to the Roma question because the EU alone has the resources to make a real difference, and I am glad to say that the wheels have started turning. This has kept me busy. I have appointed a full-time deputy to coordinate our Roma programs, Kalman Mizsei, so that we shall be better organized. But I intend to remain fully engaged. If not me, who? If not now, when?

PART V

U.S. Open Society:
Drugs, Crime, and Two Cities

Students from the Baltimore Community School, one of the Baltimore public school system's three Accelerator Schools. An Open Society Institute–Baltimore grantee launched the schools to serve students who have fallen behind or need help managing the responsibilities of getting an education and providing for their families. (© Open Society Foundations, photograph by Jim Burger)

CHAPTER 9

The Baltimore Experiment

In 1998, George Soros, Aryeh Neier, and the Open Society Foundations' U.S. Programs chose the city of Baltimore to be the subject of an unprecedented, albeit unscientific, social experiment. Soros and Neier wanted to see whether a concentrated, coordinated, collaborative philanthropic effort of sufficient magnitude in one city would act as a catalyst for systemic reforms that would produce significant and lasting societal improvements. They selected Baltimore because it is a city plagued by the entire array of societal ills that afflict so many of the country's urban areas: drug addiction, racial prejudice, crime and violence, unemployment, dysfunctional and fatherless families, high rates of incarceration, huge numbers of young people leaving school unprepared for the workforce or higher education, and, underpinning so many of these problems, a paucity of self-esteem.

The goals of the Open Society Institute–Baltimore were to inform national discussions about urban problems and to help engineer programs that would be effective in solving Baltimore's problems and could be applied in other cities. Since 1998, the foundation's financial support and advocacy have clearly helped local organizations to improve the lives of thousands of inner-city people, including persons recovering from dependency on heroin, people on parole striving to reintegrate themselves into

273

their community, and two young students who found their way from inner-city streets to victory at an intercollegiate debate tournament.

In the mid-1980s, the community of West Baltimore was being suffocated by an economic chokehold that has yet to ease. Factory, dockyard, and steel mill closings had sent thousands of blue-collar employees to unemployment lines. The affluent fled to the leafy suburbs, abandoning West Baltimore and other inner-city row house grids to mostly low-income African Americans, a few whites, and a growing immigrant population. Too many local people were poisoning themselves on heroin, cocaine, and other drugs, and too many had given up on school and normal jobs to join the drug-dealing "game." Violence and crime were rampant. AIDS, "the bug," was starting to exact its toll, mostly on drug users sharing needles. Schools decayed. Weathered plywood covered doors and windows of deserted row houses. Foot soldiers in America's so-called war on drugs—the now failed government campaign, launched in 1969 by President Richard Nixon and Vice President Spiro Agnew of Baltimore, to eradicate America's drug abuse problem by interdiction, arrest, and imprisonment—were cramming juvenile detention facilities, municipal jails, and state prisons with thousands of the city's sons, daughters, fathers, and mothers, most of them facing charges or sentences for relatively minor offenses, and many suffering an untreated medical condition: heroin and crack addiction. All the while, big traffickers continued to bag their millions.

On December 3, 1984, a heroin dealer shot and killed thirty-six-year-old Marcellus "Marty" Ward, an African-American police detective. Ward, the father of two children, was wearing a wire. A tape recorder captured the confrontation and the four gunshots that ended it. In subsequent weeks, one of Ward's friends, a public prosecutor named Kurt L. Schmoke, pored over the tape, searching for any hint that the shooter knew Ward was a police officer. If so, Schmoke could charge him with aggravated first-degree murder, a death penalty offense. Schmoke was a son of inner-city Baltimore and its public schools, a lacrosse and football star, a Yale graduate, a Rhodes Scholar, and a recipient of a J.D. from Harvard Law. As he replayed the sounds of his friend's death, Schmoke found himself radically reexamining the strategies underlying his work as a prosecutor. After all the arrests, all the long prison sentences, and all the dead victims, he asked himself, why were heroin, cocaine, and other illegal drugs less expensive, more potent, and more readily available than ever?

"I had to listen to Marty die over and over," Schmoke said in an interview. "That started me looking around for other drug control policies." In 1987, Kurt L. Schmoke became Baltimore's first African-American mayor. He soon became the first mayor of a major American city to question publicly the policies that effectively treat drug addiction as a crime. In speeches and on national television, he called for decriminalization of drugs, arguing that it would be better to consider drug users as victims of a medical epidemic. A public health problem, he argued, was best handled by the public health authorities, thus enabling the full force of local and federal law enforcement agencies to turn against real criminals: violent offenders and high-volume drug traffickers and their high-end accomplices.

Mayor Schmoke and his public health advisers proceeded to clear legal barriers and launch a needle-exchange program, targeting the city's major cause of HIV transmission. Thousands of drug users participated; eight to ten million needles came off the street. In the program's wake, there was 70 percent less incidence of HIV among those drug users who regularly used the exchange than among those who never took advantage of the program.

Schmoke's team also reformed the operations of the city's drug treatment centers after Baltimore's health commissioner, Dr. Peter Beilenson, disguised himself as a drug addict and experienced the hostile reception people seeking treatment were receiving at the city's drug treatment centers. Schmoke made more city funds available for drug addiction treatment, and his successor, Martin O'Malley, managed to bring state funds to bear on the problem as well. Schmoke, Beilenson, and others created a quasigovernmental, nonprofit organization, Baltimore Substance Abuse Systems, and put it in charge of reducing the harm associated with drug addiction and overseeing the city health department's drug abuse treatment and prevention operations.

By 1998, Baltimore had become the only city in America with an administration treating drug abuse as a medical and public health issue instead of a crime. This was a crucial factor in the decision by Soros, Neier, and the Open Society Foundations to select Baltimore to test what more could be done in this inner-city dystopia less than an hour's drive from the White House. From its inception, the Open Society Institute–Baltimore, led by Diana Morris, an experienced foundation executive, focused on three interlocking problems: untreated drug addiction, the criminal justice system's overreliance on incarceration, and the obstacles impeding Baltimore's inner-city youth from succeeding inside and outside the classroom.

*   *   *

Frostbite in Summer. Today, an estimated 60,000 of Baltimore's 650,000 residents are drug dependent. Most of these people use a number of illegal substances at the same time, but the drug of choice is heroin. About 70 percent of the 80,000 or so arrests made in Baltimore each year involve people who test positive for drugs. Over 80 percent of the felonies and misdemeanors committed in Baltimore are drug related. For years, drug overdoses annually killed about 250 to 350 people in the city, outstripping the city's homicide tally. During the tenures of Mayor Schmoke and Mayor O'Malley, the number of drug treatment slots in the city more than doubled to 11,000, enough to serve 26,000 people. The goal of the city's public health authorities, however, remains drug treatment on demand, and the best estimate of the number of people prepared to seek such treatment at any given time is 30,000 to 35,000.

Behind the statistics, however, is the Baltimore of flesh and blood and hearts and minds, where policy and treatment must ultimately have their effect. This is the Baltimore of boarded up row houses and police sirens, the Baltimore subjected to surveillance by hundreds of police cameras blinking blue atop telephone poles, the Baltimore of the cops-and-drug-dealers television series *The Wire*. Carroll C., Jacqueline W., and Kim B. were born of this world.

Carroll C. is still muscular and driven, though graying at age fifty. He started selling marijuana and cocaine in his teens. He was addicted to cocaine at seventeen. In his late twenties, he turned to selling and shooting heroin. He has been through central booking, and felt "dope sick" in the holding pen with its one toilet for forty people, half of them also "dope sick" and vomiting on the floor. There is a felony on Carroll C.'s record. "Now I know why all this happened," he said. "It had a lot to do with self-hatred. When I was a young kid, I was abused, starved, and beaten at times. I was angry. I was self-medicating. Most of the people using are self-medicating. They are suppressing something."

Carroll C. graduated from high school and college. He became financial aid director at a business college and an account representative for a computer corporation. All the while, he was addicted to heroin and dealing as well. The crack cocaine epidemic during the 1980s made the dealers and users more violent, and it tore up families. "My daughter was talking about trying to kill herself," Carroll C. said. "I know people who sold their children's toys at Christmastime just to get high. I lost everything: the home, the car, the wife, everything. I was tired of doing the same thing and not getting anywhere. I didn't want to go to prison for the rest of my life. I always used my mind. I started to pray."

Jacqueline W. was born and raised in West Baltimore and never knew her father. Her late mother was HIV positive and addicted to heroin, and Jacqueline W. says her mother injected her with heroin while she was an infant. When she was six or seven, she and her mother were living in the woods, where Jacqueline W. sustained burns in a fire. She spent the rest of her childhood and her entire adolescence bouncing in and out of foster families and group homes, suffering sexual abuse along the way. She managed to graduate on time from high school. She went to a community college and studied data processing for two years at a four-year university. She had the first of her four children at eighteen.

Jacqueline W. said her heroin use began when she was twenty-six: "I started because I was covering up my feelings. I had been abused, neglected. I didn't understand why my mother didn't want me or why she didn't want to have a relationship with me." Sometimes Jacqueline W. got her fix from the men she lived with, including one with a gun who was killed by the police somewhere in West Baltimore. She then moved from house to house, living with relatives and friends who were also drug users. For a time she earned $60 or $70 a day working ten or twelve hours on the street as a "tout," drumming up customers for dealers by shouting "DOA," "Sugar Hill," and other brand names of prepackaged "product." In the mornings, the dealers would throw out free samples. The drug users would emerge from the neighboring houses and crawl over one another to snatch a packet.

Kim B. was also born in West Baltimore. She did not finish high school, and by age twenty, she was addicted to heroin. Two years later, she was HIV positive. Both of her parents were addicted to drugs. Her aunt and her cousin are still using heroin and crack cocaine. Her brother was a heroin dealer who died of cardiac arrest at age twenty-three after swallowing his stash during a police chase.

"When I started using heroin," Kim B. said, "it just seemed like I could do anything. I felt empowered. I had three children and my own place and I was okay then. I was with my mate. I was in public housing. I was getting social services and could pay my rent. My mate eventually got arrested. He was 'boostin.' He stole stuff to sell on the street. People would tell him what they wanted, and he'd go and get it." Kim B. warned her three children—boy, girl, boy, now 26, 25, 22—about the danger of heroin. Even so, her eldest son was on the streets selling drugs and is now in prison for murder. Her daughter sold marijuana, went to jail, and was evicted from public housing. Her younger son is behind bars for selling drugs. "I was in a methadone program for five years," Kim B. said. "I didn't want to be on meth for all my life. I saw my friends who had been on meth. It deteriorates your bones. It makes you look drowsy, sleepy. I made a resolution to get off it on January 1, 2007." She went to a detoxification center for two weeks and started suffering withdrawal. "You ain't going to die, but you'll feel like it," she said. "Your body aches. Pressure rises. Loose bowels. Irritable. Sweats. Everything cold hot." To beat back the withdrawal symptoms, she started using heroin again, and crack cocaine: "I was using. I was tricking. At the end, that's how I got money."

Even on summer days, coroners performing autopsies find frostbite on the dead bodies of heroin users. Milk and saltwater appear in the bloodstream. The cause of death is overdose. A person sick with drug addiction injects heroin. In a few minutes, the user becomes sleepy and hard to rouse. The opiate tampers with a part of the brain that regulates breathing. The user inhales and exhales more slowly. The skin turns blue. The breathing stops. Trusting street myth, shooting partners sometimes plunge the victim into ice water or inject the victim with milk or saltwater. They do not call the paramedics or the police, for fear of arrest. The partners leave the dead where they lie or drag them to a porch, a sidewalk, a street, a vacant lot.

"The way you fight a disease epidemic is to make treatment as widely accessible as possible," said Dr. Robert Schwartz, a psychiatrist who oversaw the Open Society Institute–Baltimore's programs to expand drug treatment. In Baltimore, there was a need to close the gap between the number of people seeking drug treatment for heroin and cocaine addiction and the number of slots available in a sustainable, effective treatment system. First the Open Society Institute–Baltimore worked to help draw the attention of the public and policymakers to the fact that treatment is a cost-effective way to restore the health of drug-dependent people, reduce crime, and help families and communities rebuild. Then the foundation went to work to help organize efforts to increase treatment funding. Both Diana Morris and Schwartz held seats on the board of the Baltimore Substance Abuse Systems, the city's quasigovernmental agency that oversees treatment. They worked to develop a national advisory board and met with city leaders, initially to create drug treatment benchmarks and later to ensure that the system met these benchmarks by providing effective treatment.

The Open Society Institute–Baltimore also assisted Beilenson, Dr. Christopher Welsh of the University of Maryland Hospital, and collaborators at Johns Hopkins University's school of public health to implement a program to reduce the number of drug overdose fatalities. They exploited the city's needle-exchange program as a platform to train drug users in how to recognize an overdose as it is happening, how to administer cardiopulmonary and mouth-to-mouth resuscitation, and how to inject their shooting partners with Narcan, a drug that can halt an overdose in progress.

After the training, drug users received kits containing Narcan vials and a few syringes with needles. "We certified hundreds of people," Beilenson said. "I would go in and write prescriptions." City hall even convinced police not to make routine arrests in overdose cases, since this would contribute to saving lives.

By 2008, the number of overdose deaths in Baltimore had declined to levels not registered since the mid-1990s. "Baltimore was first to organize a program like this out of the health department," Welsh said. New York and other cities followed suit, as did the state of Massachusetts. "Maybe there are better programs around. But because this was done with the health department, other programs are using the Baltimore model," Welsh added.

The availability of a new drug—the street calls it "bupe" or "bupes," doctors and pharmacists know it as buprenorphine— might have contributed to the decline in overdose deaths. Buprenorphine is a partial narcotic. It can be crushed and injected and offers something of a kick. But if the orange pill is placed once a day under the tongue and held there until it dissolves, buprenorphine works effectively for detoxification by reducing withdrawal symptoms and for maintenance by reducing or eliminating cravings for heroin and other opiates. During the 1990s, doctors in France began prescribing buprenorphine to help heroin addicts overcome their dependence. Since heroin is king in Baltimore, local public health officials and doctors realized quickly how beneficial buprenorphine might be for the city. When it became clear that the Food and Drug Administration would approve its use in the United States, the Open Society Institute–Baltimore urged the city to adopt it and worked closely with the Baltimore health commissioner, Dr. Joshua M. Sharfstein, and other officials to prepare to add buprenorphine to the city's drug treatment medicine chest as quickly as possible.

Buprenorphine can contribute significantly to closing the treatment gap for heroin users, because buprenorphine can take up where methadone, the most common maintenance drug for opiate addicts, falls short. Methadone treatment can be inconvenient, since U.S. laws and regulations often require drug-dependent people undergoing methadone treatment to appear at a clinic, wait in line, and, under supervision, gulp down a daily dose of the drug. This routine can be hard to maintain for people who have jobs or family responsibilities. Moreover, the stigma of drug use carries over to methadone clinics. "Nobody wants a methadone clinic near them," said Welsh. "Diabetes is a disease, but you don't see diabetics having to do their shots in front of someone," added Beilenson. "Doctors don't want methadone in their offices."

Unlike methadone, any pharmacy can sell the orange buprenorphine pills to anybody with a prescription written by a doctor who has completed an eight-hour certification course. The Open Society Institute–Baltimore flew in health care professionals from France to educate doctors and public health officials about buprenorphine and its benefits. It provided a grant to help hospitals increase buprenorphine's visibility, to attract more physicians into the buprenorphine certification program, and to simplify the process hospitals use to identify heroin-dependent patients and channel them into buprenorphine treatment. The foundation sponsored training and other efforts to convince primary care physicians, family doctors, and HIV and AIDS program doctors to prescribe it. "More doctors have gotten the waiver than have prescribed it," Welsh said. "We want them to use it. We don't have enough methadone and buprenorphine treatment."

Carroll C., Jacqueline W., and Kim B. were already notches in statistical tally sheets on drug addiction in Baltimore, but not in the death-by-overdose column. Carroll C. received a call from a detoxification center on Thanksgiving Day, 2005. "We have a bed for you," a voice announced. "Try not to use." Carroll C. showed up the next day. He grew "dope sick." He vomited and felt his bowels ready to burst, his legs ache, his stomach cramping. He was depressed and miserable, and felt suicidal. And on the tenth day, "clean," he reemerged and asked himself what he would do now.

A day after his first dose of buprenorphine, Carroll C. was up and functioning: "That's when I knew I didn't want to go back ever again. Bupe gives you stability. I saw a therapist, and continued to see a therapist." Four years later, Carroll C. was running a peer support group he had started at a health care center. The group numbers eighty people who, using buprenorphine, have been able to resist the siren calls of the touters for years. Most of them now have jobs. "I have fears and wreckage. How do I move forward?" Carroll C. had asked himself. "We work through these questions in peer support. Many people coming off drugs dropped out of school and have no education. We try to get people into GED programs. So many people want to do better. But some, when they hit a roadblock, break down."

The last time Jacqueline W. and her mate shot heroin was on January 28, 2007. Her third attempt to get clean began the next day: "We showed up in the morning. It was an orientation group. We had to tell about ourselves. After that group was over, we got medicated. Once it was over, I said, 'Hey, you know what, I'm not even sick anymore.' It makes me feel very good, and normal.

I was able to do what I was supposed to be doing." When Jacqueline W.'s health insurance lapsed, a doctor paid for two weeks worth of buprenorphine. Then the buprenorphine stopped for an entire year. Jacqueline W. managed to stay off heroin despite living in a boarded-up, open-air drug market of a neighborhood. "I kept going to meetings and talked to certain people about how I was feeling, and they kept me going. I truly didn't want to live that life anymore. Now I'm back on buprenorphine for two months. I feel better. It makes me feel good. I clean houses, and I'm trying to start my own business cleaning houses." Her mate is remodeling homes. "Bupe makes you get back in society, where I should have been long ago," she said. "We're probably going to get married next year. We wanted it on my birthday or his birthday, but we didn't have enough funds yet."

Kim B. calls it "my end." It was four months filled with crack, heroin, and prostitution, including an arrest for soliciting. She began buprenorphine treatment at a city health center on December 14, 2007. "I was on the death bed before I came here. I used to pray for a pill that would help you. And thank you, Lord, for it. Bupe makes you feel normal. You just feel like you can function. Coming from street drugs to bupe, you don't have to go through withdrawal. It don't cloud your mind. You can think. You don't have to get up in the morning and worry about where you're going to get your fix. You can deal with your family, you can go to church, you can deal with grandchildren. If you don't tell anyone you're on it, they'll never know. Now I'm finished with the program. I get the bupe from my doctor. There is no stigma. I hadn't had a stable job since I don't know how long. I'm working now. I canvass. I try to help prevent people from being foreclosed. I am going to go to school."

*   *   *

"What will you do with your one wild and precious life?"
The "war on drugs" and similar "get tough on crime" initiatives
fueled astounding increases in the numbers of people—the vast
majority of them African-American men—locked up in prisons
across the United States, including the state of Maryland, where
half of the inmate population hails from Baltimore. Surprisingly,
this increase continued for years despite the fact that crime itself
was actually declining.

Most offenders in prison had not committed violent crimes.
Many people imprisoned for drug-related offenses were convicted of crimes that involved neither violence nor great quantities of illegal substances. The vast majority of the prisoners—
including some juveniles—were abusing drugs at the time of
their arrest. Many were school dropouts and ill-prepared to
return to their neighborhoods. Ironically, recidivism—the risk
that a person will emerge from prison and commit new crimes—
does not diminish based on the length of time a person has spent
behind bars; recidivism is linked far more clearly with the
inability of a released person to find a job or combat addiction.

Further swelling the costs of the drug war are the expense of
maintaining such a large imprisoned population. Housing,
guarding, and feeding tens of thousands of prison inmates is
expensive even before the health care bill arrives, and sky-
rocketing costs have torn into state budgets for education, law
enforcement, health, and other social services.

In view of these and other hard facts, parole systems are supposed to allow some prisoners—especially those who have not
committed violent offenses and present a low risk of committing
new crimes—to leave prison and serve the remainder of their
sentences outside.

However, the parole system is susceptible to profound
political pressure. Any governor whose administration grants

paroles in significant numbers—or even paroles a single offender who goes on to commit an act of violence that triggers a media feeding frenzy—risks exposure to public ridicule and attack by political opponents for being "soft on crime."

Perhaps as a result of such fears, researchers found that parole boards in Maryland and other states were disregarding existing guidelines and routinely denying parole even to low-risk offenders jailed for crimes that did not involve violence. The prison system also lacked effective programs—including drug addiction treatment programs—to smooth the transition prisoners must experience once they are released back into their communities.

The Open Society Foundations' Baltimore experiment has provided dozens of grants in its effort to help wean the criminal justice system from a counterproductive overreliance on incarceration for offenders who pose little risk of committing new offenses.

From 2002, the Open Society Institute–Baltimore presented grants to the Institute on Crime, Justice, and Corrections at George Washington University and to the JFA Institute, run by James F. Austin, a nationally respected researcher on the workings of the U.S. criminal justice system, to collaborate with Maryland's government in a reform of the state's parole system. The effort began with an assessment of guidelines used by the state's parole commission to decide whether to grant parole to individual inmates. The assessment led to the development and implementation of new guidelines designed to be evidence-based and fair and ultimately would increase the number of people granted parole.

Subsequent grants funded the training of parole commissioners and the establishment of a monitoring system to determine whether parole commission personnel were complying with the new guidelines. This reform helped to curtail what had seemed an ineluctable rise in Maryland's prison population, and in 2009 the state's prison population began to fall. The reform also triggered efforts to eliminate racial and gender-based disparities in parole decisions. Research showed that not only were African-American prisoners less likely than white prisoners to be released on parole, but imprisoned men who posed the same recidivism risk as imprisoned women were also less likely to be paroled.

The Open Society Institute–Baltimore also provided crucial funding as well as development and advocacy support for the Maryland Public Safety Compact, a written agreement between community-based organizations and the state department of public safety and corrections. The compact outlines a program to shorten the prison stay of some parole-eligible felons and assist them before and after their release with drug addiction treatment and other services designed to ease their reentry into society. This program is premised on research that indicates that released prisoners who are drug dependent are far less likely to return to prison if they receive drug treatment before and after they leave jail. After successfully completing a drug treatment program in prison, inmates in the program were released on the condition that they continue with drug treatment and cooperate with case managers assigned to help them find jobs, secure housing, and reconnect with their families. The state is responsible for monitoring compliance with these and other conditions of parole. The parole authorities also agreed to devise alternatives to reincarceration in instances where parolees relapsed into drug use or committed a technical violation of their parole terms.

Postrelease drug addiction treatment and other services for the parolees are paid for with a portion of the cost savings to the corrections system. These savings will amount to an estimated $3 million with the parole of the first 250 inmates, all of them from Baltimore. To initiate the flow of parolees through the system, local and national foundations provided more than $2 million for up to two years of postrelease support. "This public-private partnership has the potential to be a model for other states that are trying to reduce overcrowding in prisons while still protecting public safety," said Gary Maynard, secretary of Maryland's Department of Public Safety and Corrective Services.

The Open Society Foundations' Baltimore experiment has included scores of grants to local advocacy and service organizations and over one hundred fellowships for individuals developing and implementing small, innovative projects that had potential to expand and contribute significantly to improving the community—and making the whole of the philanthropic experiment something greater than the sum of its parts. More than 70 percent of the fellows chosen since 1998 were still operating their projects in 2009.

The mission Greg Carpenter has taken up in his work at the Episcopal Community Services, Jericho, is the fight against the revolving-door syndrome. Carpenter knows the way back from life inside a Maryland penitentiary and how easy it is to slide back into crime. After escaping from a Georgia prison, he robbed a store in Maryland and ended up spending the next seventeen years behind bars. Released on Thanksgiving weekend 1994, Carpenter subsequently accepted Islam, married a woman he met in prison, and became an assistant to a boxing trainer. In January 2007, he began working at Jericho, a faith-based grantee of the Open Society Institute–Baltimore that assists men released from prison in their struggle to establish new lives. "I'm dealing with the more violent offenders," he said. "It is so hard to find employment for them. We help people get their papers to prove their citizenship. We assist them in looking for a job, getting them appropriate clothing and haircuts, writing résumés, and preparing for interviews. We teach them to speak in a friendly manner and how to field questions about criminal background.

"Lots of people have issues from childhood and have not dealt with them. Guys want to live in a make-believe kind of world and not deal with the realities in front of them. A lot of them intoxicate themselves on drugs and alcohol, so they become more delusional. You pay to forget. Then you wake up sober with a headache and behind bars. For $5,000 a year, you can probably put someone through the program and make them a functional person. It costs $35,000 to $40,000 to house them in prison. And most come home no better than they were when they left."

Walter Lomax's mission began inside Maryland's most notorious prison, the now-defunct Maryland House of Correction, where he was nicknamed Mandela. At the time, Lomax was grinding through the twenty-eighth year of a life sentence for a crime he did not commit, a murder and robbery at a Baltimore convenience store. Lomax had begun teaching himself to read in solitary confinement. He had joined a writer's group. He had earned his GED, a welder's certificate, and an associate's degree in business and criminal justice. He had risen through the ranks of reporters to become the editor of a small prison magazine, *The Conqueror*.

He entered a work-release program for six years, but after another work-release inmate murdered his girlfriend and killed himself in Baltimore, the governor of Maryland returned Lomax and the 133 other work-release inmates to prison. There was injustice in this, Lomax concluded. He recognized that the governor was erring on the side of caution, but this decision had strayed too far into the realm of the arbitrary.

By 1995, Lomax was organizing prisoners who, like himself, had spent decades behind bars. They were all serving life sentences with the possibility of parole. They had all received positive recommendations from the parole authorities. But their parole was not even being considered. Under Maryland law, only one elected official, the governor, has the authority to grant such a parole. Lomax and his collaborators campaigned for years to have the law amended to give a three-judge panel the sole authority to parole an inmate who has served twenty years and received a favorable parole board recommendation, psychological evaluation, and risk assessment. "This is closer to the intent of the legislature when the original law was passed," Lomax said. "We want to move the parole decision away from the political process."

In 2000, an amendment bill failed by three votes. In 2005, a new governor reinstated the work-release program. In 2006, after a judge had reviewed new, exculpatory evidence presented in Lomax's murder-robbery case, the Mandela of the Maryland House of Correction walked free. He had spent thirty-nine years behind bars for a crime he did not commit.

"Tell me," the judge asked him, quoting a Mary Oliver poem, "what is it you plan to do with your one wild and precious life?" Lomax answered in deed, by continuing to press for amendment of the parole law.

The Maryland Restorative Justice Initiative, for which Lomax campaigns, received an Open Society Institute–Baltimore grant. Since his release, Lomax has organized seminars, spoken to high school and college kids, and published a book of his prison cell writings. He has visited Maryland's prisons for women and men. He has helped bring witnesses to testify before legislative committees. He knows his allies are fewer than his friends: "At first people are ideologically opposed to paroling lifers, but when they know more of the facts, their position begins to change." Walter Lomax also works to abolish capital punishment. "If I had been in Florida, Texas, or Virginia," he added, "I would have already been executed."

*　　　　*　　　　*

Lauren Abramson became one of the first recipients of the Open Society Institute–Baltimore's fellowships to help her bring to inner-city Baltimore a reconciliation process adapted from the culture of the precolonial inhabitants of New Zealand, the Maori. Abramson and her associates at the Community Conferencing Center assemble people separated by anger and antagonism. They, like the Maori, seat their clients in a circle and have them describe the events that brought them into conflict. They invite them to talk about how the situation has affected their lives. They provide a framework for the clients to negotiate their own remedy.

During the process, Abramson and her colleagues strive to act as catalysts for an emotional transformation. "Our emotions motivate us biologically," said Abramson, who has a doctorate in animal behavior and neuroscience and is a faculty member of the Johns Hopkins psychiatry department. "When someone has harmed someone else, there is conflict. If you are disgusted, angry, and terrorized, you are going to be motivated, and this is what fuels conflict." Conferencing provides a safe space for people to verbalize emotions fueling conflict, and to listen as other people involved describe their experience of it. Releasing emotions is a key to the process, Abramson said. When community conferencing works, there is an emotional shift away from anger, rage, terror, and disgust. There is crying. There is a shared sense of empathy. Many times victims even feel a sense of responsibility for the perpetrator's well-being. "This shift from negative emotions of conflict to positive emotions of reconciliation is crucial," Abramson said. "If this emotional shift does not take place, there is far less chance of a lasting positive effect."

In twelve years, the Community Conferencing Center has brought teenagers who stole cars face-to-face with the cars' owners to describe the theft and to listen to how the theft affected the lives of the car owners and their families. The Community Conferencing Center has brought imprisoned murderers together with their victims' survivors, ten or fifteen years after the crime, when the survivors realized that the criminal justice process had left them with emotional wounds that had never closed. Junior high principals have called in the Community Conferencing Center to bring together girls whose jealousies had spawned hair-tearing fights that threatened to escalate into criminal violence.

In one neighborhood near a park, after eighteen months of receiving 911 complaints about kids playing football in the street, making noise, scratching the paint on parked cars, and pouring sugar into gas tanks, the police called the Community Conferencing Center. Almost fifty people showed up for the conference: eighteen kids, ages ten to fourteen, a bodega owner, neighbors, parents, blacks, whites, Koreans, Hispanics, all in a circle, everyone angry. "Why not play in the park?" one of the neighbors growled. The kids answered that dogs were crapping at one end of the park and drug dealers were beating them up at the other. The remedy: One neighbor offered to watch over the kids during football games in the park. The next day, twenty-two kids showed up. Within three weeks there were sixty-five players—girls and boys, black, white, and everything else. Over the next eight years, the pickup games evolved into a football league: two hundred linemen and backs in pads, helmets, and colors, with cheerleading squads in uniforms. Each team set rules for participation, including finishing homework before practice. The community conference had lasted all of ninety minutes.

The Community Conferencing Center seeks to bring people together; the alternative—resorting to the criminal justice system—separates victims and perpetrators. Its task is to assign guilt and mete out punishment. Too often the result is a network of angry, alienated people.

The Community Conferencing Center has helped divert about 650 young people from the juvenile justice system—for many, the portal into a lifetime cycle of crime and imprisonment. "Our reoffending rates are 60 percent lower than the juvenile justice system's," Abramson said. "Conferencing costs a tenth of a court proceeding. Cases that would take the court four to six months or longer to process, we finish within two weeks of receiving a referral. The state attorney's office, public defenders, and courts are overwhelmed with work. Nobody has said this is a bad idea. It's not a liberal-conservative issue anymore in our legislature. Everyone realizes that the criminal justice system is not delivering outcomes we want."

The Community Conferencing Center has helped seven other Maryland jurisdictions launch similar programs. It has provided training and technical assistance for the state of Maryland. It has done training sessions and presentations in Alabama, Louisiana, Michigan, New York, Texas, Vermont, Washington, D.C., and Washington state, as well as the United Kingdom.

*   *   *

Pedagogy of the Oppressed. Social science researchers have observed few correlations as striking as the positive relationship that exists between the number of years people spend in school and the amount of income they earn over a lifetime. More education, more earnings. And with higher earnings, people have more means and energy to invest in their community. Drawing from this sociological fact of modern life, the third targeted area for the Open Society Institute–Baltimore experiment has been education: keeping kids in school and removing obstacles to their success in and out of the classroom.

The Open Society Institute–Baltimore provided an initial $6.25 million to initiate after-school education and enrichment programs that have kept thousands of children off Baltimore's streets from 3:00 to 6:00 each afternoon and improved school attendance and performance—and continues to invest in these programs. To combat the substantial learning losses children from low-income households suffer during the three-month summer break, the Open Society Institute–Baltimore helped initiate a national organization, the National Summer Learning Association, which has lobbied legislators and government officials to organize summer learning programs and to have them include activities that would enrich young minds. The Open Society Institute– Baltimore helped develop and establish new public high schools. Its advocacy and legal support helped reform unnecessarily punitive school disciplinary policies, and consequently Baltimore's inner-city public schools adopted new disciplinary measures that reduced the number of school suspensions by six thousand in its first two years. From its earliest days, the Open Society Institute– Baltimore initiated work to bring to inner-city schools an extracurricular activity once found only in the suburbs: debate.

On the morning of the Saturday before Thanksgiving 2009, the Baltimore Urban Debate League took over a middle school near former Vice President Spiro Agnew's old neighborhood and held a tournament for inner-city primary and middle school debaters. The proposition: "Baltimore's government should provide housing vouchers for the homeless." Hundreds of debaters, in two-on-two competitions, stood up one at a time, note sheets in hand, to attack and parry and rebut.

"Twenty percent of the homeless are children, and kids deserve better than living on the street," a nine-year-old African-

American girl argued while her teammate scratched down notes. "Not enough people give the homeless jobs. Everybody makes mistakes. They need a second chance. With housing vouchers, people will try to turn their lives around."

Her opponent, an African-American boy, glowered, obdurate as pharaoh or a Fox News talking head: "Let the homeless get jobs. If they had done the right thing, they would not be homeless. They'll only sell the vouchers to buy drugs and alcohol, and then taxes will rise for everybody else. They had money, but they spent it on useless stuff. My brother gave money to a homeless man, and he saw him go right to the liquor store."

During rebuttal, the little girl pounced: "And what is your evidence of this? What are your sources?"

After a pizza break and cafeteria hubbub, arguments and counterarguments proceeded throughout the afternoon.

Debate galvanizes a young mind. "It can take kids who are ready to give up on school and allow them to feel success, to feel part of a community that believes in them, and then they begin to believe in themselves," said Pam Spiliadis, director of the Baltimore Urban Debate League. "They have a desire to win, a desire to be part of a team. They get a family feeling by going to practice and pushing themselves. In a year or two, there is a radical expansion of what they and others assumed they were capable of doing."

The debate league organizes workshops, camps, training, and public debates in the public market, on the streets, and even on public buses. "Our definition of success is moving kids toward opportunities they never had," Spiliadis said. "Learning to read, graduating, going to college, getting themselves the degree and a job they wanted, becoming leaders in the community. Success is about all of these things. And sometimes it's about being champion debaters."

In 1999, the Open Society Institute–Baltimore founded the Baltimore Urban Debate League. By 2009, the league had 6,000 alumni, and the number of kids enrolled had grown to 800 or 900 per year. "This was something that was totally unexpected," Spiliadis said. "But in Baltimore, we realized that in too many instances, even though kids in debate were developing skills they needed to be successful, the world around them did not sufficiently value these skills. The kids didn't have the support systems to capitalize on the skills they had developed. So I became focused on our need to provide guidance, especially for college."

The program was still in its infancy when Deven Cooper, born in 1986, and Dayvon Love, born a year later, joined their high school debate teams. They grew up in neighborhoods maimed by the drug trade. Family members fell victim to drugs. Love had friends who were dealing: "I didn't get involved. And my friends, for the most part, respected me. My friends told me, 'You can do it. You can make it.' They didn't think they could make it themselves. But they were my friends. Real friends. They cared. A lot of them are still where they were when I graduated. Doing the same things. Some have kids. A few are dead. A few went to jail. One was shot down."

Cooper took his first foray into debate as a freshman at a free, two-week debate camp in Atlanta, where he won five out of the six rounds in the final tournament. Despite his early success, he hesitated to try debate again as a sophomore: "I didn't think I would be any good at it."

Before classes one freezing morning in that same year, 2002, Love wanted to get into the building to get warm. Students had to have a reason to go inside. "They asked where I was going, and I said debate. I went in and met the coach and just kept doing it." The incentive: "In the mornings they used to have Krispy Kreme. And I think I took home two boxes of pizza from the first tournament."

After winning an award at a debate camp in New York City, Love believed that he really had a chance of landing a college scholarship. "I have two years to be really good at this, focus, get a scholarship," he told himself. "I hadn't been doing well at school before that. Debate for me was a place where I felt intelligent. I always felt smart. My grades didn't reflect it. But debate did reflect it. In debate, people took me seriously. In debate, they were evaluating me on the basis of what I brought to the table instead of what I was expected to say based on what someone else had told me."

Cooper and Love rose to the heights of the Baltimore Urban Debate League. They won college scholarships. Cooper went to the University of Louisville for a year before transferring to Towson State, near Baltimore. Love had talked him into coming home and debating with him on Towson's team. They drew inspiration from Frantz Fanon, a mixed-race psychiatrist who, with his writings on the psychological effects of colonization, became an icon of anticolonial liberation struggles, and Paulo Freire, the renowned Brazilian educator whose *Pedagogy of the Oppressed* is a classic on teaching the illiterate poor by respecting the knowledge they bring to the classroom.

In March 2008, Cooper's junior year, they traveled to Wichita, Kansas, and competed at a five-day national championship—debate's March Madness: sixty-four teams, two-person squads. The brackets included Dartmouth, NYU, and Harvard, a past champion, as well as teams from big state universities in Kansas, Missouri, Michigan, and Iowa. They figured their chances of winning were slim. But they were not about to let down their coaches, themselves, or the spirit of Fanon and Freire.

So they resorted to the quixotic. They chose to forgo the assigned topic—United States engagement in the Islamic world—and divert the debate into an examination of how the competitive debate system itself and the debate community to which they both belonged were flawed by exclusion, racism, sexism, and homophobia. "We have a responsibility to talk about these things," Cooper said, before he and Love drove home their point using hip-hop clips and song lyrics. "We were completely off topic," Cooper later chuckled. "We didn't expect to get far." But during the early rounds, their strategy blindsided opponents and captivated the judges, most of whom were white.

Deep into the tournament, emotions flared. Cooper and Love took 2–1 and 3–0 decisions. Members of defeated teams sobbed. Shouting matches erupted. Television cameras broadcast obscene gestures. In the semifinals, one of their opponents, the tournament's champion public speaker, lost his composure and blurted out offensive comments. Cooper and Love rolled into the finals on Cooper's birthday.

In desperation, their opponents resorted to an "everybody should love everybody" position. "It did have a philosophical dimension," Love said. "But it wasn't competitive." By a 7–4 score over the Jayhawks of Kansas, Deven Cooper and Dayvon Love of Towson in Baltimore became the first African-American team ever to win a national debate championship.

Cooper and Love returned to the finals of college debate's March Madness in 2009, putting an end to whispers that their championship had been a tainted fluke. It was their last tournament as a team. Cooper graduated and went off to graduate school in California. Love, who had a year to go to finish his degree, was working with Americorps and returning to his high school to work as a mentor and debate coach. He wanted to stay in Baltimore, to do something, "I don't know what," to improve his community. Cooper returns home from time to time and judges debate tournaments with his cochampion. "I'll come back to stay," Cooper said, "when Dayvon becomes mayor."

*   *   *

The Baltimore experiment continues. Having contributed more than $60 million to the city, George Soros is the single largest outside philanthropic investor in Baltimore's history to dedicate funds to the city's most needy residents. Yet he has not gone it alone.

From the beginning, Soros's philanthropy has been collaborative, requiring grantees to obtain funding from a variety of sources to ensure the sustainability of their programs. From 2006, the Open Society Institute–Baltimore had to do just that. By February 2010, under Morris's leadership, the foundation staff and board have raised $14 million toward a $20 million challenge. Soros pledged to match all gifts on a 1 to 2 basis, up to $20 million. All funds raised from new investors go directly to key initiatives. Soros covers all administrative costs and overhead.

The fund-raising task comes with a singular challenge. As Diana Morris said, "It is not easy to raise money from other donors when you work for a billionaire." But raising money has also had value beyond the purely financial. It has allowed Morris and her staff to engage many more community members in the issues. She noted that "fund raising has had a surprising outcome—it has convinced many more people how critical this work is to the future health of Baltimore."

New Orleans residents, driven out by the floodwaters of Hurricane Katrina, mourn the destruction of their neighborhood. The Open Society Foundations support groups working to build a better, stronger city through criminal justice reform, government transparency and accountability efforts, and arts and cultural activities that advance social change. (© Kadir van Lohuizen/NOOR)

CHAPTER 10

The New Orleans Challenge

The people of the United States of America comprise the largest, most complex open society humanity has ever known. Despite many flaws both glaring and hidden, American society has long been a beacon of freedom and opportunity for people around the globe. The country's constitution has withstood the shame of slavery, a civil war, widespread racism and racial segregation, the integration of huge influxes of immigrants, societal upheavals brought on by the industrial revolution and urbanization, and unrest fueled by traumas sustained during economic downturns and foreign wars. In the United States today, vast numbers of people with wildly diverse opinions partake in political, economic, and cultural life. Public issues are hashed over in public debate, even if it is often ill informed. The U.S. Constitution and derivative laws and institutions largely protect fundamental human rights and underpin the rule of law. Society promotes prosperity, though not its equitable distribution.

But in the United States at the turn of the new millennium, crucial legal protections and other rights and social benefits taken for granted by many Americans were failing to reach significant segments of the population. In places like Louisiana—the state with the largest per capita prison population in a country that puts more people behind bars than any other—

people routinely found themselves at the mercy of juvenile justice systems that, unmonitored for decades, ensnared young people convicted of only minor, nonviolent offenses and proceeded to destroy them with brutal beatings; sexual molestation; solitary confinement; and systemic neglect of education, medical and psychological care, and the most fundamental personal protection.

In August 2005, after levee breaks had flooded New Orleans and stranded thousands of people without drinking water, food, shelter, medical care, and emergency rescue, police officers and vigilantes gunned down African Americans who were trying to escape the disaster area by walking along public thoroughfares. A federal indictment refers to one gunman saying he would shoot anyone with skin darker than a brown grocery store bag who was fleeing across the Mississippi River bridges into a predominantly white area untouched by flood waters.[1] Matters did not improve during the postflood reconstruction effort, as thousands of immigrant workers were recruited from South Asia, Latin America, and other regions of the world only to be held in what was effectively indentured servitude by unscrupulous construction companies and other firms that were refusing to hire local people in desperate need of jobs to rebuild their lives. Societal failings of this order of magnitude motivated the Open Society Foundations to support organizations working to find solutions across the United States.

The idea was to build upon American values of openness and democratic decision making to extend and strengthen the reach of grassroots organizations working to cure societal ills. The Open Society Foundations in the United States funded projects that helped people organize and draw attention to increasingly punitive national security, criminal justice, and immigration policies. Funding fostered organized demands for greater government transparency and accountability at a time when political leaders were discounting both. These programs nurtured grass-roots efforts to fight against entrenched, structural racism; to reduce obscenely high, and increasing, rates of incarceration; and to repair the image of the United States in the world.

Through its grantees and partners, the Open Society Foundations have sought to break down barriers that exclude people from fully participating in public life. These include laws that have disenfranchised felons and thereby effectively denied many African-American men the right to vote. They include zero-tolerance rules that force children out of school and, in too many instances, shove them down a slippery slope to long-term incarceration. They include immigration policies that punish rather than reward the hard work of new Americans. They include criminal justice policies whose outcome has been the incarceration, on any given day, of more than two million Americans—a hugely disproportionate number of them African Americans and members of other minority groups.

With these goals in mind, Soros and the Open Society Foundations in the United States took aim at a wide range of targets. Soros created the Emma Lazarus Fund in 1996, in response to a public-welfare reform by Congress and President Bill Clinton, which unfairly cut off millions of legal immigrants and refugees' access to food stamps and other programs. In 1999, the Foundations launched the Medicine as a Profession initiative to support efforts by physicians to improve the quality, distribution, and accessibility of health care in the United States. From 1994 to 2003, Soros funded the Project on Death in America, which sought to transform the culture and experience of dying and bereavement in the United States by promoting innovations in care for the dying as well as changes in professional and public education and in public policy. While the Project on Death in

America ended its work in 2003, the Open Society Foundations' International Palliative Care Initiative has continued to promote the practice of palliative care in Central and Eastern Europe, the former Soviet Union, and South Africa.

The Open Society Foundations were the first philanthropic organization to have a dedicated youth media program, supporting, for example, youth radio in Oakland, California, which produced commentaries for National Public Radio, and New America Media's Beat Within, which published a magazine written by young people in juvenile detention. Soros funded a nonprofit organization dedicated to enhancing the quality and availability of after-school programs in New York City, creating a model for the state of New York and other states and cities.

The Foundations worked in the United States to expand access to legal assistance for people in low-income and marginalized communities, to strengthen and protect judicial impartiality, and to promote professional responsibility and public-interest values—as opposed to solely profit criteria—in the legal profession. The Arts Initiative supported policy initiatives related to free expression and increasing participation in arts activities for all citizens. The "Seize the Day" Fund promoted organizations working to bring issues such as mass incarceration, immigration, drug policy, and structural inequality onto the national agenda; to ensure transparency, accountability, and fairness in the development and implementation of economic recovery plans; and to increase participation of people of color, immigrants, and members of low-income communities in public policy reform efforts. From mid-2005, the Open Society Foundations sought to build sufficient public and political will to adopt and implement effective domestic policies to deal with climate change and to restore American leadership in international efforts to solve the climate change problem.

By the end of 2010, the total of George Soros's giving to promote the strengthening of open society in the United States had reached over $1.2 billion. His efforts in New Orleans are but one element of that larger effort.

*   *   *

Stimulating Expansion of Open Society in Louisiana and New Orleans. "The Big Easy," New Orleans, revels in its reputation as a wide open river town. It boasts about Bourbon Street's bars, its steamboats, its riverfront casino, clanking street cars, and the gumbo-spiced dialect of the Saints' rallying cry— "Who dat?"—and finds it outrageous that some of the newcomers gentrifying Faubourg Tremé, the neighborhood of shotgun houses that gave birth to jazz, have complained about the brass-band music wafting from the legendary Candlelight on Wednesday nights.

New Orleans is a city where the races mix with the racists, where drug violence and shoot-ups have marred parades of feather-costumed Mardi Gras Indians and traditional Second Line funerals. It is a place where friends celebrate the lives of the deceased with trumpet, tuba, and trombone solos and dances with canes and parasols, sometimes atop the lid of the casket.

Yet New Orleans is also a city where public institutions have suffered from corruption and a lack of transparency and accountability. The administration of justice has been inherently unjust. Unnecessary mass incarceration of blacks and members of other minority groups has helped perpetuate racial inequality. The decrepit levees that burst in August 2005 exposed the authorities' failure to have invested in the construction of new public works projects and in the maintenance of existing public infrastructure. Television images broadcast to the world showed the failure by the local and national authorities to rescue and protect people trapped in flooded neighborhoods and seeking shelter and assistance in the Superdome. Local gadflies like Karen Gadbois have torn away the veneer covering gross official corruption in the reconstruction effort. Music lovers and activists have bemoaned the lack of official support for the unique, generations-old local culture of music, costume, and art whose carriers—most of them impoverished—had attracted the millions of revelers from around the world who put money into the pockets of hotel, casino, and restaurant owners; land developers; the owners of the mass media outlets; and others.

The Open Society Foundations' initiatives in Louisiana are a highly concentrated sampling of the work the Foundations have undertaken across the United States, and they amount to a demonstration of the realm of the possible for grassroots efforts in other urban American dystopias. More than half a decade before the New Orleans levees burst, Soros's grant-making in Louisiana began with fellowships for activists and funding for organizations at work on reforming the state's shameful system of imprisoning minors. After New Orleans flooded in 2005, the Open Society Foundations broadened their efforts to include help for organizations working to reform the city's criminal justice system, support for groups working to ensure fairness in the recovery and reconstruction efforts and to bring transparency to government, and assistance for groups striving to recover and strengthen the culture that gave New Orleans its unique soul and made it "The Big Easy." George Soros provided about $10 million in grants and fellowships in Louisiana from 1999 to 2010.

*   *   *

Supporting the Organization of Criminal Justice Reform Efforts. The initial thrust of the Open Society Foundations' funding in Louisiana was directed at strengthening a small grass-roots effort that had been calling for reform of the legal machinery and the gulag of brutal, in some instances for-profit, youth prisons that state officials referred to as a "juvenile justice" system. After Hurricane Katrina and the levee breaks that flooded New Orleans, members of the juvenile justice reform effort—many of them Open Society fellows—decided that the time had come to press for sweeping reforms of the broader criminal justice system.

Juvenile Justice Reforms. Few Americans know much about the realities of juvenile justice in the United States. Press attention is minimal. Public scrutiny is constrained by privacy considerations. Public relations efforts routinely assure people, including parents of prosecuted young men and women, that juvenile detention facilities provide rehabilitation, counseling, educational opportunities, and mental health and substance-abuse treatment. As Grace Bauer recalled her ordeals with Louisiana's juvenile justice authorities, she repeatedly remarked on how she trusted the system. Her mother had worked for the state's penal authority. Bauer placed as much faith in the state's probation officers, school officials, and juvenile judges as she placed in her church pastor.

Bauer's only son was an eleven-year-old junior high honor student who had never posed discipline problems before the day in 1998 when he was caught stealing a three-dollar pack of cigarillos. Bauer paid for the cigarillos and apologized to the store's owner, who saw no reason to press charges. Months later, however, the police of her county in southwestern Louisiana—a place not too far from the banks of the legendary river that transported the incorrigible delinquent Huckleberry Finn and his slave friend Jim into the soul of American culture—pursued a prosecution.

Bauer's son was placed on six months of unsupervised probation whose terms effectively gave the regulations of his junior high the punitive power of criminal law. A few months into his probation, he skipped out of school rather than attend a pep rally for the girls' volleyball team. For this, the juvenile authorities placed him on supervised probation and required him to undergo drug tests, even though he had committed no offense involving drugs. Later, school officials caught him carrying "smoking paraphernalia": a cigarette lighter. He now had to spend two weeks in a detention center for shoplifting the pack of cigarillos. Grace visited him. The boy, still age eleven, came out wearing the same garb as a convicted felon serving time in a penitentiary: an orange prison jumpsuit, shackles on his feet, hands cuffed to a chain around his waist. After release, his probation expired, but his "record" was not expunged. He was barred from returning to public school.

At age fifteen, Bauer's son was picked up with two older boys in connection with the theft of a stereo from a truck. The two older kids, one of them the son of a judge, were given probation. But, because of his previous record—read: taking a three-dollar pack of cigarillos, cutting a pep rally for the girls' volleyball team, and getting caught with a cigarette lighter at school—a probation officer deemed Bauer's son to be "ungovernable" and advised her that it would be in her son's best interests to send him into the state juvenile system, where he would receive, the officer assured her, drug and mental health treatment.

Bauer had yet to consult a defense attorney. Lawyers were expensive, and Bauer trusted the system. Other probation officers assured her that her son would be home in ninety days. They convinced Bauer that she was a failure as a parent. They asked

whether the family attended church regularly; when Bauer answered yes and told them her son attended vacation Bible school,
they inquired whether Bauer had a personal relationship with
Jesus Christ.

When he entered the facility, her son was a diminutive fifteen
year old. Instead of finding treatment and counseling inside the
state juvenile prison, he was treated like a hardened criminal,
beaten, mostly by guards, and bullied by kids serving time for
violent offenses. On her first visits, Bauer saw bruises on her
son's body. His lips were puffed and busted. There was a slash
above one eye. His eyebrows had been shaved off. The skin over
his rib cage bore the imprint of a guard's boot. She called to
complain. Her complaints were ignored. She was told she had
no rights regarding her son, who was now bounced to other
state youth prisons, one a five-hour drive from the Bauer home.
Guards held him under water until he resisted and then beat him
for resisting. He would panic when he had to leave the solitary
confinement cell.

Finally, Grace Bauer engaged a lawyer. He explained that her
son would not return to her in ninety days and probably not until
he had turned eighteen; he told Bauer that her son had been
sucked up into a system that most white people like Bauer do not
notice because it mostly catches black kids and other young
people of color. This lawyer, an officer of the court in the United
States of America at the turn of the new millennium, told Bauer
that he could do nothing.

Grace Bauer watched her son's weight drop to below eighty
pounds. He was suffering physical and psychological trauma.
She felt an abject fear that her son would die if he remained
confined. She succeeded in engaging another lawyer who,
seemingly against all odds, made Bauer's son the first person ever
to be "paroled" from Louisiana's juvenile justice system.

The boy returned home at age sixteen. He screamed in his sleep. After months in state custody, he required drug treatment and medical attention, mental health treatment, and counseling to deal with anger. At age seventeen, he earned his high school diploma with a near perfect grade-point average and began taking courses at Louisiana State University. His probation ended when he turned eighteen. But with the end of probation, he no longer qualified for free mental health and drug treatment. He was subsequently arrested for burglary and was returned to jail. He remained imprisoned until the age of twenty-four. Then, after Hurricane Rita had wiped out her home, Grace Bauer got him out of the state of Louisiana.

The Open Society Foundations began supporting grassroots efforts to reform the juvenile justice system in Louisiana at roughly the same time Grace Bauer spotted the bruises and cuts on her son's face and the mark of a guard's boot on his chest. The Foundations began by funding the Juvenile Justice Project of Louisiana, an advocacy organization founded in 1997 to reduce the inordinate number of young people incarcerated in Louisiana's youth prisons—many, like Grace Bauer's son, for nonviolent offenses—and to end the brutality and neglect they were suffering inside these prisons. "The Open Society Foundations' funding was critical," said David Utter, one of the founders of the Juvenile Justice Project of Louisiana. "They also stuck with us."

Utter said that race was an "indelible factor" in his dealings with Louisiana's juvenile justice authorities. He once represented a thirteen-year-old African-American boy from the city of Lake Charles who was given a "juvenile life" sentence on the same purse-snatching charge for which his white codefendant was given probation. Utter subsequently worked on the defense of African-American teenagers from Jena, Louisiana, who were initially charged with attempted second-degree murder for beating up a white high school student during a period of racial tensions after someone strung nooses from the branches of a schoolyard tree.

Under David Utter, the Juvenile Justice Project of Louisiana spearheaded a campaign to end for-profit management of the state's youth prisons; the campaign succeeded in closing two privately run juvenile prisons, at Jena and Tallulah. "In all of these places, brutally violent guards were beating up the kids," Utter said. "But Jena was unique, because it was where the guards would spew racial epithets." The Jena prison was run by Wackenhut Corporation, a security services firm. "They were sensitive to negative publicity," Utter continued. "When we filed the lawsuit, they were brought in via a motion for preliminary injunction. The Wackenhut attorney wanted a gag order. He told me that every time I used their name in the press, the price of their stock fell."

The Juvenile Justice Project of Louisiana was instrumental in rallying public and political support for passage of the state's Juvenile Justice Reform Act of 2003, which shifted Louisiana's juvenile justice system away from a reliance upon incarceration in youth prisons and toward community-based alternatives for low-risk offenders. When the reform effort began, Louisiana was holding about 1,900 juveniles behind bars; ten years later, the number had declined to about 500.

The Juvenile Justice Project of Louisiana also served as an incubator for other grassroots organizations, including Families and Friends of Louisiana's Incarcerated Children, which emerged from the campaign to shut down the Tallulah detention center. The organization helped secure a strict separation between the state's youth services office and the adult Department of Corrections and monitored, on a continuing basis, implementation of the juvenile justice reform legislation. As the years passed, parents and grandparents of children suffering in Louisiana's youth prisons began calling the Juvenile Justice Project's office seeking help. Among those callers was Grace Bauer.

Bauer worked as a volunteer for Families and Friends of Louisiana's Incarcerated Children before being hired to build a chapter of the organization in southwestern Louisiana. After moving to Baltimore, she began working with the Washington, D.C.–based Campaign for Youth Justice. In 2010, she appeared before a Congressional committee to urge passage of the federal Juvenile Justice and Delinquency Prevention Act, which would provide protections for young people incarcerated in juvenile and adult facilities across the country. Bauer helped a 2010 Open Society Foundations fellow, Zachary Norris, to build a nationwide effort to organize and support families of incarcerated youth.

Much work remained. The Juvenile Justice Reform Act left on the books the provisions that had given school regulations the power of criminal law for juveniles on probation. Young people in Louisiana's state juvenile prisons were still reporting acts of physical, sexual, and psychological abuse and insufficient access to the court system and the possibility it offered to gain early release. As Hurricane Katrina approached New Orleans in August 2005, the juvenile justice authorities dumped a load of their wards at the adult Orleans Parish Prison and then took off, as did much of the prison's staff. The kids were shackled when the water reached chest level. Some were surviving on food picked from flood waters that contained raw sewage and decomposing bodies. A week of hunger and terror passed before they were evacuated. Clearly, the post-Katrina reform effort would have to target the entire criminal justice system.

The Post-Katrina Effort: Reform of the Criminal Justice System.
In October 2005, David Utter and staff members of the Juvenile
Justice Project of Louisiana, Families and Friends of Louisiana's
Incarcerated Children, and the Louisiana Justice Institute—all
of them driven into temporary exile by Hurricane Katrina—
gathered in Atlanta to strategize about how best to take
advantage of the unprecedented media attention that Katrina,
the levee breaks, and the subsequent chaos were drawing to New
Orleans. The Atlanta meeting spawned the formation of a kind
of brain trust bent on organizing a quintessentially open society
effort to reform criminal justice in New Orleans. "If the Open
Society Foundations had not already invested in increasing
community leadership indirectly, by granting young people
fellowships, I do not think we would have had the capacity to
push for reform after Katrina hit," said Derwyn Bunton, who was
then associate director of the Juvenile Justice Project. "Had they
not given direct funding to nurture grassroots organizations, we
would not have been able to develop internally the capacity to
give a decisive push to the reform effort that arose."

"This was a huge moment in New Orleans," said Xochitl
Bervera, an Open Society fellow who had also finished law school
at New York University on a Soros-funded scholarship. "There
were no judges or public defenders in the city. The police department had been given a green light to arrest and to shoot without
any oversight or due process. Juveniles had been dumped at the
parish prison for adults, where the prisoners had been left to
drown. For months after the storm, the criminal justice system
was being used to keep poor black people from returning to
New Orleans. It was frightening, but at the same time, there was
a power vacuum which left open great possibilities. We saw an
opportunity to change totally the way the criminal justice system
operated in New Orleans."

The meeting's participants decided to mount an effort to overhaul the dysfunctional system Louisiana was using to provide legal assistance to indigent criminal defendants. The meeting participants also decided to organize an effort in New Orleans to reduce the huge numbers of people held behind bars awaiting the filing of charges or a trial, or serving time for relatively minor and nonviolent offenses.

The brain trust—Utter, Bunton, and Bervera, as well as Norris Henderson, an Open Society fellow who had served twenty-seven years in the state's most-notorious prison, the Louisiana State Penitentiary at Angola, for a crime he did not commit, and Gina Womack, the codirector of Families and Friends of Louisiana's Incarcerated Children—initiated an entirely new organization: Safe Streets/Strong Communities.

In the weeks that followed, the Open Society Foundations allowed Norris Henderson to alter the terms of his fellowship in order to get Safe Streets/Strong Communities running. The team called out to allies across the country, including Open Society fellows elsewhere, to come to New Orleans and help launch investigative efforts into the breakdown of the juvenile justice system, into killings by vigilantes and members of the police department, and into the failure of the public defenders system. Families and Friends of Louisiana's Incarcerated Children began coordinating a nationwide effort to reconnect young people incarcerated in the state's juvenile justice prisons with their family members who had fled the storm or were evacuated after the disastrous levee breaks and having trouble finding their way home.

"We were scared to death doing this work," said Xochitl Bervera. "The police had carte blanche to arrest anyone and were not above doing unethical and drastic things. And here we were campaigning against corruption and police violence. We took precautions. We traveled around the city only in groups for our own security. We did not want to be found alone or give the police any pretext to arrest us."

Confronting Police Violence and Misconduct. Police violence is commonplace in all large American cities. Yet New Orleans may well go far beyond the norm. At Mardi Gras time—though not only Mardi Gras time—New Orleans police officers beat up people placed under arrest and, if they react, seek resisting-arrest charges against them. But there is a much darker dimension. In 1996, a New Orleans police officer was convicted of hiring a hit man to kill a woman who had submitted a police brutality complaint against the officer. In September 1995, a police officer was convicted of killing, execution style, a brother and a sister working at a Vietnamese restaurant as well as an off-duty city police officer hired to be a security guard. A subsequent attempt to purge the police department resulted in the arrests of over one hundred officers and the suspensions of six hundred others.

Police brutality reemerged after the levee breaks of 2005. Though many New Orleans police officers carried out their duties under harrowing conditions—in the chaos a police officer was shot in the head—credible, corroborated allegations have arisen that high-ranking police officials issued orders to shoot looters on sight.[2]

According to federal court records, on September 2, 2005, four days after Katrina, a police officer wounded thirty-one-year-old Henry Glover as he ran from a parking lot in Algiers, a New Orleans neighborhood across the Mississippi from the central city. William Tanner, a passerby driving a Chevrolet Malibu, picked up Glover and, seeking help, drove him to the makeshift headquarters of a police SWAT team; the officers allegedly handcuffed and beat Tanner, who later reported seeing an officer with a flare sticking from his pocket drive off in the Malibu with Glover, wounded but alive, in the back seat; Glover's charred remains were later recovered in Tanner's burned Malibu at the base of the Mississippi levee.[3]

Another federal criminal indictment states that, on Sunday, September 4, on the city's Danziger Bridge, police officers shot and killed nineteen-year-old James Brissette and forty-year-old Ronald Madison and wounded four other African Americans. The victims were not looting. None were armed. Madison, a mentally disabled man from a respected New Orleans family, was shot in the back.[4] Even so, the police department would maintain for years that the victims in the Danziger shootings were armed and had first opened fire on police officers.

Safe Streets/Strong Communities demanded investigation of the Danziger Bridge shootings. "We reached out to the Madison family," Henderson said. "We went with them when they went to the authorities with their story." William Tanner, the Good Samaritan in the Glover killing case, came to the Safe Streets/ Strong Communities office with his account of how a police officer had driven off in his Malibu with Glover, still alive, inside. "We started to see what we could find out," Henderson said. "Nobody believed that those cops did what they did."

In the spring of 2006, members of Safe Streets/Strong Communities and people who had suffered police brutality testified before the newly elected New Orleans City Council and demanded passage of a resolution calling for the creation of an independent monitor to gather complaints about police misconduct and present these complaints to the police department's official internal-investigation division. Two months later, Safe Streets/Strong Communities undertook a survey that provided a stark report on just how little trust the city's African Americans had in the police.

Safe Streets kept demanding investigations of police violence. "We were going to make as much noise as we could," Henderson said. "We were repeating ourselves over and over like a Louis Armstrong record with a skip. Every time we registered an incident, we called. We complained. Then some cops beat up the son of one of our own workers inside a bar he owned. They beat him up and then came outside and asked, 'Hey where's the guy who owns the bar?' thinking they had just done him a favor."

Police violence continued. On May 9, 2006, the family of a mentally ill man named Ronald Goodman requested police assistance when they discovered that he had locked himself inside their house in Algiers and was in need of his medicine. The police dispatched a SWAT team. "Normally you'd have a crisis team, a psychiatric team, but all that had shut down after Katrina," Ronald Goodman's brother, Robert, said later. "A SWAT team is trained to react with violence, not to resolve these kinds of problems." The team showed up at the house at seven in the evening and removed the family from the scene; at two in the morning gunfire erupted. Ronald Goodman was shot in the back of the head, his brother said, adding that police personnel told the Goodmans that the officers could tell from outside the house that he was breaking things: "My mother said, 'That's his house, he can do what he wants.'" Robert Goodman showed up at Safe Streets with his mother, met with Henderson, and began volunteering for the organization.

On January 2, 2007, police officers involved in the Danziger shooting were indicted for murder and attempted murder. Nineteen months later, District Judge Raymond Bigelow dismissed the charges, citing misconduct by the prosecution. "When Bigelow threw out the case against the police, we went nuts," Henderson said. "The prosecution had warned us in advance. They wanted support."

In 2007, the Open Society Foundations awarded Safe Streets/ Strong Communities a grant to organize local residents and forge alliances with local and national organizations to mount pressure to push through criminal justice reforms. "We started lobbying for the Department of Justice to take up the case," Henderson said. "The Bush administration really didn't give a damn. But after Obama was elected, things changed."

The Federal Bureau of Investigation and the Civil Rights Division of the Federal Department of Justice began investigating the post-Katrina police shootings in September 2008. Seven months after the Obama inauguration, federal agents mounted a surprise raid on the New Orleans Police Department's homicide unit and removed computers and other records. Police violence had continued even after the federal investigation had begun. At three hours after midnight on January 1, 2009, police officers in the French Quarter shot Adolph Grimes III fourteen times, twelve of the bullets in the back. The police said Grimes fired first and deemed the shooting justifiable.[5] The family of Adolph Grimes showed up at Safe Streets. "We're trying to get the feds to look into this case," Henderson said. "They are supposed to look into all the post-Katrina shootings."

By August 2010, the federal authorities had issued indictments against eighteen police officers in connection with the Glover killing and the shootings on the Danziger Bridge. Some of the charges involved elaborate schemes to cover up police responsibility for the shootings.[6] By the time these indictments were filed, the New Orleans City Council had passed the legislation establishing the city's Office of Independent Police Monitor. This was a crucial step in creating a credible deterrent to police violence.

Safe Streets/Strong Communities and the Juvenile Justice Project of Louisiana became two of the organizations officially authorized to collect citizen complaints about police misconduct and present these complaints and supporting material to the Office of the Independent Police Monitor so the office could present them to the police for further investigation and, if appropriate, undertake disciplinary or legal action. No longer could the police stonewall and avoid accountability by saying they had received no complaints or by repeating ad nauseam that such cases were under review.

Reform of the Public Defenders Office. In 1963, the United States Supreme Court issued a unanimous, landmark decision, ruling in *Gideon v. Wainwright* that states are required under the Constitution to provide free-of-charge counsel in criminal cases for defendants unable to afford their own attorney. Before that time, indigent people facing criminal charges in Louisiana found themselves with few public defenders the likes of the fictional hero, Atticus Finch, over in the Alabama of *To Kill a Mockingbird*.

However, between the decision in *Gideon v. Wainwright* and the destruction of Hurricane Katrina, cost-free public-defender services for indigent defendants in Louisiana were, as Derwyn Bunton said, "at best a hustle and at worst a fraud." The Orleans Parish's indigent-defender board had contracts with lawyers to represent poor people before the parish criminal court and the municipal criminal and traffic courts. These lawyers maintained private practices, while simultaneously handling, on a part-time basis, a workload of six hundred to one thousand cases each year. It was commonplace for these attorneys to ignore conflicts of interest, for example, by representing two defendants in the same criminal case. They had no dedicated staff of investigators. There was little money for expert assistance. There was little or no timely representation for defendants during the period right after their arrests, and the authorities were holding vast numbers of persons in pretrial detention. Clients received almost no visits from their attorneys. There were also few client files and data-tracking mechanisms.

None of this boded well for defendants like Shareef Cousin, who faced a capital murder charge in connection with the killing of a tourist outside a restaurant. Cousin was in his early twenties and had been fingered by police informants. The appointed public defender did only a cursory personal investigation. The case went to trial. Cousin was convicted and sentenced to death. The public defender believed his client to be innocent. He eventually learned that the district attorney had failed to disclose evidence, including a time-stamped videotape showing Cousin playing basketball at the time the murder took place. The court threw out the conviction. But the ineffectiveness of the original defense effort was embarrassing.

Hurricane Katrina disclosed the extent of the rot in the city's indigent-defense system. The New Orleans jail flooded. The police department did not know how to track accused people being held in pretrial detention. Funding sources, especially from traffic fines and fees, dried up.

Safe Streets/Strong Communities undertook an investigation into the scandalous collapse of the indigent-defense system, interviewing inmates in prisons across the state. The system had left more than six thousand detainees behind bars for more than nine months with no representation. "One local judge, Calvin Johnson, set up a call-in line for public defenders to inquire about the whereabouts of their clients," said Bunton. "Not a single public defender ever called."

With Open Society Foundations support, Safe Streets demanded the resignation of the entire board overseeing the existing indigent-defense program. But for one holdout, it quickly achieved its goal. Public pressure convinced judges to appoint a new public-defender board, which began instituting reforms based upon standards set by the American Bar Association. Derwyn Bunton was appointed to oversee the operation of the Orleans Parish indigent-defense program. "We began to initiate reforms," Bunton said. "We made indigent defense a full-time endeavor, with offices, recruitment, and training. We became client centered. Some judges—including Judge Bigelow—were angry. They called us incompetent. We sued them."

The state authorities in Baton Rouge grew weary of being embarrassed day after day by media coverage of the scandals pouring out of New Orleans after Katrina. The governor allocated $20 million in state funds for overhauling the indigent-defense system. The state legislature passed a new law that eliminated the local indigent-defense board in New Orleans and created a more-structured, statewide system.

In 2009, Derwyn Bunton became the chief public defender of Orleans Parish: "We are a political subdivision of the state and housed in the executive branch. This means the judges have no jurisdiction operationally over our office. We receive a distribution from the state each year: state tax money and local fines and fees." The Open Society Foundations have funded training for new public defenders at the Southern Public Defender Training Center, a contract with Juvenile Regional Services, an organization that provides comprehensive services to indigent youth, and a full-time staff position committed to community outreach. In its first year, the office's caseload was about 15,000, Bunton said. In 2009, it was about 25,000. For a time, Orleans Parish had the highest per capita ratio of exonerations in the United States.

Ultimately, however, even repairing the public defender system is only one piece of the puzzle. That's why it was crucial for the Open Society Foundations to address the root of problems in Louisiana's justice system: a troubling fixation on detention as the solution to all ills.

Ending the Overreliance upon Detention and Incarceration. Louisiana's criminal justice system has had a decades-long addiction to detaining and incarcerating people. Too many people arrested for minor misdemeanors in Orleans Parish have found themselves lingering in jail for as long as forty-eight days before prosecutors filed charges or decided not to file charges. Those arrested for felonies might sit behind bars for sixty days before prosecutors decided whether or not to charge them with a crime. The authorities' overreliance upon detention and incarceration has ruined lives and exacerbated racial tensions. It has helped depress entire New Orleans neighborhoods. It has drained public funds and arguably benefited only the bureaucracies and political leaders who manage the criminal justice system. Before August 29, 2005, the local county jail, the Orleans Parish Prison, had by far the largest inmate population in the country, calculated on a prisoner population to local population basis. The vast majority of the prisoners were detainees awaiting the filing of charges or a trial.

"One of the silver linings of Katrina was that it tore down the jail for us and allowed for a rethinking of detention in New Orleans," said Jon Wool, director of the Vera Institute of Justice's office in the city. "Now, this city has to build a jail. The question is whether it will build a jail that continues the tradition of mass detention. If you build a jail with too many beds, it will be impossible to improve the system in other ways."

In 2006, a number of local activists, including Dana Kaplan, a former Soros Justice Fellow at the Center for Constitutional Rights in New York who became executive director of the

Juvenile Justice Project of Louisiana, recommended to New Orleans City Council members that they call upon the Vera Institute of Justice to examine incarceration trends in the city, identify problem areas, and recommend reforms. In the spring of 2007, the Vera Institute produced a report on the state of criminal justice in New Orleans, along with a number of recommendations on what might be done to improve the dismal situation. With the support of local city council members and local and national foundations, including the Open Society Foundations, Vera began working with public agencies, local criminal justice reform advocates and nongovernmental organizations, and New Orleans business and civic leaders. It brought together the city's criminal justice leaders—members of the city council, the superintendent of police, the district attorney, the sheriff, judges of the criminal district court and municipal court, the city attorney, and the public defender—and developed a statement of commitment to a set of criminal justice reforms, including the expedited screening of arrests to speed up the decision on whether or not to file charges and the development and implementation of a pretrial release system. All of the principals signed the statement.

"Vera works in partnership with government," said Jon Wool. "One of the things we noticed was that it was taking an absurd amount of time between when someone was arrested and when that person was charged with a crime." Police officers sometimes turned in arrest reports to their supervisors weeks after an arrest was made. The department then had officers drive each report to the district attorney's office, where there was a thirteen-day backlog at the desk of the typist who entered the case into the record. All of this expanded the case backlog. It often took sixty days for people with no money to post bail. "If a poor person gets arrested for having a joint," Wool said, "it should not require waiting days, let alone weeks, for a judge to say, 'If you plead guilty, I'll let you go home.'"

Vera worked with the district attorney and other agencies to arrange for these cases to be heard in the municipal court system, where they began to be processed within one day of an arrest. Vera also facilitated the agencies' development of a system designed to expedite the screening of people who are placed under arrest. This system, which was implemented in 2008, reduced the time between an arrest and the filing of charges to about five days for cases based on state charges for incidents not involving a civilian victim. "It demonstrated to officials in key agencies that, by working together, they could advance practices to everyone's mutual benefit," Wool said.

Vera then went to work on other reforms to wean the authorities in New Orleans from their overdependence upon detention. These reforms included the development of a pretrial services system to make it easier for persons who had been arrested for nonviolent crimes and who did not present a significant flight risk to await trial in the community rather than behind bars. They also included a new city ordinance expanding the use of summonses to deal with minor misdemeanors, as well as examination of funding structures in the justice system, including the funding mechanism for the Orleans Parish Prison.

"In most places jails are funded through the normal budget process in a way that rewards efficiency and positive outcomes," Jon Wool said. "In Orleans Parish, the jail is funded by a per diem system. For every prisoner handed over by the city, the city must pay the parish sheriff $22.39 per day, plus $4 million annually for medical care, plus another $5 million for other expenses, for staff, unemployment, compensation, health insurance, etc. This creates perverse incentives and invites perverse outcomes. It forces the sheriff to try to incarcerate as many people as possible in an endless struggle to make payroll. We need to detain fewer people but to provide more resources per detainee. To do so, we need to shift the incentive toward quality and away from volume. That is how we advance justice as well as efficiency and public safety."

*   *   *

Support for Organizations Working Beyond Criminal Justice Reform. In the months and years after Hurricane Katrina and the disastrous levee collapses, the Open Society Foundations broadened the targeting of their funding to strengthen citizen participation in government and improve the transparency of government and to assist organizations promoting cultural activities crucial to preserving the soul of New Orleans.

The anarchy that descended upon New Orleans after the levee breaks galvanized the city's returning residents. People who had never taken an interest in community affairs now sought to participate in neighborhood organizations, independent watchdog organizations, and other organized efforts to exercise their constitutional right to monitor the decision making of their elected officials and the operations of public agencies. In every area of public affairs from the management of schools to municipal contracting and budgeting to post-Katrina reconstruction efforts, ordinary people in New Orleans discovered that their efforts were frustrated by a lack of government transparency. Basic data on city revenues and spending were not being collected. Nearly three hundred independent commissions—in effect a shadow government—were acting with little or no accountability. Bureaucratic ineptitude and stonewalling were effectively voiding open records laws already on the books.

The Open Society Foundations supported a multipronged response to the challenge of enhancing government transparency and accountability in New Orleans. The first prong was support for the New Orleans Coalition on Open Governance, a network of community organizations and good-governance and data-collection organizations. A second prong was support for Karen Gadbois, an award-winning gadfly reporter; Ariella Cohen, an investigative journalist; and their colleagues at a web-based news outlet, *The Lens*, to continue ferreting out corruption. Gadbois was undergoing cancer treatments during Katrina when she fled the city with her husband and daughter.

Soon after returning on New Year's Eve, 2005, Gadbois saw that the mass media—television and print, local and national— were reporting untruths as facts. "Heavy rains did not flood the city," she said. "We're not all below sea level. You can't move the city up the Mississippi. And the people here carried out the most successful prestorm evacuation in history."

Gadbois began writing a blog about how the reconstruction effort was destroying the heritage of New Orleans. She reported on the use of federal money to demolish private housing and joined forces with a community of people interested in pre-serving neighborhoods. "We started tracking meetings taking place with no public notice. Absentee landlords were seeking demolition of properties they did not want to repair, because the rents they could collect were so low. Other landowners were trying to build things their neighborhoods had opposed. In other areas, the government, with no procedure, condemned proper-ties and earmarked them for demolition."

Working without pay, Gadbois began interviewing people and identifying houses that were being demolished. "We looked at inspection sheets and found that page after page was empty," she said. Next Gadbois unearthed a scam involving $5 million in federal funds that were supposed to help elderly people repair their homes. She obtained a list of the houses that had been awarded assistance, found that many of them belonged to public officials, and photographed them to demonstrate that none of them had been repaired. "Not one had even been cleaned," she says. "That blew the thing up. I was writing about it in a very oblique way. I didn't want to get sued or killed." The story galvanized the city and earned Gadbois national and local journalism awards. Karen Gadbois, who was fighting cancer as she was doing her reporting, had never worked in journalism before.

The Open Society Foundations helped Timolynn Sams and fellow members of the Neighborhoods Partnership Network in their efforts to convince twice-shy inner-city residents that it was in their interests to organize and demand change in the way government in New Orleans works. The Foundations helped photographers Chandra McCormack and Keith Calhoun to restore flood-damaged photographs that document the cultural richness of the city's ravaged Ninth Ward, the home of Fats Domino and other musicians, a grid of shotgun houses built by local men and women who pulled the cypress boarding from scuttled river barges along the adjacent wharves. The Foundations also supported the Ashe Cultural Arts Center's work to revive an historically significant neighborhood in central New Orleans and to develop arts and cultural programming that encourages advocacy on acute community problems.

Neighborhood organizers, gadfly reporters, tenured sociologists, budget watchdogs, federal prosecutors, public defenders, judges, rights advocates, and reform-minded elected officials contributed significantly to help New Orleans begin to recover from the levee breaks and to rethink the timeworn ways the city had of doing things. But "The Big Easy" would have slipped away with the receding floodwater had there not been a focused local effort to bring home a critical mass of the people who keep the city's heart beating to its signature cadence: the city's musicians, its Mardi Gras Indians, and marching members of old-time African-American funeral and insurance societies known as Social Aid & Pleasure Clubs. These men and women are the living repository of a tradition that has set New Orleans apart from every other city in the United States. It is a tradition of feathered costumes, fedora hats, white shoes, and a big brass sound swaying to four-to-the-bar rhythms laid out on drums and banjos. It was not a foregone conclusion that enough of them would return. It took a homegrown assistance effort with funding from individuals, small private donors, and a number of foundations, including the Open Society Foundations, to restore the soul of "The Big Easy" and to organize it in a way that can make it better able to weather stormy weather, human and natural. The mainspring of this effort was Sweet Home New Orleans.

Since its founding after Hurricane Katrina, Sweet Home New Orleans has provided more than $3 million to help four thousand musicians, Mardi Gras Indians, and Social Aid & Pleasure Club members reestablish themselves and their families in New Orleans. From the Open Society Foundations, Sweet Home received a grant to support the work of one caseworker who dealt with several hundred clients. This caseworker turned out to be Joe Stern of The Original Prince of Wales Social Aid & Pleasure Club, a Clevelander who had become "White Boy Joe," the first non–African American ever to parade in an African-American Social Aid & Pleasure Club. Stern was one of the marchers who had to find his way home. "I had water to my ceiling," he said. "I lost a whole collection of suits and shoes."

The average household income of Sweet Home's clients was about $21,000 on the day Hurricane Katrina hit; after the storm, incomes collapsed, and they had only recovered to about $18,000 by 2010. "This is a working poor community," said Jordan

Hirsch, Sweet Home's former executive director. "They engage in music, which has a cultural value that is not compensated in the way that it is for a professional musician in New York or Nashville, because the mechanisms for turning music into personal income have not been developed in New Orleans in the same way. These people are leaders in their community and drivers of the city's tourism and hospitality industry. Everyone feeds off them. And they struggle to feed their families."

Sweet Home has adjusted its focus to make the city's musicians; its "gangs," the local term, of Mardi Gras Indians; and its Social Aid & Pleasure Clubs more sustainable in hard times. "Our role as advocate is no longer tied to Katrina and the flood," said Gabriela Hernandez, who replaced Hirsch as Sweet Home's executive director. "We're expanding our capacity to address challenges our clients are now facing, such as a lack of playing dates and outside employment. We are also developing ways to help them transmit the culture to younger people. Ultimately, our goal is the advancement of culture as a mechanism to attain social justice for our constituents."

Mardi Gras Indian suits are now protected by copyright, and their owners can exercise a greater degree of control over their own photographic representations in advertisements and other media. A number of Social Aid & Pleasure Clubs have registered as corporations in the state of Louisiana. Musicians are working with advocates to copyright their work and to conclude better contracts. "As members of this community see the way they handle the business of their art as something crucial to the well-being of their families, we have been able to offer some new opportunities for them to develop professionally," Hirsch said.

In 1947, Louis Armstrong and Billie Holiday first performed "Do You Know What It Means to Miss New Orleans?" for a film. In 2010, Jeffrey Hills lipped the mouthpiece of his nickel-plated tuba as the bell of the horn uttered the song's opening phrases. The tones were identical to those of Hills' own voice, controlled and understated. From the porch of his apartment, Hills had watched the floodwater submerge the corner of Lafitte Street and Claiborne Avenue after the levees broke. Past experience had taught him to act fast and to take cash, some food and drinking water, and his family members' personal documents. He put the kids and the older folks into a recycling container and floated them over to a ramp sloping upward to the I-10 viaduct, which led to dry land.

In his living room, well above the flood waters, Hills left behind his nickel-plated tuba, disassembled, its bell, its valves, and its cup-shaped mouthpiece set out in a corner. It was the first tuba Hills had ever owned, an instrument he had received in 1989, when he was thirteen years old. Danny Barker, a New Orleans banjo player who had made music with Louis Armstrong, Dizzy Gillespie, Charlie Parker, Jelly Roll Morton, Sydney Bechet, and Cab Calloway, found out that Hills, who was still in junior high school, needed an instrument. Barker rummaged through his house and came out with a nickel-plated sousaphone—a marching-band tuba—that was practically as old as jazz itself. "Don't let anybody take it from you," Barker said. "It's yours." Hills played the instrument through junior high and high school. He played it on football fields and in band concerts. He played during Mardi Gras parades, wedding marches, and Second Line funerals. He began carrying it on tour around Europe, Africa, and Asia with the families Marsalis and Neville even before he had graduated from high school in 1997. "The music kept me on the straight and narrow," he said. His mother had died. His father, a Vietnam veteran, worked building bridges and held down odd jobs to support the family. Hills worked on crews for the sewage and water department and

Exxon. He delivered pizzas and did landscaping. But it was his nickel-plated horn that put two sisters through school and one sister through college.

The sun was beating on the deck of the I-10 viaduct on the day Hills left his home. The floodwater below was already stinking of sewage as the family headed to the Superdome. Hills tried to walk across the Mississippi to Algiers, but his skin—the skin of the son of a Vietnam veteran—was darker than a brown super-market bag. Back in the Superdome, elderly people were dying of dehydration. "Everyone was looting," he said. "We needed water." After forty-eight hours of pandemonium and thirst, Hills and his family managed to board a commandeered city bus, passed through the phalanx of police and vigilantes in Algiers, and found their way out of New Orleans.

Hills had made it to Arizona before he thought of the nickel-plated sousaphone he had left behind in pieces. He received a tuba from a New Orleans foundation, played gigs with the Nevilles, toured Africa and the Middle East, and performed at New York's Lincoln Center before starting home for New Orleans. He made it as far as an aunt's house in Houston. After a few months, Joe Stern arranged for a trailer to move Hills home from Houston, but the music was dead in New Orleans for the time being, and he withdrew for a few more months to Mississippi. Hills finally moved home, again with Sweet Home's help: a deposit and a first month's rent on a place near Elysian Fields Avenue.

By then, the police had cordoned off the housing project Hills had called home before Katrina. Looters had ransacked the apartments before the authorities allowed their residents to return to reclaim their property. (The projects, largely undamaged, were demolished; in August 2010, an overgrown vacant lot spread northward from the corner of Claiborne and Lafitte.)

Hills' sister managed to retrieve his musical instrument. The looters had seen only a moldy bell and valves and other pieces of some old horn, not a nickel-plated sousaphone with a history. Everything else in the Hills' apartment—records, autographs, photos, jewelry, and a television set and other electronic goods—had been stolen. "The thing that made all the money, they didn't take," he said. Hills came to his sister's home to retrieve his tuba—tarnished, stuck valves, and crusty with mold.

"Of course I cried," he said. "And my sister cried, too. That's a sister. And we know what it means to miss New Orleans."

*   *   *

GEORGE SOROS

For several years, I felt that by entering into Baltimore we merely became part of the scenery without making any real difference. Conditions were still deteriorating. Perhaps we were helping to reduce the rate of decline; but I often asked myself whether that was enough to justify our presence. But perseverance pays off. After more than five years, I could see some real progress on our issues, particularly the drug situation. At the expiration of our ten-year commitment, I decided to continue funding the Baltimore experiment, but insisted that our support had to be matched by other contributions. Increased fund-raising activities have made the effort even more successful. Now the citizens of Baltimore can really call it their own, and they are actively engaged in making it successful.

On a visit to Baltimore, I was shocked to discover that most of the children that end up in the juvenile justice system were put in there directly from the schools, which were eager to meet the standards of the No Child Left Behind Act. The new school superintendent, Andrés A. Alonso, made it a priority to reduce the number of dropouts and to discourage the practice of handing over children to the justice system. His efforts are actively supported by the Open Society Institute–Baltimore. On a subsequent trip, I visited a school where the foundation provides a number of supplemental services such as tutoring, family counseling, and mentoring by former gang members, released from prison, on how to stay out of gangs. I was impressed with the spirit prevailing in the school. The results are beginning to show up in the statistics. Baltimore has recorded the biggest improvement in school completion rates in the country in the last three years.

I am so pleased with the Baltimore experiment that I want to extend it to other cities. New Orleans is a prime candidate. The need is great. Based on our record in Baltimore and New Orleans, we sought to be able to secure matching funds from the start. Such an arrangement makes funders more firmly grounded in local communities.

The destruction resulting from Katrina exacerbated problems in New Orleans, but they existed long before the hurricane struck. I think that it is probably inappropriate to re-build New Orleans the way it was. The old New Orleans has washed away. The new New Orleans must reconcile itself to being a smaller city. At the same time, there is tremendous local enthusiasm for restoring New Orleans, which we are support-ing. It is very fertile ground. Again, it is a slow process, so one doesn't quite see the results, but a lot of progress is being made. When you actually go there and talk to the people, you see the positive developments even if the city as a whole is not fully recovered.

Aryeh Neier and George Soros in Croatia, 2002. The two men led the efforts of the Open Society Foundations to help countries in South Eastern Europe recover from years of war and prepare for membership in the European Union. (© Beka Vučo/Open Society Foundations)

Afterword

Aryeh Neier

George Soros begins his essay in this book by describing himself as both selfish and self-centered. Almost certainly, he would reject another label for himself that seems inconsistent with those traits: modest. Yet his account of his role in establishing and shaping his network of foundations greatly understates the innovative role that he played.

Before getting to those innovations, it may be worth making a point that should be obvious to anyone familiar with philanthropic foundations. That is, all but a small number are named for their donors. Rather than advertise himself, George Soros has chosen to call attention to our mission by designating us as the Open Society Foundations. He has also refrained from using his own name for the university he founded and endowed. It is the Central European University. Though he has given away billions of dollars, he has never asked that his name should be attached to a building or used to label a program that he has funded.

As for his innovations, certainly among the most significant was to recognize that he could help to undermine the Soviet system from within. He did not do so by operating clandestinely. Rather, he empowered a few individuals in Communist countries who shared his commitments to open society values, and he exploited the self-interest of some officials in those countries who had their own reasons for favoring greater contact with the West. He also saw the value of the work being done by others who sought to promote change from within and became a leading supporter—and sometimes the leading supporter—of their efforts. These included the intellectual exchanges arranged by Annette Laborey that gave many independent thinkers in Eastern Europe their first exposure to the West and the efforts by Helsinki Watch (which evolved into Human Rights Watch) to establish and support Helsinki committees in Communist countries such as Poland.

When the Berlin Wall fell in 1989 and the Soviet Union disintegrated in 1991, George Soros moved rapidly to establish foundations throughout the region. He saw it as a revolutionary moment in which he had an opportunity to have a disproportionate impact in fostering transitions from closed societies to more open societies. Unfortunately, he largely failed to persuade Western governments also to seize this opportunity. The consequence has been far less headway in developing open societies in parts of the former Soviet empire than might have been possible.

An important Soros innovation was to entrust those from the countries in which he established foundations to make crucial decisions about programs and funding. No other substantial philanthropy, public or private, operates in this way. George Soros decided that his main concern in operating in a particular country should be to identify individuals committed to open society values who are qualified to make decisions affecting their own country. They would make better decisions, he thought, than he could from afar. The distinctive network of foundations that operates today is the legacy of his readiness to trust and respect local decision making. Other philanthropic institutions have staff based in different parts of the world who make funding decisions within bounds set at the organization's headquarters. Only the Open Society Foundations have staff in different countries who report to local boards of directors who have the final say on their grant-making and their other activities.

A consequence of the establishment of substantially autonomous foundations in many countries is that their role is not limited to the disbursement of funds. The foundations themselves are often significant institutions of those countries, and they play a role in struggles over such critical issues as the treatment of racial and ethnic minorities, the transparency of public decision making, and electoral regularity. They not only give grants to others but also operate their own programs; in addition, they may speak in their own names on issues important to the development of a more open society. This combination of grant-making, operational programs, and advocacy also is the way that the Open Society Foundations operate at the international level.

On many occasions, George Soros has recognized the significance of innovations by others and has built on their efforts and, thereby, greatly expanded the work that they may have launched on a small scale. An example is the question of transparency for the revenue that governments derive from the exploitation of natural resources. The pioneering work in this field was done by a small, London-based organization, Global Witness. In addition to helping to make it possible for Global Witness to greatly enlarge its operations and to enhance its effectiveness, George Soros took up the issue with governments and intergovernmental bodies and also helped to launch new institutions, such as the Revenue Watch Institute, to address aspects of the issue that were not included in the efforts of Global Witness. Largely as a consequence, there is now a worldwide movement concerned

with this issue—and transparency for revenues from natural resources, and their expenditure, have become a significant policy
question for many governments in different parts of the world.

Not everything that is innovative about the Open Society
Foundations is directly attributable to George Soros. Yet the
spirit with which he has infused the network plays an important
part in the creativity of others. One reason is his commitment to
trial and error. He often has ideas that he wants to push but that
are not fully worked out. By always holding himself open to criticism, and making adjustments, he has often achieved far more
through the programs sponsored by the Open Society Foundations than seemed possible at the outset. There is never an
advantage that anyone in the foundations network derives from
parroting his thoughts. Nor does he resent those who bring him
bad news about his pet projects. Indeed, he prizes the views of
many of those who are most likely to enter into an argument with
him. In this way, he carries out in practice his view that all human
endeavor is fallible and that the way to make progress is to
correct mistakes as one goes along.

The unique institution created by George Soros has had its
share of failures. Outside the United States, it has spent far more
money in Russia than anywhere else but has been disappointed
grievously by its inability to help make Russia more of an open
society. George Soros does not regret his expenditures in Russia.
He still believes that some of the seeds he planted are bearing
fruit. But he knows that the emergence of an open society is not
on the horizon.

There have been many other disappointments, but there
have also been successes. Today, thanks in significant part to the
work of the Open Society Foundations, close to ninety countries
in all parts of the world have freedom of information laws, and
they are increasingly implemented to make governments operate

more transparently. Budget transparency and, as noted, transparency for the vast wealth derived from the extraction of natural resources, often used corruptly and abusively, have been a particular focus.

The Open Society Foundations have also been the leading supporter of efforts to protect rights and promote opportunities for minorities suffering from discrimination. As is apparent, these are efforts that must be pursued over the long term, and they usually meet with substantial resistance. The struggle supported by the Open Society Foundations in Central Europe and South Eastern Europe to deal with the marginalization of the Roma minority is an example. Yet, over time, the foundations network has helped to bring about significant advances. In addition to efforts focused on racial, ethnic, and religious minorities, the Open Society Foundations have also launched programs to deal with abuses and discrimination against the mentally and physically disabled, those addicted to drugs, sexual minorities, the dying, and others requiring such assistance.

Another issue on which the Open Society Foundations have led the way internationally is in providing legal assistance to criminal defendants and in addressing a closely related issue, the pretrial detention—often for very extended periods—of those not represented by counsel. Recently, this work has been supplemented by efforts to promote legal empowerment of the poor in civil matters. In parts of the world where there are few lawyers, the Open Society Foundations have supported programs in which paralegals provide crucial assistance.

The Open Society Foundations have played a leading role in the development of the international human rights movement. Because of my own background, George Soros has largely deferred to me to guide the network's activities in this area. Thanks to the resources he has made available, we are today the largest

supporter of the human rights movement worldwide. It is—
along with the international environmental movement—one of
the two largest, best organized, and most influential global citizen movements. This is a field in which another donor, the Ford
Foundation, became a major factor even earlier than the Open
Society Foundations and continues today to play a leading role.
Also, a handful of other philanthropies in Europe and the United
States are making immensely valuable contributions to the field.
The Open Society Foundations have entered into partnerships
with almost all the other major supporters of the human rights
movement. These partnerships have enhanced the effectiveness
of our own contributions.

The human rights movement has devoted substantial effort in
the past three decades to advocacy with respect to the foreign
policies of governments so as to take advantage of their influence
over each other to protect rights. In the past decade and a half,
the Open Society Foundations have extended our efforts to
shape foreign policy to other issues by becoming the leading
supporter of such organizations as the International Crisis
Group and the European Council on Foreign Relations. George
Soros has himself played a central role in the work of such
organizations. Often, his own thinking about public policy has
been shaped by his participation in the deliberations of these
groups, and the consequence has been manifest in initiatives
he launches within the foundations network. An example is his
decision a few years ago to launch programs in Nepal following
the ouster of that country's king. It was his exposure to the
reporting of the International Crisis Group on Nepal that persuaded him that the Open Society Foundations could make a
contribution to the development of a more open society in the
former monarchy that had recently suffered from a disastrous
internal armed conflict.

When I joined the staff of the Open Society Foundations in 1993, it quickly became apparent to me that George Soros was far better informed about its already far-flung activities than anyone else. That continued to be true for a number of years thereafter. More recently, however, his knowledge of its activities has become far more selective. He focuses on particular aspects of its work in which he himself is deeply engaged and leaves it to me and to others to try to ensure that other parts of the network operate effectively. At the same time, he often says that the best things done by the Open Society Foundations are things he does not know about.

The main reason it is possible for him to be sanguine about continuing to expend vast sums of money supporting an enormous range of activities that he cannot himself fully follow is that he is aware that he has imbued the entire foundations network with his own philosophical commitments to open society values and his own trial-and-error approach that produces constant corrections of course. He does worry, of course, that the spirit of innovation which he has brought to his Open Society Foundations, as to everything else he has done, will decline as inevitable transitions of leadership take place. He is concerned that the Open Society Foundations will become like other philanthropic institutions which sometimes seem preoccupied with self-perpetuation and less inclined to take risks. I am less worried about this than George Soros because I think that his influence on the thinking and the behavior of many young persons in key positions in the Open Society Foundations is more profound than he realizes. I expect them to ensure that the institution will retain the distinctive characteristics with which he has endowed it for a long time to come.

Notes

CHAPTER 1

1. This background summary draws liberally on *Publishing What We Learned*, by Mabel van Oranje and Henry Parham, who describe in detail the birth and development of the global transparency and accountability movement in the natural resources business.

CHAPTER 2

1. See BBC News, "DR Congo colonel Kibibi Mutware jailed for mass rape," February 21, 2011, http://www.bbc.co.uk/news/world-africa-12523847.

CHAPTER 5

1. Global Witness website, www.globalwitness.org.
2. Christina Fink, *Living Silence: Burma Under Military Rule* (London: Zed Books, 2001), pp. 29, 30, 31.
3. Global Witness website, www.globalwitness.org.
4. Tomás Ojea Quintana, *Report of the Special Rapporteur on the Situation of Human Rights in Myanmar*, United Nations Human Rights Council, A/HRC/13/48, March 5, 2009.
5. Global Witness website, www.globalwitness.org.
6. Women of Burma, *CEDAW Shadow Report: In the Shadow of the Junta*, 2008, www.womenofburma.org.

CHAPTER 6

1. Will Dunham, "TB Killed 1.7 Million Globally in 2006, WHO Says," Reuters, March 17, 2008.

2. Lee B. Reichman and Janice Hopkins Tanne, *Timebomb : The Global Epidemic of Multi–Drug Resistant Tuberculosis* (New York: McGraw-Hill, 2002), p. 88.
3. P. E. Farmer et al., "Recrudescent Tuberculosis in the Russian Federation," in *The Global Impact of Drug-Resistant Tuberculosis*, pp. 53–54.
4. Farmer et al., "Recrudescent Tuberculosis," p. 53.
5. Farmer et al., "Recrudescent Tuberculosis," p. 57.
6. Reichman and Tanne, *Timebomb*, p. 121.
7. Farmer et al., "Recrudescent Tuberculosis," pp. 54, 56.

CHAPTER 7

1. Buhrer Tavanier, Yana, "Institutions Remain Dumping Grounds for Forgotten People," in the newsletter of the European Coalition for Community Living, No. 10, October 2009.
2. Laura Ahern and Eric Rosenthal, et al., *Hidden Suffering: Romania's Segregation and Abuse of Infants and Children with Disabilities* (New York: Mental Disability Rights International, 2006).
3. Laura Ahern and Eric Rosenthal, et al., *Torment not Treatment: Serbia's Segregation and Abuse of Children and Adults with Disabilities* (New York: Mental Disability Rights International, 2007).
4. www.glas-javnosti.rs/clanak/glas-javnosti-28-11-2007/hazari-sude -srbiji.

CHAPTER 8

1. "Europe's Spectral Nation," *The Economist*, May 10, 2002.

CHAPTER 10

1. *United States of America v. Roland Bourgeois, Jr.* See http://media .nola.com/crime_impact/other/rolandbourgeois ind.pdf.
2. "New Orleans Cops Say They Got Orders Authorizing Them to Shoot Looters in the Chaos after Hurricane Katrina," August 25, 2010, http://www.nola.com/crime/index.ssf/1010/08/ new_orleans_cops_say_they_got.html.
3. "New Orleans Police Officer Under Investigation in Shooting in Days after Katrina," February 13, 2010, http://www .propublica.org/nola/story/new-orleans-police-officer-under

-investigation-in-shooting-0210; United States of America v. David Warren, et al., http://graphics8.nytimes.com/packages/pdf/us/20100612-glover-charges.pdf.

4. "Six More Charged in New Orleans Danziger Bridge Shootings," ProPublica, July 13, 2010, http://www.propublica.org/nola/story/six-more-charged-in-new-orleans-danziger-bridge-shootings/.

5. "Family Wants Police Charged in New Orleans Killing," CNN Justice, January 9, 2009, http://articles.cnn.com/2009-01-09/justice/new.orleans.shooting_1_police-department-orleans-parish?_s+PM: CRIME.

6. "Six More Charged in New Orleans Danziger Bridge Shootings," ProPublica, July 13, 2010, http://www.propublica.org/nola/story/six-more-charged-in-new-orleans-danziger-bridge-shootings/.

Acknowledgments

This description of George Soros's philanthropic endeavors would not have been possible without the patience, understanding, and perseverance of Ari Korpivaara, who questioned, ferreted out errors, and suggested numerous improvements, as well as Laura Silber and Michael Vachon, who coordinated the work.

In addition to those persons acknowledged and quoted in the body of the text, this book owes a significant debt of gratitude to the following people: in New York—Rachel Aicher, Maureen Aung-Thwin, Kritika Bansal, Ann Beeson, Leonard Benardo, David Berry, Mary Callaway, Will Cohen, Francoise Girard, Tracey Gurd, Julia Harrington, Rachel Hart, Thomas Hilbink, Phillip Howse, Steve Hubbell, Erlin Ibreck, Rebecca Iwerks, William Kramer, Alexander Krstevski, Heather Marciniec, Leonard Noisette, Amie Patel, Paul Silva, Svetlana Tsalik, Elizabeth Tydeman, Robert Varenik, Amy P. Weil, Laura Wickens, and Zaw Zaw; in Budapest—Dora Felegyhazi; in Washington, D.C.—Gabi Chojkier, Sandra Dunsmore, Ambassador Morton Abramowitz, and Katie Redford; in London—Luis Montero, Mabel van Oranje, and Henry Parham; in Senegal, Mauritania, and Sierra Leone—Aubrey Wade and Souleymane Sagna; in Cambodia—Heather Ryan, Nget Sovannith, and Johanna Macdonald; in South Africa—Sisonke Msimang, Cedric de Beer, and Heidi Holland; in Haiti—Sacha Telfort, Samson Charles, Sibrun Rosier, Lucie Couet, and Maude Malengrez; in Costa Rica, José Zaglul, Kristine Jiménez, Wendy Judy, and the faculty members of Universidad EARTH; in Switzerland—Nena Skopljanac; in Nigeria—Anthony Nwapa; in Lesotho—Salmaan Keshavjee and Dr. Hind Satti; in

347

Negotino—Borče, Božidarka, and Kika; in Kumanovo—Sebihana Skenderovska; in Zagreb—all the people at the Association for Promoting Inclusion; in the Czech Republic—Simona Reichlová, Kumar Wiswathan, and Štěpán Ripka; in Baltimore—Debra Rubino, Monique Dixon, Pamela King, Justin Schaberg, Tania Cordes, Joanne C. Kess, Nikki Glass-Brice, Cindy Lemons, David Williams, and Chris Baron; in New Orleans—Charmaine Neville, Lolis Elie, Carol Bebelle, Ann Silverberg Williamson, Eddie Ashworth, Lydia and her crew at the Avenue Garden Hotel as well as the breakfast and lunch shifts at the Saint Charles Tavern and the Voodoo Barbeque; in Bloomington, Indiana—Jerzy Kolodziej; and at PublicAffairs in New York—Peter Osnos, Susan Weinberg, Pete Garceau, Brandon Proia, and Niki Papadopoulos.

Index

Chuck Sudetic is a former reporter for the *New York Times* and the author of *Blood and Vengeance*, which was named a *New York Times* Notable Book and a "Book of the Year" by *The Economist* and the *Washington Post*. He has written for *The Economist*, *Atlantic Monthly*, *Rolling Stone*, *Mother Jones*, and other periodicals, and is a writer for the Open Society Foundations. (© Pamela Chen)

PublicAffairs is a publishing house founded in 1997. It is a tribute to the standards, values, and flair of three persons who have served as mentors to countless reporters, writers, editors, and book people of all kinds, including me.

I. F. Stone, proprietor of *I. F. Stone's Weekly,* combined a commitment to the First Amendment with entrepreneurial zeal and reporting skill and became one of the great independent journalists in American history. At the age of eighty, Izzy published *The Trial of Socrates,* which was a national bestseller. He wrote the book after he taught himself ancient Greek.

Benjamin C. Bradlee was for nearly thirty years the charismatic editorial leader of *The Washington Post.* It was Ben who gave the *Post* the range and courage to pursue such historic issues as Watergate. He supported his reporters with a tenacity that made them fearless, and it is no accident that so many became authors of influential, best-selling books.

Robert L. Bernstein, the chief executive of Random House for more than a quarter century, guided one of the nation's premier publishing houses. Bob was personally responsible for many books of political dissent and argument that challenged tyranny around the globe. He is also the founder and was the longtime chair of Human Rights Watch, one of the most respected human rights organizations in the world.

.   .   .

For fifty years, the banner of Public Affairs Press was carried by its owner Morris B. Schnapper, who published Gandhi, Nasser, Toynbee, Truman, and about 1,500 other authors. In 1983 Schnapper was described by *The Washington Post* as "a redoubtable gadfly." His legacy will endure in the books to come.

Peter Osnos, *Founder and Editor-at-Large*